Investment Mathematics

for

Finance and Treasury Professionals

About TMA

The Treasury Management Association (TMA) is the world's leading professional association representing more than 12,000 treasury executives from 6,500 leading companies and organizations.

TMA enables treasury professionals to perform effectively in a changing business world and prepares them for future challenges through professional development and executive education opportunities, certification programs, career services, publications and technical information, original research, industry standards, and representation before legislators and regulators.

Membership in TMA is open to corporate treasury practitioners as well as those who sell products and services to the treasury management profession, such as bankers, consultants, and academics. The mission of the Association is enhanced value of the treasury profession through professional knowledge, respect and recognition for the profession, a favorable business environment, and professional conduct.

Investment Mathematics
for
Finance and Treasury Professionals

A Practical Approach

Gregory Kitter

JOHN WILEY & SONS, INC.
New York • Chichester • Weinheim • Brisbane • Singapore • Toronto

To Sharon and Valaria.
Without you, none of this means anything.

This book is printed on acid-free paper. ∞

Library of Congress Cataloging-in-Publication Data:
Kitter, Gregory V.
    Investment mathematics for finance and treasury professionals:
a practical approach / Gregory V. Kitter.
        p.   cm.
    Includes bibliographical references and index.
    ISBN 0-471-25294-8 (cloth : alk. paper)
    1. Investments—Mathematics. I. Title.
HG4515.3.K58   1998
332.6'01'—dc21   98-29520

Printed in the United States of America.

10 9 8 7 6 5 4 3 2 1

PREFACE

My best friend and another close friend are what I would term "rocket scientists" in that both are PhDs, one in mathematics and the other in geophysics. Yet, when learning a new investment concept or technique, they like to first hear an explanation in plain English. "I can figure out the math," one of them will remind me, "just tell me what you are trying to achieve." This approach—along with participation in many academic and business seminars, and study of numerous "practical, hands-on" investment texts—led me to some stark realizations about the study of investment mathematics.

There are three types of people who really need to understand investment mathematics. First, there are the mathematicians (scientists) who create the formulae to do the calculations. Next, the computer programmers must translate the algorithms the mathematicians have created into usable computer files and applications. Finally, there are the teachers of the mathematicians and the programmers. The rest of us mortals just need to understand the concepts and learn which buttons to push on the computer to get the job done.

Second, the majority of investment texts I have studied delve deeply into the theoretical constructs of different investment applications, spending what I consider to be an inordinate amount of time going through the various algorithms, where an understanding of the Greek alphabet is not only helpful but is sometimes necessary to follow what the author(s) is trying to get across to the reader.

Third, in many cases, examples are included in many investments texts. Their format and presentation, however, are not always straightforward. The reader must spend a considerable amount of time simply translating the text into understandable, bite-size pieces.

Finally, the large majority of the available texts are anthologies on one particular market or type of financial instrument. Aside from getting too deeply involved, for many readers' tastes, in the subject topic or instrument, the cost of getting a survey of the financial markets in general requires taking out a home equity loan, or cutting into

v

one's college tuition trust fund. I won't even mention the aggravation many people suffer at the hands of budget-conscious bosses and/or accounting gurus.

The structure of this book identifies, in logical order, the mathematical concepts associated with the investments sector of Treasury management. The bulk of applications falls into the fixed-income arena (the money and capital markets), but studies of the foreign currency and equities markets are relevant and are also included. Finally, the various derivatives that markets use as both speculative and hedging tools are addressed, with emphasis on the more generic types of instruments, such as futures contracts, options, and interest rate swaps. For readers who require the in-depth formulae for one or more of the concepts discussed, reference texts for these algorithms are cited.

A brief summary of each chapter follows.

Chapter 1 begins with a discussion of present and future value. These are core determinants used in calculating yield. This is followed by a discussion of price yield changes. When yield goes up, why does price go down? Then, an overview of the securities traded in the money and capital markets is presented. Different types of yield calculations are reviewed, along with those instruments using that yield to measure investment returns.

Chapter 2 looks more closely into the concept of yield to maturity. How is it calculated and used as a measuring tool? Does it really tell the user what it purports to calculate? What are the inherent faults in the application? What can the user do to mitigate the problems associated with yield to maturity? Concepts discussed include realized compound yield, total dollar return, true yield, constant maturity yield, yield to call, yield to worst, reinvestment rates, and horizon analysis. How does the user apply these concepts to everyday investment decisions and analyses?

Chapter 3 covers yield spread analysis, the core of value determination in fixed-income securities. There are more than two million fixed-income securities outstanding, relatively few of which trade on a regular basis. How does the user determine the value in these issues? The principles of yield spread analysis are discussed with respect to relative value calculations and market conventions on pricing. Readers learn the importance of using yields as relative measuring tools. The concept of "rich/cheap" analysis is also covered, with examples and with a quick-and-dirty, yet effective method of calculation. Readers are also taken through yield comparisons of valuing the relationship between similar-maturity securities with different yield calculation methods.

Virtually all individual fixed-income securities have a unique relationship to price/yield sensitivity. (How much does the price change, given a specific change in yield?) Determining these relationships represents a major principle of risk management. "What is my risk in owning this individual security/portfolio of securities?

Chapter 4's discussion includes the more popular technique of price/yield sensitivity analysis. The focus is on why and how securities behave the way they do with regard to incremental changes in price/yield, coupons, maturity, and the different types of risk measured with these techniques. Readers study the definitions of and the differences between interest rate risk and basis risk. Examples cover the practical use of the various price/yield sensitivity measures in both individual and comparative yield analyses.

Chapter 5 addresses different types of yield curves and how they are structured. This segues into the concept of the term structure of interest rates and zero coupon securities, specifically the U.S. Treasury STRIPS (Separate Trading of Registered Interest and Principal on Securities) market. The calculation of the value of a STRIP is discussed, using specific examples. How is the "implied" zero curve used to price other cash and derivative fixed-income securities? What are the differences between the implied and actual STRIPS yield curve and the standard coupon curve?

Chapter 6 examines the world of fixed-income securities with stochastic, or uncertain, cash flows. Returns on these securities, most often represented by callability or convertibility features, have a somewhat different method of calculation from securities with fixed cash flows because of one or more specific factors creating an uncertain cash flow stream over the life of the security. An overview of issues containing these features is presented, with a breakdown of the components of the issue to be valued. How much is a one-year call feature on a two-year security actually worth? How is the coupon on a bond affected by a convertibility feature? A practical explanation of fair value pricing for both callable and putable securities, as well as mortgage-backed securities (MBS), is included.

Chapters 7 through 10 are devoted to the derivatives markets. After a brief introduction to derivatives, Chapter 7 focuses on interest rate forwards and futures contracts. Forward rate agreements and Eurodollar futures contracts are examined, as are the U.S. Treasury futures markets. Valuation techniques and various examples for both sectors are included.

Chapter 8 covers the foreign currency spot and forward markets as well as the foreign exchange (FX) futures markets. The concept of covered interest arbitrage is explained in detail, along with a valuation for FX futures.

Chapter 9 is devoted to the world of plain put and call options. Definition of terms, hedging, and spread trading strategies are covered using examples and profit and loss (P/L) charts. The theory behind option pricing (not too much math, I promise) is explained in detail, using as few Greek letters and symbols as possible. The reader will emerge from this section with a basic understanding of how an option is priced. Option price sensitivities (the "Greeks") are also covered. The final section is devoted to LEAPS (long-term options).

Chapter 10 explores other types of derivative instruments. The first section, covering different types of exotic options, looks at structures such as split-fee, barrier, and Asian options. Interest rate caps, floors, and collars are also examined. The next section looks at interest rate swaps. Definitions of terms, different types of swap structures, pricing, and swaps examples are included. The last section of the chapter is devoted to inverse floater securities. Definitions of terms, coupon logic, and security structure are covered.

Chapter 11 looks into the overall concept of risk/return. Traditional models, including the capital asset pricing model (CAPM) and arbitrage price theory (APT) are discussed. The basic principles of value at risk are also reviewed.

Chapter 12 basically says, "Now that you're so smart, where do you find all the necessary information to use what you've learned?" Listings and brief descriptions of real-time information services vendors, investment analytics spreadsheet add-in vendors, economic forecasting services, available data from government sources, and print media offerings are noted.

The book's appendixes represent supporting data. Tables include: historical interest rate and yield spreads, Treasury bond conversion factors, the normal distribution function, selected futures contract specifications, and more. The goal was to amass a series of useful data that would otherwise require many sources to compile.

As I mentioned at the outset, the basic concept of this book is to provide a practical understanding of the borrowing, lending, and investment techniques used to measure and value securities in the marketplace. Over the years, I have come to believe that one doesn't need to be a mathematical wizard to understand the applications of investment mathematics. What is needed is a "survival guide" that cuts through the mathematical jargon and notations, and presents the important concepts and applications in plain English. This book is intended to satisfy that need.

If you want to reach me with questions or comments, my e-mail is Gkitter@aol.com.

ACKNOWLEDGMENTS

The successful completion of a book of this type can't be accomplished without the help of many talented people. I thank the Treasury Management Association (TMA) for its support over the life of the project. The TMA's emphasis on education of its membership is extremely important to the continuation of professional excellence in the treasury management function. I would also like to thank the TMA's book Development Advisory Board, who reviewed this book for technical accuracy, especially Ira Kawaller, Ph.D., President of Kawaller & Company, LLC; James Washam, Ph.D., CCM, Assistant Professor of Finance, Arkansas State University; and Fran Carson, Manager of Pension & Thrift Management, Asea Brown and Boveri.

I want to specially acknowledge the following individuals who made a significant difference in the quality of this book. Eileen Klecka, you're the best. Jeff Maron, someday we'll work together again, if I'm lucky. Dr. Steve Hellinger, you were invaluable. Ron Ryan, for placing the em-*pha*-sis on the right syl-*la*-ble. Mike Arbolino, for catching an important omission. Jeffrey Falk, without whom this book would have been largely only text. And Dr. Mel Mullin, who not only contributed but made me believe what I said actually made sense. Thanks to all of you.

GREG KITTER

September 1998

CONTENTS

1 INSTRUMENTS IN THE BAND

A fixed-income security is simply that: fixed. Unlike equities, where there is no maturity date or guaranteed rate of return, an investor purchasing a fixed-income security and holding it until its maturity will earn a fixed rate of return. This fixed rate is a function of the nominal rate of interest, or coupon, assigned to the security. Periodically (usually every 6 months), the security issuer will remit the coupon payment to each investor owning the security. The amount of payment is determined by multiplying the coupon rate, adjusted for the number of payments each year by the face value of the security. The final payment will also include return of the principal or face amount of the issue. This will be discussed in greater detail in Chapter 2.

The present value of a security is its value today. If an investor pays $100 for a 1-year security with a face or par value of $100 and 6% coupon interest payable in one year, the present value is $100. The future value is $106 ($100 principal + $6 coupon interest). This is the value of the security on its maturity or redemption date.

For fixed-income securities, the most important word is *yield*. The reason is simple: Yield is the rate of return to an investor, or what the borrower effectively pays to borrow. It measures the return on investment over a stated time period. Yield is the measuring stick on which many, if not all, fixed-income securities are evaluated. The calculation of yield, although relatively simple in some cases, can be very complex in others. It is a function of the creditworthiness, amount, degree of certainty, liquidity, and maturity of the cash flow stream associated with a security. Chapter 6 will examine yield as a function of the degree of certainty in cash flows. In this chapter, the focus is on creditworthiness, maturity, amount, and liquidity.

Creditworthiness is directly related to yield through the concept of risk/return. If an investor was simultaneously offered like amounts of a 5-year U.S. Treasury note and a 5-year junk bond, both with a yield to maturity of 6% and similar cash flow streams, which one should the investor choose? Unless the investor is a glutton for punishment, the lower-risk 5-year Treasury note is the appropriate choice. Why take more risk than is necessary for the same return?

Maturity, like creditworthiness, is a function of the risk/return tradeoff. If an investor is simultaneously offered like amounts of 2- and 10-year U.S. Treasury notes at the same yield, which one should the investor choose? To answer this question, think about the concept of a yield curve. This is a graphic representation of the yields on securities with similar creditworthiness but different maturities. Under what are termed normal circumstances, the longer the maturity the higher the yield.[1] The reason is simple: Being able to forecast interest rate levels becomes more and more difficult as one looks further ahead in time. Why should the investor be satisfied with the same rate of return on a security that has a maturity 8 years longer than another security of similar creditworthiness?

Amount is simply a function of arithmetic. If an investor were offered two 5-year U.S. Treasury notes at the same price, but one has a 6% coupon, and the other a 9% coupon, presuming a strategy to hold the investment until maturity, the investor would obviously select the higher coupon issue.

Liquidity is a little more indirect with respect to affecting yield. Several factors impact the liquidity of a particular security. The age of the security and the amount outstanding are two important factors. The life cycle of a fixed-income security runs from birth in an underwriting or initial offering, to placement in investor portfolios, clipping of coupons (where applicable), and final maturity. The longer a security has been outstanding, the more likely the issuing underwriters will have placed all of the issue in portfolios as investments rather than securities held for short-term trading purposes. Additionally, the smaller the size of an offering, the smaller the number of investors who are likely to own the issue. This usually translates into increased difficulty in locating an owner of the security after it has been placed with investors during the initial offering period. Generally speaking, the more difficult it is for a trader to locate a particular issue, the wider the bid/ask spread will be.

Stripping, or the detachment of coupons from the principal, or corpus, of a fixed-income security for individual sale, also reduces the amount outstanding in original form. In the U.S. Treasury market, this has become a popular practice. Billions of dollars in securities are stripped and *reconstituted* (coupons are reattached to the principal) every month. We will look more closely at the mathematics associated with stripping in Chapter 5.

PRICE/YIELD RELATIONSHIP

In the world of fixed-income securities, the relationship between an issue's price and yield is inverse. In other words, as price rises, yield falls, and vice versa. The logic of this is simple. As mentioned at the beginning of this chapter, a fixed-income security is exactly that: fixed. The purchaser receives a fixed or stated return on investment over a stipulated period of time, as stated in the legal documentation supporting the security. For example, a 6%, 20-year bond with semiannual interest payments will generate a cash flow of 3% of the principal value each 6 months, with a return of the principal, or face amount, on the maturity date of the security. These cash flows will not change over time.

When investors purchase this bond, they will require a certain rate of return, or yield to maturity, to purchase the security. The yield to maturity is a market-driven function determined by various fundamental and technical factors related to maturity, creditworthiness, liquidity, and cash flow certainty. As a result, the actual required yield is subject to change as market conditions shift. Despite dynamic market conditions, the cash flows on our bond are not altered. The fixed nature of the security creates the inverse relationship between price and yield.

EXHIBIT 1.1   6% coupon, 20-year maturity, noncallable, semiannual compounding

Yield to Maturity	Price	Change
4%	127.36	
5%	112.55	14.81
6%	100.00	12.55
7%	89.32	10.68
8%	80.21	9.11

When the coupon rate and the yield to maturity are equal, the price of the security is par, or 100% of face value. The interest on the security is accruing at the same rate as the market-required factor used to discount the future value of the cash flow back to present value. If, however, our 20-year bond has a yield to maturity of 6½%, this required yield is higher than the nominal or coupon rate of 6%. To achieve the higher yield, the investor would pay less than par, or 100%, of face value for the securities. Accreting this price difference over the life of the security represents the return required to make up the yield spread between the 6% coupon and the 6½% yield to maturity. The lower the yield to maturity, the higher the price necessary to achieve this required yield to maturity, because the discount factor (denominator) used to reduce the future value of each cash flow to present value gets smaller as the yield to maturity declines.

Exhibit 1.1 reflects the change in price as yield to maturity is adjusted. It shows how price and yield are inversely related in a fixed-income security. Another interesting factor in this exhibit is the structure of the price/yield relationship: the lower the yield, the faster the price rises. We will return to this relationship in much greater detail in Chapters 4 and 5.

FIXED-INCOME SECURITIES

This section summarizes different types of fixed-income securities. (For a detailed treatment of these securities, see Appendix F, which gives references to other texts.)

In the United States and other industrialized countries, there are five major issuers of fixed-income securities:

1. Governments.
2. Federal agencies.
3. Municipalities.
4. Corporations.
5. Banks.

These issuers operate in two market segments with respect to time. *Money markets* represent securities with an initial final maturity of less than one year. *Capital markets* (page 15) cover securities with an initial final maturity of one year or more.

Money Market Securities

Three basic types of yield calculations are important to fixed-income securities. In the money markets, *discount rate* and *money market* yield calculations are the most popular forms of measurement. In the capital markets, *yield to maturity* is most commonly used. We will examine each of these yield calculations.

Discount Rate Yield Calculation

Discount rate is the return on a security, calculated as a percent of par value or the face amount of the security. It is applied to money market securities, which are issued at a discount from par or face amount and are redeemed at par. To the issuer, there is only one cash inflow (purchase cost) and one outflow (redemption proceeds). Discount rates are calculated based on the actual number of days in each month and on a 360-day year. The following money market securities are quoted using a discount rate.

1. *Treasury Bills (T-Bills).* These short-term unsecured obligations of the U.S. Government are issued:

- In three maturities: for 13 weeks, for 26 weeks (issued weekly), and for 52 weeks (issued every 28 days). All T-Bills mature on a Thursday (unless a holiday).

- Via auction process through the Federal Reserve.
- In a minimum denomination of $10,000, then in increments of $1,000.
- In registered book entry form (nonphysical) through the Federal Book Entry System.
- With approximately 33 different T-Bill maturities outstanding at any one time (one each week for 26 weeks, and every 28 days thereafter, out to 52 weeks).

2. *Federal Agency Discount Notes.* Federal agencies are quasi-governmental entities established to lend money to specific industries such as housing and agriculture. The debt of most of these organizations is not guaranteed by the U.S. Government, although an *implicit guarantee* is understood. There have been a few scary moments, but no federal agency has ever defaulted on its securities. Nevertheless, there is a small risk-adjusted yield spread between federal agency debt and U.S. Treasury debt of similar maturity and structure.

There are two types of federal agency debt. One is unsecured, but guaranteed by the full faith and credit of the agency. The other is collateralized by different types of home mortgages. This latter type of debt, more commonly referred to as mortgage-backed securities, will be treated in Chapter 6. We will focus here on the noncollateralized debt.

The most active issuers of noncollateralized agency securities (and the industries they lend to) are:

- **F**ederal **F**arm **C**redit **B**ank (agriculture).
- **F**ederal **H**ome **L**oan **B**ank (savings and loan lender).
- **F**ederal **N**ational **M**ortgage **A**ssociation and **F**ederal **H**ome **L**oan **M**ortgage **C**orporation (housing).
- **S**tudent **L**oan **M**arketing **A**ssociation (education).

The money market securities of federal agencies are issued:

- In maturities from overnight to 360 days, on a daily basis, by the issuing agencies. Rates are available through information services providers such as Bloomberg, Bridge Information Systems, and Reuters.
- In a minimum denomination of $10,000, then in increments of $1,000.

- In registered book entry form (nonphysical) through the Federal Book Entry System.

3. *Commercial Paper (CP)*. This short-term unsecured debt is issued by corporations, using one of two methods. *Direct paper* is sold directly by the issuing corporation to investors. *Dealer Placed paper* is sold by the issuer to an investment banker (dealer), who resells the paper to investors. The difference between using the two methods centers on the CP's program size and credit rating. Larger corporations with higher credit ratings are more likely to issue CP directly, rather than paying an investment banker what amounts to a placement fee. Commercial paper is issued:

- In maturities ranging from overnight to 270^2 days, on a daily basis.
- In varying minimum amounts, but the minimum is usually no less than $25,000.
- In both physical and book entry form.

4. *Bankers' Acceptances*. These securities are issued by banks in conjunction with a letter of credit (LC), usually for international trade. The steps in the process are shown in Exhibit 1.2:

(a) The importer gives a letter of credit to the exporter, covering the value of the goods being shipped. In exchange, the exporter gives the importer the necessary shipping documents to retrieve the goods.
(b) The letter of credit is delivered to the exporter's bank, which draws a time draft on the importer's bank, based on the LC.
(c) The importer's bank pays the exporter's bank some discounted amount of the face value of the draft [which becomes a banker's acceptance (BA) after the time draft is stamped "accepted" by the importer's bank] and either holds it in the bank's portfolio until it matures, or sells it in the open market. The open market purchases and sales comprise the BA market.
(d) On the maturity date of the BA, the importer's bank charges the importer's account for the face amount of the BA.

EXHIBIT 1.2   Creation of a banker's acceptance

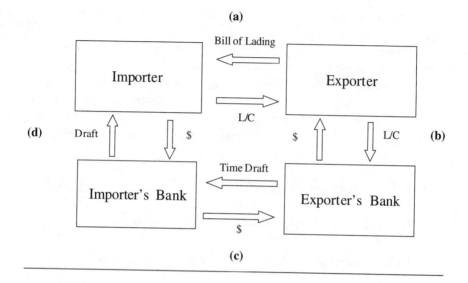

Bankers' acceptances are issued:

- In maturities from overnight to 270 days, on an "as needed" or "as created" basis.
- In no minimum amount, although small BAs with similar maturities are bundled together to create larger units. BAs with par value in the millions are sometimes sold on a participation basis; investors can buy a piece of the acceptance.
- In both physical and book entry form.

Exhibits 1.3, 1.4, and 1.5 introduce the basic formulae used to calculate discount yield, price, and discount amount. (In each exhibit, a different factor is given.)

Discount Rate (DR); Purchase Price given (Exhibit 1.3):

$$DR = \frac{\text{Face amount} - \text{Purchase price}}{\text{Face amount}} \times \frac{360}{\text{Days from settlement to maturity}}.$$

EXHIBIT 1.3 Discount yield, price, and discount amount: $1,000 face amount, $980 purchase price, 90 days to maturity

$$.08 = \frac{\$1,000 - \$980}{\$1,000} \times \frac{360}{90}.$$

Discount Price (DP); Discount Rate given (Exhibit 1.4):

$$DP = 1 - \left(DR \times \frac{\text{Days from settlement to maturity}}{360} \right).$$

EXHIBIT 1.4 Discount yield, price, and discount amount: 8% discount rate, 90 days to maturity

$$\$0.98 = 1 - \left(.08 \times \frac{90}{360} \right).$$

Discount Dollar Amount (DDA); Purchase Price or Discount Rate given (Exhibit 1.5):

$$DDA = \text{Face amount} - \text{Purchase price}.$$

or

$$DDA = \text{Face amount} \times DR \times \frac{\text{Days from settlement to maturity}}{360}.$$

EXHIBIT 1.5 Discount yield, price, and discount amount: $1,000 face, 8% discount rate, 90 days to maturity

$$\$20 = \$1,000 \times .08 \times \frac{90}{360}.$$

Money Market (Interest Add-On) Yield Calculation

Money market yield is the return on a security calculated as a percentage of the dollar return divided by the purchase price. Securities using this type of yield are interest bearing. They are issued at par, or face value, and they are redeemed at par plus accrued interest, usually with one cash outflow and one inflow. As with the discount rate, most securities using money market yield are money market securities. Accrued interest is calculated on an *actual/360-day basis.* As with the discount rate calculation, this means the actual number of days between purchase (or settlement) and maturity is used to determine the interest earned.

The most popular money market securities using this type of yield are domestic and Eurodollar certificates of deposit and time deposits. Other investments include federal funds, municipal notes, and coupon-bearing securities.

1. *Certificates of Deposit/Time Deposits. Certificates of deposit (CDs)* are issued by banks as funding vehicles for loans and other investments. They are negotiable; that is, they can be resold in the secondary market. *Time deposits (TDs)* are nonnegotiable. Once purchased, they must be held until maturity. There are two types of deposits, depending on their size. All deposits *under $100,000* are referred to as *retail* and are nonnegotiable. Certificates of deposit *over $100,000* are negotiable and are referred to as institutional or jumbo CDs. As a practical matter, negotiable CDs usually trade in blocks of $1 million, and TDs are issued in minimum blocks of $5 million. Although maturities on both CDs and TDs can stretch out beyond 5 years, the most popular expiration terms are 1, 2, 3, and 6 months.

When comparing a domestic and a Eurodollar deposit, the primary difference rests in the domicile of the funds. Domestic CDs and TDs are generated by monies held on deposit in domestic banks. Eurodollars represent U.S. dollars held outside the United States. In the 1980s, there was a difference in the rates on domestic and Eurodollar deposits, due in part to different reserve requirements on both securities. The rates were eventually standardized and, in 1991, reserve requirements on all term deposits were eliminated. One could argue a credit risk difference between domestic and Eurodollar deposits, but, in most cases, the monies actually never leave the United States. They are simply transferred from one set of bank books to another.

EXHIBIT 1.6 Calculation of interest on overnight loan of federal funds

Investor A lends \$50,000,000 in federal funds overnight at a rate of 6%.

Interest calculation: $\$50,000,000 \times .06 \times \dfrac{1}{360} = \$8,333.33.$

2. *Federal Funds.* Federal funds are uncommitted reserves that banks and other institutional players borrow and lend among themselves. Maturities of these investments may extend as long as 3 months, but a large majority of the volume is executed on an overnight basis. Interest calculation is actual/360. A trading unit among larger institutional market participants is \$25 million, although \$1 million to \$5 million increments are also available. (See Exhibit 1.6.)

3. *Municipal Notes.* Municipalities usually issue these notes in anticipation of collecting some form of revenue, tax, or bond proceeds. A RAN, or revenue anticipation note, is a popular type of municipal discount note. It is issued in conjunction with an expectation of revenue, usually from the state or federal government, and it is paid off from the receipt of the revenue. A note called a TRAN is a combination of tax and revenue anticipation. A TAN, a tax anticipation note, is issued in anticipation of receiving taxes payable, and it is paid off from the tax receipts. A BAN, a bond anticipation note issued prior to a bond issuance by a municipality, is considered to be the riskiest short-term municipal note. It is contingent on the municipality's ability to issue bonds. BANs are paid off from the proceeds of the bond sale.

4. *Coupon-Bearing Securities.* The following basic formulae are used to calculate money market yield (MMY; Exhibit 1.7) and price (Exhibit 1.8).

Money Market Yield; Price given (Exhibit 1.7):

$$MMY = \frac{1 + \left(\text{Coupon interest} \times \text{Days to maturity} / 360\right)}{(\text{Price} / \text{Par value})} - 1 \times \frac{360}{\text{Days to maturity}}.$$

Price; Money Market Yield given:

$$Price = \frac{1 + \left(\text{Coupon interest} \times \text{Days to maturity} / 360\right)}{1 + (\text{MMY} \times \text{Days to maturity} / 360)} \times 100.$$

EXHIBIT 1.7   Money market yield formula: $1,000 face amount, 90-day maturity, 6% coupon interest, price 99½

$$MMY = \frac{1 + \left(.06 \times \frac{90}{360}\right)}{.995} - 1 \times \frac{360}{90},$$

$$MMY = \frac{1.015}{.995} - 1 \times 4 = 8.04\%.$$

Often, money managers must determine a money market equivalent yield by comparing alternative investments for which the yields are calculated differently. For example, suppose a money manager is offered a 90-day CD with a money market yield of 6.05%, and a 90-day T-Bill with a discount rate of 6%. Which security provides the best return? To determine the difference in yields, we must convert one format to the other. By converting the 6% discount rate on the T-Bill we get:

Money market equivalent (MME) on discount rate (DR) =

$$\frac{DR \times 360}{360 \times (DR \times \text{Days to maturity})}$$

$$\frac{.06 \times 360}{360 - (.06 \times 90)} = 6.0914\%.$$

Despite the apparently higher rate on the CD, the money market equivalent yield on the T-Bill is more than four basis points above the

EXHIBIT 1.8   Price formula: $1,000 face amount, 90-day maturity, 6% coupon interest, price 99½

$$Price = \frac{1 + \left(.06 \times \frac{90}{360}\right)}{1 + \left(.0804 \times \frac{90}{360}\right)} \times 100,$$

$$Price = \frac{1 + (.015)}{1 + (.0201)} \times 100 = .995\,°.$$

(°Rounded)

CD. The key point here is that yield comparisons must be calculated on the same basis.

A *bond equivalent yield* (BEY) is a concept normally used when comparing the return on a discount or money market instrument against that of a coupon-bearing security, when both have a similar amount of time to maturity. The reasons for this calculation are:

- Coupon-bearing securities use a different method or day-count basis to determine interest accruals and yield. (Securities use the discount or money market yield formula.) Therefore, to accurately compare two or more securities quoted in different yield formats, it is necessary to convert all issues to the same yield basis.

- Money market securities with maturities in excess of 182.5 days require a different method of yield calculation than money market securities with 182.5 days or less to maturity. In both cases, market convention dictates a conversion to a bond equivalent basis. There are two conversion formulae: one for discount to bond equivalent yield, and the other from money market to bond equivalent yield.

The following securities use yield to maturity to measure returns. To convert a discount rate to a bond equivalent yield for securities with a maturity less than 182.5 days (see Exhibit 1.9):

Formula; Discount Rate (DR) given:

$$BEY = \frac{DR \times 365}{360 - (DR \times Days\ to\ maturity)}.$$

The above formula and Exhibit 1.9 presume a maturity period of *less than 182.5 days*. Another calculation wrinkle must be added for discount securities with 183 or more days to maturity. A coupon security with 183 or more days to maturity will generate more than one cash flow at maturity. For example, an old Treasury note with only 9 months left to maturity will generate one coupon payment in 3 months and a principal and coupon payment at the end of 9 months. A T-Bill with 9 months to maturity still has only one cash inflow to the investor. Therefore, when comparing the return on the old Treasury note to the T-Bill, an implied cash flow must be added to the T-Bill at the end of 3 months to make it similar in design to the Treasury note. The following formula presumes that the discount accreted (earned) on a T-Bill between the purchase

EXHIBIT 1.9   Example of formula, discount rate given

A portfolio manager is attempting to compare returns on a T-Bill with an old T-bond; both have 120 days to maturity. The discount yield on the T-Bill is 5%. The yield on the T-bond is 5.10%. Which one offers the better return? The manager must convert the return on one of the securities into the same basis as the other. Market convention is to convert the T-Bill discount rate into the same yield basis as the T-bond. T-bonds are calculated using the actual number of days in the year.

$$BEY = \frac{.05 \times 365}{360 - (.05 \times 120 \text{ days})} = 5.1554\%.$$

In this case, the bond equivalent yield on the T-Bill provides a more attractive return than the T-bond. Keep in mind, this isn't simply a numbers game. It is the calculation of actual returns on two different securities using the same calculation method. Converting a money market yield to a T-bond equivalent yield for securities with maturities less than 182.5 days would only require multiplying the money market yield by 365/360.

(settlement) date and the coupon payment date of the Treasury note is reinvested at the discount rate quoted on the purchase date. If, for example, a 9-month T-Bill is quoted with a discount rate of 5.05%, the bond equivalent yield presumption is that, when the T-Bill has 6 months left to maturity, the earned discount will be reinvested at the 5.05% rate. The following formula converts the discount rate (DR) on a discount security with more than 182.5 days to maturity into a bond equivalent yield (BEY):

$$Yield = \frac{\dfrac{2t_{sm}}{t_{basis(BEY)}} + \sqrt{\left[\dfrac{t_{sm}}{t_{basis(BEY)}}\right]^2 - \left[\dfrac{2t_{sm}}{t_{basis(BEY)}} - 1\right]\left[1 - \dfrac{1}{P}\right]}}{\dfrac{2t_{sm}}{t_{basis(BEY)}} - 1}$$

where: $P \text{ (price)} = 1 - \dfrac{t_{sm} \times DR}{t_{basis(BEY)}}$

t_{basis} = number of days over which the discount rate applies,

$t_{basis(BEY)}$ = number of days in the year in which the settlement date falls (the year is measured from 3/1 to 2/28 (or 2/29 in leap year),

t_{sm} = number of days between settlement date and maturity date,

DR = discount rate quoted for T-Bill.

The Yield Curve

The study of interest rates generally centers around a series of securities with equal creditworthiness but different maturities. The graphic representation of the yields on these securities is known as a *yield curve*. Yield curves will be discussed in greater detail in Chapter 5.

As an example of *riding the yield curve*, an investor has made a determination to purchase 3-month T-Bills. At present, the discount rate for a 3-month T-Bill is 5%. The investor could select an alternative investment: purchase a 6-month T-Bill with a discount rate of 5.10% and sell it at the end of 3 months. The risks in this trade are straightforward. The investor can earn an additional 10 basis points by purchasing the 6-month T-Bill. The question is: What will the discount rate be when the 6-month T-Bill is selling as a 3-month T-Bill in 3 months?

If the investor believes the yield curve out to 6 months will either remain the same or move lower in the next 3 months, the best strategy would be to choose the 6-month T-Bill alternative and sell the T-Bill in 3 months. This is called *riding the yield curve*. The idea is simple. If the investor is correct and interest rates remain constant, the 6-month T-Bill will be sold in 3 months as a 3-month T-Bill at a discount rate of 5%. Not only will the investor earn 5.10% for 3 months, but a capital gain will be realized by selling the security at a lower yield than when it was purchased. Exhibit 1.10 reflects the calculations for the 6-month T-Bill purchase, the sale in 3 months, and the profit on the trade.

There are a number of sources for viewing composite pricing for many of the instruments we discussed above. Telerate has created a composite real-time page of money market securities, along with the on-the-run Treasury notes and bonds. The screen shown in Exhibit 1.11 is the most widely viewed page on the Telerate network and the one most imitated by other real-time information services vendors.

Capital Market Securities

The formulae shown earlier in the chapter were applicable to securities with one cash outflow (purchase) and one inflow (redemption). Coupon-bearing securities need to be treated in a different manner because multiple cash-flow securities presume reinvestment of the interim payments prior to maturity. Few people (if any) take their coupon payments and stuff them into or under a mattress. Investors reinvest

EXHIBIT 1.10 Riding the yield curve

Date	Security	Discount	Price
March 2, 1998	3-Month T-Bill	5.00%	98.75
	6-Month T-Bill	5.20%	97.40
May 31, 1998 (90 days forward)	3-Month T-Bill	5.00%	98.75

The price of the 6-month T-Bill, if the discount is still 5.20%, would be 98.70

```
            98.75
           -98.70
           ---------
           $ .05
```
Additional income generated
from riding the yield curve

EXHIBIT 1.11 Telerate's (formerly Dow Jones) page 5

Overnight Federal Funds   On-the-Run T-Bills   Eurodollar Time Deposits   Repurchase Agreements

```
05/29    12:13 EDT   [DOW JONES TREASURY & MONEY MARKETS]              PAGE 5
[FEDERAL FUNDS    12.14][T-BILLS    12.14  YIELD][EURO$DEP 12.08][GOV RP 12.00]
BID/5 11/16 OPEN 5 11/16  3M  4.88-86 -.04  4.988  5 9/16\ -5/8   O/N 5.63-55
ASK 5   3/4 HIGH 5   3/4  6M  5.12-10 -.01  5.308  5 5/8   -11/16 1WK/5.55-52
LST 5   3/4 LOW  5 11/16  YR  5.14-12  UNC  5.401  5 3/4   -13/16 2WK 5.51-45
FUNDS SOURCE:G. GUYBUTLER [FOR ECONOMIC CALENDAR SEE PGS 21 & 22] 1MO 5.48-43
[TSY CPNS   N Y   EDT 12.14  YLD ASK][GSCI  2564.97+   3.12-DJIA 8960.99 - 9.21
05.500 05/00  99.30-31 +02        5.517][11.35 YANKEE CDS   DOM BAS][LIBOR 11.00
05.625 05/01 100.07-09 +03        5.519][BID][EARLY][LATE][EARLY][LATE] 1M 5.65625
05.500 05/03  99.25-27 +04        5.536 JUL  5.56   5.56   5.53   5.53  2M 5.68750
06.500 05/05 104.28-00 +04        5.621 AUG  5.58   5.58   5.51   5.51  3M 5.68750
05.625 05/08 100.18-22 +06        5.534 SEP  5.59   5.59   5.50   5.50  4M 5.71875
06.125 11/27 104.21-25 +16        5.785 OCT  5.61   5.61   5.50   5.50  5M 5.75000
[SPOT FOREX][CMT 4Y 5.522 7Y 5.624]      NOV  5.63   5.63   5.50   5.50  6M 5.75000
JPY 138\47| 30Y MBS JUN DELIVERY         DEC  5.65          5.50         1Y 5.87500
DEM 1.7835|GNMA 6.5   99.17-19 +05 [DEALER COMML PAPER OFFER 11.38][BANK RATES]
GBP 1.6317|GOLD 6.5   99.16-18 +04  15   5.58   60   5.51  120   5.49 PRIME  8.50
CHF 1.4819|FNMA 6.5   99.12-14 +04  30   5.52   90   5.50  180   5.48 BKR   | 7.25
```

On-the-Run Treasury Notes & Bonds   Broker Loan Rate

these proceeds in other securities to generate incremental cash flows over and above the return on the initial investment. To calculate the yield on these kinds of securities, it is necessary to consider the reinvestment or compounding activity of the security throughout its entire life. The yield calculation used to measure these returns is called yield to maturity.

Calculating Yield to Maturity

Yield to maturity represents a discount or present value rate applied to each cash flow in a fixed-income security. The sum of the present values of these cash flows, all using the same discount rate, will equal the current purchase price of the security. As mentioned, the calculation is most often used to determine the returns on coupon-bearing securities. We noted above that, according to market convention, both discount and money market yields are translated into yield to maturity, or bond equivalent yield, when comparing securities using one of the money market yield calculations with a coupon-bearing security using a yield-to-maturity calculation. The calculation, strengths, and weaknesses of yield to maturity are discussed in Chapter 2.

The following securities use yield to maturity to determine a rate of return.

1. *U.S. Treasury Notes and Bonds.* U.S. Treasury notes have a minimum maturity of 1 year and a maximum maturity of 10 years. Treasury bonds have maturity dates greater than 10 years and (at present) no longer than 30 years. The 30-year bonds came into existence in 1977. Prior to that time, the longest maturity issued by the Treasury was 20 years. As it does for Treasury Bills, the U.S. Government has an auction schedule for various note and bond maturities.

As of May 15, 1998, the Treasury issues notes and bonds on the following schedule:

- Two-Year Treasury Note is issued at the end of each month.
- Five-Year Treasury Note is issued in the middle of each calendar quarter.
- Ten-Year Treasury Note is issued in the middle of each calendar quarter.
- Thirty-Year Treasury Bond is issued on 2/15, 8/15, and 11/15.

These four maturities, along with the 13-, 26-, and 52-week T-Bills, represent the active, or *"on-the-run"* Treasury issues.

Treasury securities are usually quoted in 32nds of a point, although shorter-term coupon securities can be quoted with spreads as narrow as 1/256 of one percent of par [this is equal to $39.0625 per million par value ($1,000,000/100 = $10,000 /256)].

Interest on U.S. Treasury Notes and Bonds is accrued on an actual/actual basis (actual days in the month and actual days in the year). As a result, each coupon period may be slightly different from the previous one, although the coupon payments remain constant. The formula for calculating accrued interest during a normal coupon period is shown in Exhibit 1.12.

Odd-period accrued interest calculations may be necessary. Some securities have coupons with nonstandard coupon periods, usually either the first or last coupon period. These accrued interest calculations are similar to a standard coupon period, but there are some differences. Appendix B lists both short and long coupon period accrued interest formulae.

2. *Treasury Inflation Protection Securities (TIPS).* In January 1997, the Treasury began issuing Treasury Inflation Protection Securities, or TIPS. Their purpose is to provide investors with what amounts to an inflation-adjusted or real rate of return on investment. The securities

EXHIBIT 1.12   Calculation of accrued interest

$$\text{Accrued interest} = \frac{\dfrac{\text{Annual}}{\text{coupon rate}}}{\text{Freq}} \times \frac{\substack{\text{Days on last coupon} \\ \text{to settlement date}}}{\substack{\text{Days in current} \\ \text{coupon period}}} \times \text{Par value}$$

where: Freq = Number of coupon periods per year

Given: $1,000,000 par value 6% Treasury Note due 5/15/2005

Interest payment date = 5/15/98
Settlement date = 3/15/98
Previous coupon date = 11/15/97
Days in coupon period = 181

$$\text{Accrued interest} = \frac{6\%}{2} \times \frac{120}{181} \times \$1,000,000 = \$19,889.50$$

are structured with an inflation adjustment clause: the principal or par value of the issue is increased by the rate of inflation semiannually, on a 3-month time lag, as measured by the Consumer Price Index (CPI). To illustrate, on January 2, 1998, an investor purchases $1,000,000 par value of TIPS. During the following six months, the CPI rises a total of 3%. The par value of the security increases to $1,030,000 (3%) on October 1, 1998. The coupon on the issue remains constant. Given this relationship, the yield on the security can be viewed as an inflation-adjusted or real rate of return. This is why the yield and coupon on these securities are significantly lower than yields on noninflation-adjusted Treasury securities.

As of May 18, 1998, the following yields were offered on inflation-adjusted and non-inflation-adjusted Treasury securities:

Coupon	Maturity	Price	Yield	Inflation-Adjusted
3.625	1/15/2008	$98^{30}/_{32}$	3.76	Yes
5.500	2/15/2008	$98^{27}/_{32}$	5.66	No
3.625	7/15/2002	$98^{27}/_{32}$	3.93	Yes
6.000	7/31/2002	$101^{8}/_{32}$	5.65	No
3.625	4/15/2028	99	3.66	Yes
6.125	11/15/2027	$102^{29}/_{32}$	5.91	No

As you can see, the inflation-adjusted securities have a much lower yield than the non-inflation-adjusted issues. The reason lies in the floating value of the principal on the inflation-adjusted issue. Clearly, it is in the best interest of the U.S. Government to promote a low level of inflation when issuing these securities, because the effective cost of borrowing may be significantly reduced. Currently, tips are issued in a quarterly cycle on January 15, April 15, July 15, and October 15.

3. *Federal Agency Securities.* The composition of capital market securities of federal agencies has changed in recent years. The traditional method of financing was to periodically offer different maturity securities through a selling group made up mostly of primary dealers of U.S. Government securities. This form of financing has largely been replaced by smaller and more specialized financing techniques largely divided into structured notes and medium-term notes (MTN). Structured notes (a hybrid of medium-term notes) are essentially offerings as small as $25 million–$100 million. Typically, an investment banker

brings together a borrower and a small group of institutional investors. The structure of the notes is created to fit the needs of both the borrower and lenders. Fixed and floating rates, interest rate swaps, step coupons, call and put options, sinking funds, and other different twists may be included in these structures. Both the size and the unique structure of many of these notes make them difficult to trade after initial issuance.

Medium-term notes, like discount notes, carry the daily offering rates posted by the issuing agencies. The rates on these securities are largely a function of the issuing agency's financing needs at that particular point in time. For example, if a particular agency has a strong need for three-year money, it may be willing to pay a higher rate than the other agencies for that particular maturity. The notes are tradable in the secondary market, but the method and size of the original issuance make the limited liquidity of each issue a drawback.

Quoting conventions on federal agency securities are similar to those for U.S. Treasury issues. Accrued interest is calculated on a 30/360-day basis. The formula for accrued interest is:

$$\text{Accrued interest} = \text{Par value} \times \frac{\text{Annual coupon}}{\text{Number of coupons per year}}$$

$$\times \frac{\text{Days on last coupon to settlement date}}{\text{Days in coupon period}}$$

An example is shown in Exhibit 1.13.

EXHIBIT 1.13   Accrued interest example

Given: $1,000,000 6% FNMA due 6/21/03

Settlement date = 3/15/98
Next coupon date = 6/21/98
Days in coupon period = 180
Previous coupon date = 12/21/97

$$\text{Accrued interest} = \$1,000,000 \times \frac{.06}{2} \times \frac{84}{180} = \$14,000.00$$

4. *Corporate Bonds.* Both domestic and international corporate notes and bonds issued with the full faith and credit of the corporation are in the form of debentures or medium-term notes. Maturities range from 1 year to 100 years. In fact, one issuer, Safra Republic Holdings, issued debt in 1997 with a maturity of 1,000 years! The securities mature in the year 2997. Talk about leaving debts to your children!

Among other forms of corporate bonds, the most popular are mortgage bonds (not to be confused with mortgage-backed securities). Mortgage bonds, usually sold by utilities, are used to finance plant and equipment purchased by the utilities. The mortgages are on these fixed assets. Maturities range up to 40 years. Other collateralized corporate securities include railroad equipment trust certificates. Corporations also issue debt securities with floating coupon rates, put and call options, and a sinking fund, or a periodic paydown of principal over the life of the security. Convertible debt gives the investor the opportunity to convert bonds into common stock of the issuing company at a predetermined price established at the time of the bond issuance. It also allows the corporation to move company funding from the liability side of the balance sheet to stockholders' equity, albeit at the cost of further diversifying ownership. See Chapter 6 for an in-depth discussion of convertible bonds and securities issued with uncertain or contingent cash flows.

Corporate medium-term notes, like the federal agencies, are issued on a day-to-day basis. They are authorized through a shelf registration process; the issuing company can sell a certain amount of these securities for a period of two years. Offering rates are established daily, in line with borrowing needs. Maturities on these securities, traditionally set up to 10 years, have changed with the financing needs of the issuers. At least one MTN issuer recently sold a maturity of 100 years.

Corporate bond quoting is usually in eighths of a point. For example, a GM bond could have a quote of 98⅜–98⅝. Medium-term note offerings by a corporate issuer are usually posted on a yield-to-maturity basis. Like federal agency securities, interest on corporate debt securities is calculated on a 30/360-day basis (see Exhibit 1.14).

5. *Municipal Notes and Bonds.* The most popular form of municipal bond is the noncollateralized General Obligation (GO) bond, backed by the full faith and credit of the municipality. A revenue stream backs some issues, known as Revenue bonds, from a specific municipal project.

EXHIBIT 1.14   Accrued interest on a corporate bond

Given: $1,000,000 ABC 6% due 5/1/2001
Settlement date = 3/1/98
Next coupon date = 5/1/98
Last coupon date = 11/1/97

$$\text{Accrued interest} = \$1,000,000 \times \frac{.06}{2} \times \frac{120}{180} = \$20,000.00$$

Corporations team up with municipalities and issue tax-exempt bonds for funding projects that benefit both the corporations and the municipalities. These are called Industrial Revenue or Industrial Development bonds.

Like federal agency and corporate debt, the coupon rate on a municipal bond can be fixed, or floating with periodic resets. The securities are quoted with either a dollar price or a yield to maturity minus some discount. For example, a price of 6.75% − ¼ translates into a price based on yield to maturity of 6.75% less ¼ point, or $2.50 per $1,000 bond. Accrued interest is usually calculated on a 30/360-day basis.

Appendix A summarizes the day count basis for accrued interest calculations on U.S. capital markets securities and some of the major international capital market instruments.

Other Measures of Yield

Yield to Call

Like yield to maturity, yield to call calculates an annualized return using the same input parameters. The only difference is the maturity date, and perhaps a higher redemption value as an investment incentive, to reflect any call privileges stipulated in the securities indenture. For example, a 10-year note may be issued with a 3-year call feature. This means that, at the end of 3 years, the issuer may choose to call (redeem) the security at some predefined price. There is a reasonably reliable way to determine whether a security with discrete, or fixed, call dates will be redeemed early. If the current yield to maturity is lower than the stated coupon rate of the security (trading at a price above 100), investors are willing to accept a lower rate of return for this security than when the security was first issued. Suppose, for example, a 10-year security, callable in 3 years at a price of 100, was issued with a coupon rate of 8%. On the call date, the current yield to maturity required by the marketplace to purchase the issue is 6%. The security would theoretically trade at a premium to par, or at more than 100% of face value.[3] The issuer could redeem the bonds and reissue them at a lower coupon rate with a similar final maturity date.[4] (See Exhibit 1.15.)

Yield to Worst

This is simply a way to determine the worst return that can be earned on a callable security. Yield to maturity and any yield-to-call dates are calculated. The lowest of the yields is considered yield to worst.

True Yield

The calculation of the various types of yield mentioned above presumes that cash flows will be received on their appointed dates. In most cases, this does occur. But what happens if a payment date falls on a weekend or holiday? Issuers do not pay additional interest, nor interest on interest, when payment is delayed as a result of a weekend or holiday. For example, if an issue is scheduled to mature on Saturday, October 11 (10/11), the investor will not get paid until Tuesday, 10/14. Sunday, 10/12, is a weekend day, and banks are closed to celebrate Columbus Day on Monday, 10/13. The investor loses the use of the money for three days, so the actual yield on this security needs to be adjusted to reflect the loss of three days' interest. The true yield on the security needs to include the three non-interest-bearing days.

It is important to know how to quickly recognize the degree of impact of weekends and holidays on streams of cash flows. The rule of

EXHIBIT 1.15 Redemption and reissue of callable bonds

Bond XYZ: 8% due 10/15/2007; issue date: 10/15/1997
Callable on 10/15/2000 at 100
Yield to maturity on 10/15/2000 = 6% (the 10-year note is now a 7-year note)

The issuer should redeem the 8% bonds at 100 and reissue 7-year notes at a yield of approximately 6%. This saves 2% (200 basis points) per annum in funding costs.

thumb is simple: The further out in time a cash flow is scheduled for payment, the less impact any delay in that payment will have on present value and yield.

Exhibit 1.16 reflects the yield differential between the standard yield calculation and true yield. If 9/6 had been a business day, the investor would have received both the final coupon and the principal payments on 9/6. The issuer is obligated to pay interest only through 9/6. The standard yield formula would calculate the 5.376% return based on 9/6 being the repayment date. In this case, however, 9/6 is a Saturday, so the investor won't receive payment until Monday, 9/8. The investor will receive no interest for 9/6 and 9/7. The actual return calculation needs to add two days to maturity, using the cash flow that should have been received on 9/6. Remember, simply adding two days to the standard formula will automatically presume interest earned for that additional period.

In Exhibit 1.16, the yield will be based on the $4,430.56 earned between 8/7 and 9/6 but payable over the period from 8/7 to 9/8. The difference between the standard yield calculation and true yield is:

Standard yield:	5.376%
True yield:	− 5.03%
	.346% or 34.6 basis points

The investor is actually earning 34.6 basis points less than the standard yield calculation. A good way to estimate the difference between true

---

EXHIBIT 1.16   Standard yield versus true yield calculations

An investor purchases a FNMA bond with only one month remaining to maturity.

Maturity date = 9/6/1997 (Saturday)
Par (face) values = $1,000,000
Coupon rate = 5½%
Settlement date = 8/7/1997
Price = 100 + accrued interest
Yield = 5.376%°
True yield = 5.03%

° The annualized rate of return on this issue takes into account total purchase price (principal + accrued interest).

yield and standard yield to maturity is to divide the number of days an investment is actually earning interest by the actual number of days until that cash flow is received. In Exhibit 1.16, the FNMA bond is earning interest for 30 days, but the interest and principal will not be returned for 32 days. If the yield to maturity is multiplied by 30/32, or .9375, the adjustment for true yield is 5.04%—only one basis point different from the actual calculation.

As mentioned above, the impact of weekend or holiday dates on interest and principal payments gets smaller as the time is extended. As a practical matter, any bad end dates past 2 years from the settlement date will have little if any effect on actual rates of return, because of the declining impact of changes in present values on more distant coupon or principal payment dates.

Current Yield

Current yield is simply the annual rate of return divided by the price of the security. If a security has an annual interest coupon of 6% and a price of 98, the current yield is 6.16%:

$$\text{Coupon price} = \frac{6}{98} = 6.16\%$$

Current yield should not normally be used to calculate rates of return on fixed-income securities because it doesn't account for present valuing or reinvestment of cash flows.[5] If, in this example, the maturity of the security were 3 years, the yield to maturity would be 6.748%. A 10-year maturity would be 6.272%.

SECURITIES FINANCING

Purchasing securities from funds on hand requires withdrawing necessary funds and transferring them to the seller. However, purchasing securities with no available funds entails a little more ingenuity. Many traders finance their purchases through the *repurchase agreement* market. "Repos," as they are called on the street, represent collateralized lending agreements. The owner of securities puts them up as collateral

EXHIBIT 1.17   Overnight securities financing

Buy $1 million U.S. Treasury bonds 6⅜% due 11/15/2027 @ 103.125 for settlement 5/1/98

Overnight repo cost = 5%

$$\begin{aligned} \text{Principal} &= \$1,031,250.00 \\ \text{Accrued interest} &= 28,256.22 \\ \text{Total} \quad &\$1,059,506.22 \end{aligned}$$

Overnight funding cost $= \text{Repo rate} \times \text{Principal} + \text{Interest} \times \dfrac{\text{Number of days}}{360}$

$$= 5\% \times \$1,059,256.22 \times \left(\frac{1}{360} \right) = \$147.15$$

Accrued interest (AI) for 1 day = $169.20 = AI on 5/2/98 − AI on 5/1/98 (see Exhibit 1.8)

Net positive carry = $169.20 - 147.15 = **$22.05 per million par value.**
The trader is earning $22.05 per million par value per day at this funding rate.

to borrow a dollar amount roughly equivalent to their market value.[6] The tenor, or length of the borrowing is usually very short; many agreements last only overnight. Repurchase agreements lasting more than one business day are called "term repos." Repos can also be viewed as a short-term investment. An investor may be willing to lend funds against securities for one or more days, if given a favorable interest rate. The borrower of funds is entering into a repurchase agreement. The lender of funds is conducting a *reverse repurchase agreement.*

The interest calculation on repurchase agreements is accrued on an actual/360-day basis. The net interest cost or *carry* to the borrower is the difference between the accrued interest on the security and the cost of financing. The carry is positive if the accrued interest is greater than the financing cost. Negative carry occurs when the financing cost exceeds the accrued interest. Exhibit 1.17 reflects the formulae and calculation of accrued interest and carry on an overnight repo.

SUMMARY

This chapter has covered the concept of yield. It began with an outline of the factors that determine yield, and discussed the reasons for the inverse relationship between price and yield in a fixed-income security. Discount, money market yield, and yield to maturity were defined. Various other yield measurements used to represent returns were defined, as were the money market and capital market instruments that are measured using these yields. True yield, or yield adjusted for weekend and holiday principal and interest payment dates, was was defined. The shorter the maturity, the more impact true yield has on actual returns. Positive or negative carry is a function of the relationship between accrued interest and funding costs.

NOTES

1. This is one form of yield curve. See Chapter 5 for a further discussion and comparison of this structure to yield curves that have other shapes.
2. Privately placed CP is issued in maturities up to 360 days.
3. When relationships like this occur, the marketplace will normally reprice a security using the call date as the maturity date. See Chapter 6 for additional information on callable securities.
4. Refinancing costs must also be taken into consideration.
5. Current yield is used for preferred stock. Although this is considered an equity, a certain annual dividend must be paid.
6. Securities used as collateral are subject to what is referred to as a "haircut"—a reduction in the value for collateral purposes. Each collateral position is marketed to market on a daily basis. The more creditworthy the security, the higher the collateral value after the haircut. U.S. Treasury securities have a collateralized value above 90% of market value.

2 THE CONCEPT OF YIELD

As discussed in Chapter 1, yield to maturity represents the discount rate that is applied to all cash flows of a security. This rate reduces the value of each future cash flow (future value) back to its present value. The sum of these present values equals the purchase price of the security. Yield to maturity represents the basic calculation used to measure and evaluate other functions and risk factors in fixed-income analysis. Although it is widely used in the investment industry, there are some inherent weaknesses in the calculation. It is very important to understand these weaknesses when evaluating the validity of the returns projected by the yield to maturity concept.

CALCULATING PRICE AND YIELD ON CAPITAL MARKET SECURITIES

To understand the yield to maturity calculation, it is first necessary to note how the price of a coupon security is calculated, given its yield to maturity.

The Price formula (given the yield to maturity) for a noncallable security with a bullet (single) principal payment at maturity is:

$$\text{Price} = \sum_{t=1}^{nc}\left[C_t / (1 + (i/n))^t\right] + \left[P / (1 + (i/n)^{nc})\right] - \text{AI}$$

where: t = time period a cash flow is received (purchase date = T_0),
nc = total number of compounding periods in the security,
n = number of compounding or interest payment dates per annum,
C = coupon payment received,
i = yield to maturity,
P = principal payment received on the maturity date of the security,
AI = accrued interest per \$100 par value (price includes accrued interest).

Exhibit 2.1 shows how the price of a bond is determined. This calculation is reasonably straightforward, but a number of additional considerations must be taken into account. The following list highlights all the information necessary to calculate price or yield on a coupon-bearing security:

- *Coupon.* The coupon or nominal interest rate of the security.
- *Maturity.* The final maturity date of the security.

EXHIBIT 2.1   Pricing a 5-year corporate bond

Given: Corporation ABC bond, \$1,000,000 par value with a 7% coupon, maturity date of 2/1/2003, purchase (settlement) date of 2/1/1998, and yield to maturity of 7.5%. The price of the security is:

Cash Flow	Date	Present Value Factor @ 7½%	Present Value
\$ 35,000	8/1/98	.963855	\$ 33,734.94
35,000	2/1/99	.929017	32,515.60
35,000	8/1/99	.895438	31,340.34
35,000	2/1/00	.863073	30,207.56
35,000	8/1/00	.831878	29,115.72
35,000	2/1/01	.801810	28,063.34
35,000	8/1/01	.772829	27,049.01
35,000	2/1/02	.744895	26,071.33
35,000	8/1/02	.717971	25,128.99
35,000	2/1/03	.692020	24,220.72
1,000,000	2/1/03	.692020	692,020.00
Present value =			\$979,467.55

The price of the bond is \$97.946755.

- *Settlement Date.* The day the purchaser pays for the securities. In the case of a new issue, the dated date (the day the security begins accruing interest).
- *First Coupon Date.* Some securities, particularly in the first or last coupon period, are structured with long or short coupon periods. This will have an impact on the discount factor and present value of the cash flow associated with that time period. As a practical matter, any difference in the first coupon period will have a greater effect on the price than a difference in the final coupon period. For example, prior to the implementation of monthly 5-year Treasury note auctions, the 5-year notes were issued quarterly with a first coupon period lasting about 7½ months. This clearly had an impact on the present value of the first coupon payment on the issue date of the note.
- *Interest Accrual Basis.* As discussed in Chapter 1, interest can be accrued on a bond in a number of ways. The presumed number of days in a month and a year can be different. *30/360* assumes 30-day months and 360-day years. *Actual/360* assumes the actual number of days in each month, but 360 days per year. *Actual/Actual* assumes the actual number of days in each month and the actual number of days in the year.
- *Number of Days in Each Month and the Current Coupon Period.* This is important for securities that use the actual/actual and actual/360 interest bases. The numbers will vary.
- *Redemption Value.* The final maturity value of the principal amount of a security.
- *Number of Coupon Periods per Annum.* The number is two for nearly every fixed-income security. Mortgage-backed securities pay interest twelve times per year, coordinating with the principal and interest payments made by the mortgagees. We will consider the implications of compounding frequencies in a later section of this chapter.
- *Price* (excluding accrued interest). Used to calculate yield.
- *Yield.* Used to calculate price, excluding accrued interest.

There are several additional considerations regarding the price formula on page 29.

1. The formula presumes one principal payment on the final maturity date of the security. Some securities (e.g., sinking fund bonds) periodically pay down the principal over the life of the security. In these cases, each principal payment needs to be present valued by the discount factor for the period in which the payment is received.

2. Price and yield are calculated as of a purchase, or settlement, date. This is the day the investor pays for the securities, and interest on them begins accruing to the purchaser. Because many purchases are not made on a coupon payment date or the issue date of the security, the discount factors will actually reflect portions of periods.

3. Most fixed-income securities have a maturity value of 100. If, however, a security is priced to a call or put date, or if the principal value of the security is tied to some index (such as the inflation-indexed Treasury securities noted in Chapter 1) the redemption value may not be 100.

4. As mentioned above, different types of securities have different day-count bases. This variety doesn't directly affect price, but it does impact the accrued interest calculation. For example, for accrued interest purposes, the number of days between 2/15/98 and 2/15/99 is: 360 days under the 30/360 method and 365 under the actual/actual method. The annual interest payment remains the same, but the daily accrual factors change as a result of the calculated number of days in the year.

As noted above, the yield to maturity serves as a singular discount rate applied to all the cash flows in the security. The price an investor pays to purchase a fixed-income security is simply the sum of the present value of its cash flows (all coupons plus principal payments), plus any accrued interest. In the formula on page 29, the denominator, or the factor used to convert future value to present value, is equal to 1 plus the yield to maturity, divided by the payment frequency per annum. This value is multiplied by itself the same number of times as the period in which the cash flow will be received. If a cash flow were due in the fifth period, it would be divided by 1 + the yield to maturity, divided by the payment frequency per annum. This expression is then raised to the fifth power to reflect compounding. (See Exhibit 2.2.)

EXHIBIT 2.2   Present value calculation of a specified cash flow within a coupon bearing security

A cash flow (coupon of 8%) of a semiannual paying security, received in the fifth period (2½ years after issuance) on $1,000 par value with a yield to maturity of 7% equals:

$$\frac{\$40}{\left(1+\left(\frac{.07}{2}\right)\right)^5} = \frac{\$40}{\left(1+\left(\frac{.07}{2}\right)\right)\left(1+\left(\frac{.07}{2}\right)\right)\left(1+\left(\frac{.07}{2}\right)\right)\left(1+\left(\frac{.07}{2}\right)\right)\left(1+\left(\frac{.07}{2}\right)\right)}$$

$$= \frac{\$40}{1.187686}$$

$$= \$33.68$$

The *longer* the maturity of the cash flow, the *larger* the discount factor and the smaller the present value. The principal cash flow would be discounted by the last or highest period, because redemption occurs at the maturity date of the issue. It is important to note that the majority of real-world price and yield calculations are performed between coupon periods. This means interest has been accrued and must be added to the equation to get the actual or full purchase price of the security. The accrued interest (AI) was added into the price formula for that reason. It also means that the value of the time used to determine the discount factor will be a combination of whole coupon periods and fractions of periods.

Another set of definitions for price on a fixed-income security uses the terms "clean" and "dirty" prices. The clean price is the sum of the present value of all the future cash flows. The dirty price includes accrued interest.

Exhibit 2.3 shows how price plus accrued interest is calculated for a coupon-bearing corporate security.

The yield to maturity calculation is somewhat more involved. There is no simple formula, as there is for price, that one can use to calculate yield. The price of a security is equal to the sum of the cash flows, where each is discounted by the same rate. Being able to calculate yield requires knowing the present value of each cash flow associated with a security. To mitigate this problem, an iterative technique is used to essentially perform a scientific "hunt-and-peck" search to find the yield that equates to the given price. What actually occurs is repetitive price

EXHIBIT 2.3

Issuer: XYZ Corporation	Number of coupon periods per annum: 2
Coupon: 6%	First coupon date: 5/15/1998
Maturity: 11/15/2000	Redemption value: 100
Dated date: 11/15/1997	Settlement date: 12/15/1997
Par value: $1,000	Yield to maturity: 6.25%

The first coupon payment on 5/15/98 represents a discount factor calculated between the settlement date and the coupon date. For a corporate bond accruing on a 30/360-day basis, the number of days of accrued interest between 11/15/97 and 12/15/97 is 30:

11/15/97 – 11/30/97 = 16   (includes the dated date)

$\dfrac{12/1/97 - 12/15/97 \ = 14}{30}$ (doesn't include the settlement date, which is the date the new owner begins accruing interest)

There are 150 days remaining in the first coupon period. Therefore, the first discount factor would be $1/(1 + (.0625 \div 2))^{150/180} = .974683$. Because the day-count basis is 30/360, the next discount factor would add 180 days to the numerator of the first period exponent, or 330/180.

Date	Cash Flow	Amount		Present Value Discount Factor	Present Value
5/15/98	Cpn Int	$ 30.00	150/180	.974683	$ 29.24
11/15/98	Cpn Int	30.00	330/180	.945147	28.35
5/15/99	Cpn Int	30.00	510/180	.916506	27.50
11/15/99	Cpn Int	30.00	690/180	.888733	26.66
5/15/00	Cpn Int	30.00	870/180	.861802	25.85
11/15/00	Cpn Int	30.00	1,050/180	.835687	25.07
11/15/00	Principal	1,000.00	1,050/180	.835687	835.69
Total (purchase price) =					$998.36

$998.36 – 5.00 (accured interest) = $993.36 principal value.

Each of the discount factors reduces the future cash flow to its present value. Remember, the price of a fixed-income security is nothing more than the sum of the present values of all cash flows included in the security.

calculations using different yield values, where each one creates a price that is compared to that given by the user. Each calculation, or iteration, gets closer to a yield that will generate a present value equal to the given price. Once a price is statistically close enough to satisfy the equation parameters (usually, between five and nine decimal places), the yield is posted. A number of different iterative routines can be used to derive yield. Two of the more popular techniques are the Newton-Raphson method and the Secant method.[1]

The iteration process works in two stages. The first stage estimates the yield on a security.[2] This estimate is then plugged into the iteration formula. The second stage is essentially a routine where different yield-to-maturity values are plugged into the price formula. Then, through either a linear or nonlinear routine, the yield estimates move closer to an acceptable level of difference between the price generated by the estimated yield and the input price. The formulae allow for a difference of perhaps less than .00000001 between the yield estimate and the current estimate, which is sufficiently close.

Yield to Maturity: Fact or Fantasy?

As previously mentioned, yield to maturity is a reasonable tool for evaluating future returns to the investor. One flaw, however, must be addressed. The yield to maturity formula assumes reinvestment of all cash flows at the same rate as that calculated from the purchase price on the purchase date. In other words, if an investor purchased a 30-year Treasury bond at a yield of 6½%, the reinvestment rate for every coupon payment received over the life of the bond is presumed to be 6½% for the period from receipt of the first coupon payment until the maturity date of the bond. If you believe that, have I got a bridge to sell you!

REALIZED COMPOUND YIELD

The good news is that the investor can do something to mitigate this potentially misrepresentative calculation. *Realized compound yield* (RCY), a term first used by Sidney Homer and Martin Leibowitz,[3] is a total return concept where the investor is allowed to specify one or more external rates of return on the cash flows received from a fixed-income security. RCY helps to adjust return calculations to the reality of the marketplace.

Let's assume the current yield to maturity on a five-year U.S. Treasury note is 5.5%. According to the yield-to-maturity formula, a purchase at this yield would earn a 5.5% return on all coupon payments received from this security. Actually achieving this return is remote at best, but we can look at what the marketplace is expecting these rates of return to be as of today. The process is a little involved, but the exercise is valuable in seeing the potentially large danger in accepting a yield to maturity as a valid rate of return over the life of a security.

There are two ways of determining expected rates of return in the future: (1) the interest rate futures and forward rate markets represent expectations for rates of return to be received in the future, or (2) the U.S. Treasury yield curve itself can be a barometer of future value. In both approaches, it is necessary to understand the concepts of *break-even* forward interest rates and *market efficiency* to be able to read expected futures interest rates. The rates for the term between today and the start of the forward period, and between today and the end of the forward period can be used to calculate break-even forward rates. The concept of market efficiency means that the determination of market price and yield of each security takes into account other related interest rates. If some form of available arbitrage would lock in a profit with no change in risk, market prices would readjust to eliminate this arbitrage. For example, if the combination of a 1-year cash purchase and a 1-year forward purchase beginning in 1 year would generate a higher return than purchasing a 2-year maturity, the marketplace would either increase the prices of the 1-year cash and forwards or reduce the price of the 2-year cash, or effect a combination of both. The U.S. Treasury market can also be used to determine forward rates. For example, if a 2-year note yields 5.75% and a 3-year note yields 5.90%, the 1-year Treasury rate starting 2 years from now can be derived. Like the deposit example above, the logic is simple. If an investor could purchase a 2-year note today and lock into a 1-year rate of return starting in 2 years, the combination of which would generate a higher overall rate of return than simply purchasing a 3-year note today, the investor would logically buy the 2-year note and 1-year forward rate. Therefore, to eliminate any arbitrage potential, the 1-year forward rate in this case must be at a level that would make the investor indifferent to transacting either alternative. These concepts will be discussed in greater detail in Chapter 7.

Let's get back to realized compound yield. By substituting expected forward interest rates for the yield to maturity in each coupon period, an investor can get a better sense of what the actual yield to maturity will be. Keep in mind that realized compound yield can be a function of what the marketplace believes future interest rates will be as of today. If the investor can lock in these rates today, then realized compound yield becomes a reality. In most cases, however, this process is somewhere between difficult and impossible. There is the issue of basis risk, or the impact of small mismatches of cash flow payment dates and corresponding reinvestment opportunities. There is also the uncertainty of being able to lock in every required forward rate associated with a particular security. The longer and more distant the start date and final maturity of the required forward rate period, the more illiquid the forward market becomes. These rates may be available through a customized financing package from a securities dealer, but, like anything else you purchase, the more customization, the more expense.

Let's say the investor does purchase a customized reinvestment package, and, somewhere in the middle of the maturity period, needs to sell or reverse the transaction. The only outlet the investor can realistically enlist to sell the reinvestment package is the dealer who put it together. Given the nature of the transaction, the spread between bid and offer will most likely be very wide, probably resulting in some level of loss, or at least an additional opportunity cost.

The bottom line is: It is difficult to efficiently lock in forward reinvestment rates on most coupon-bearing securities. As mentioned above, many investors make an educated guess as to what the *average reinvestment rate* for a security will be. They then use this rate as an externally specified reinvestment rate in calculating yield to maturity. The difference in the calculation is that the yield to maturity at purchase date is replaced with the external rate for all cash flows expected to be received prior to the maturity date.[4] Exhibit 2.4 reflects the impact of using realized compound yield in place of yield to maturity. The wider the difference between the reinvestment rate and stated yield to maturity, the wider the difference in returns.

HORIZON ANALYSIS

When yield to maturity is calculated on a security, it is assumed that the security will be held until maturity. In many instances, this is not the case. There are many reasons why an investor may not hold an investment until maturity. Suffice it to say that determining the return for

EXHIBIT 2.4   Impact of externally specified reinvestment rates on yield to maturity

Coupon = 8%
Maturity = 4/1/2003
Settlement date = 3/1/98
Yield to maturity = 8.242%

Reinvestment Rate	Realized Compound Yield	Difference from Yield to Maturity
5.242%	7.699%	−.543%
6.242	7.876	−.366
7.242	8.057	−.185
8.242	8.242	—
9.242	8.431	+.189
10.242	8.659	+.417
11.242	8.857	+.615

the time the investment is owned is just as important. This time period, which yields a *holding period return,* can be calculated using a technique known as *horizon analysis.*

Aside from the standard parameters needed to calculate a coupon security price or yield, a holding period return calculation requires a horizon (sale date) price and a coupon reinvestment rate (if applicable). The horizon dollar return is equal to the sum of: the difference between the purchase price and the sale price, the coupon interest income, and interest on the coupon interest paid out during the holding period. As we noted above, using the yield to maturity as the reinvestment rate can generate returns that are significantly different from actual experience. The more slope there is in the yield curve, the more this is true. Consider the following example. On 11/15/92, an investor purchases a U.S. Treasury bond at a yield of 8½%. The coupon is 8%, and it matures on 11/15/2021. The investor holds the bond until 11/15/1997 and then projects that it will be sold at a yield of 7½%. It is actually sold at a yield to maturity of 6½%. During the holding period, the investor received 10 semiannual coupons. The actual reinvestment rate for the coupons turned out to be 5½%.

Exhibit 2.5 compares holding period returns using both 7½% (projected rate; case 1) and 6½% (actual rate; case 2) as sale date assumptions. A no-change scenario for the horizon date yield to maturity

EXHIBIT 2.5   Impacts of changes in reinvestment rate and horizon date yield to maturity on holding period return

Purchase with Yield to Maturity = $8\frac{1}{2}$%; Coupon = 8%

Assumptions	√ Case 1	√ Case 2	√ Case 3	Case 4
Reinvestment rate	5.50%	5.50%	5.50%	8.50%
Horizon (sale date) yield to maturity	7.50	6.50	8.50	8.50
Horizon return (realized compound yield)	9.38	10.98	7.93	8.50

√ = Externally specified reinvestment rate.

is in case 3. Case 4 assumes reinvestment at the original yield to maturity and no change in the horizon (sale date) yield to maturity.

As you can see, reducing the reinvestment rate on the coupon payments reduces the actual holding period return. The lower the yield on the sale, or horizon, date, the bigger the capital gain on the transaction. You probably noticed that estimating the reinvestment rate to determine the holding period yield is equivalent to calculating the realized compound yield on a security held to maturity. The only difference is in the length of the holding period.

Horizon analysis is a helpful tool for analyzing both individual holdings and portfolios of securities. Investors can periodically review their securities positions and can estimate the reinvestment rates on the cash flows generated from those investments and the horizon (or maturity) sale prices to determine the realized compound yield on the portfolio. Most large, real-time information services vendors and spreadsheet add-in software developers have functions that make this procedure relatively painless. Some of these vendors and their products are reviewed in Chapter 12.

CONSTANT MATURITY YIELD

Every week and every month, the Federal Reserve publishes statistical releases (designated H.15 and G.13, respectively[5]) titled "Selected Interest Rates." In each report, money market, U.S. Treasury, and several other benchmark fixed-income yields are posted (see Exhibit 2.6).

EXHIBIT 2.6   Sample page from a Federal Reserve statistical release

FEDERAL RESERVE statistical release

These data are released the first Tuesday of each month. The availability of the release is announced on (202) 452-3206.

G.13 (415)

SELECTED INTEREST RATES

Yields in percent per annum

For immediate release
August 4, 1998

Instruments	Week Ending					Jun	Jul
	Jul 3	Jul 10	Jul 17	Jul 24	Jul 31		
Federal funds (effective) [1][2][3]	5.88	5.47	5.49	5.50	5.54	5.56	5.54
Commercial paper [3][4][5][6]							
Nonfinancial							
1-month	5.53	5.50	5.50	5.51	5.52	5.51	5.51
2-month	5.53	5.50	5.50	5.50	5.50	5.50	5.50
3-month	5.48	5.48	5.48	5.48	5.50	5.48	5.48
Financial							
1-month	5.55	5.52	5.51	5.52	5.54	5.53	5.52
2-month	5.54	5.51	5.51	5.51	5.51	5.52	5.51
3-month	5.51	5.50	5.50	5.50	5.51	5.50	5.50
Bankers acceptances (top rated) [3][4][7]							
3-month	5.53	5.50	5.50	5.49	5.49	5.50	5.50
6-month	5.48	5.45	5.49	5.44	5.46	5.47	5.46
CDs (secondary market) [3][8]							
1-month	5.59	5.56	5.57	5.57	5.57	5.57	5.57
3-month	5.60	5.59	5.59	5.59	5.60	5.60	5.59
6-month	5.67	5.64	5.64	5.65	5.65	5.65	5.65
Eurodollar deposits (London) [3][9]							
1-month	5.55	5.51	5.51	5.51	5.51	5.53	5.51
3-month	5.59	5.56	5.56	5.56	5.56	5.57	5.57
6-month	5.64	5.63	5.63	5.63	5.63	5.62	5.63
Bank prime loan [2][3][10]	8.50	8.50	8.50	8.50	8.50	8.50	8.50
Discount window borrowing [2][11]	5.00	5.00	5.00	5.00	5.00	5.00	5.00
U.S. government securities							
Treasury bills							
Auction average [3][4][12]							
3-month	5.00	4.96	4.98	4.95	4.92	4.99	4.96
6-month	5.06	5.01	5.03	5.05	5.02	5.12	5.03
1-year			5.10	5.13	5.10		
Secondary market [3][4]							
3-month	4.94	4.94	5.01	4.96	4.95	4.98	4.96
6-month	5.03	5.02	5.04	5.04	5.01	5.12	5.03
1-year	5.10	5.07	5.08	5.08	5.09	5.13	5.08
Treasury constant maturities [13]							
3-month	5.11	5.08	5.15	5.08	5.07	5.12	5.09
6-month	5.23	5.23	5.23	5.25	5.21	5.32	5.23
1-year	5.38	5.34	5.36	5.36	5.37	5.41	5.36
2-year	5.48	5.43	5.46	5.47	5.48	5.52	5.46
3-year	5.49	5.44	5.48	5.47	5.48	5.52	5.47
5-year	5.46	5.41	5.47	5.47	5.51	5.52	5.46
7-year	5.51	5.47	5.54	5.52	5.56	5.56	5.52
10-year	5.44	5.41	5.49	5.46	5.50	5.50	5.46
20-year	5.73	5.71	5.82	5.79	5.83	5.80	5.78
30-year	5.63	5.61	5.71	5.68	5.73	5.70	5.68
Composite							
Over 10 years (long-term) [14]	5.71	5.69	5.80	5.77	5.81	5.78	5.76
Corporate bonds							
Moody's seasoned							
Aaa	6.51	6.48	6.58	6.56	6.60	6.53	6.55 *
Baa	7.11	7.09	7.17	7.15	7.20	7.13	7.15 *
A-utility [15]	6.87	6.89	6.98	6.92	7.04	6.98	6.93
State & local bonds [16]	5.09	5.12	5.17	5.16	5.16	5.12	5.14
Conventional mortgages [17]	6.98	6.91	6.94	6.96	6.97	7.00	6.95

* These rates were not available in time to appear on the H.15 release published on August 3, 1998.

(Continued)

EXHIBIT 2.6   (Continued)

G.13 (415)
Selected Interest Rates
Yields in percent per annum

Federal Reserve Board
August 4, 1998

	Fed funds	Comm paper 1-mo.	— Treasury bills — 3-mo.	6-mo.	1-yr.	Treasury constant maturities 3-mo.	6-mo.	1-yr.	2-yr.	3-yr.	5-yr.	7-yr.	10-yr.	20-yr.	30-yr.
Jul 1	6.35	5.53	4.96	5.02	5.09	5.09	5.22	5.37	5.46	5.47	5.43	5.50	5.44	5.73	5.63
Jul 2	5.62	5.51	4.94	4.97	5.07	5.07	5.17	5.35	5.44	5.46	5.43	5.47	5.42	5.70	5.60
Jul 3 *	5.41														
Jul 6	5.54	5.50	4.93	4.98	5.07	5.09	5.23	5.34	5.43	5.43	5.40	5.45	5.39	5.68	5.57
Jul 7	5.46	5.50	4.95	5.04	5.08	5.08	5.24	5.35	5.44	5.46	5.43	5.48	5.42	5.70	5.60
Jul 8	5.44	5.50	4.96	5.05	5.07	5.09	5.25	5.34	5.44	5.46	5.43	5.49	5.43	5.73	5.63
Jul 9	5.51	5.50	4.94	5.03	5.06	5.07	5.23	5.33	5.43	5.42	5.40	5.46	5.41	5.71	5.60
Jul 10	5.43	5.50	4.93	5.02	5.06	5.06	5.22	5.33	5.41	5.42	5.40	5.47	5.42	5.73	5.63
Jul 13	5.50	5.50	4.96	5.05	5.08	5.13	5.23	5.35	5.44	5.46	5.45	5.52	5.46	5.80	5.68
Jul 14	5.45	5.49	5.02	5.04	5.08	5.16	5.24	5.36	5.46	5.48	5.47	5.54	5.49	5.82	5.72
Jul 15	5.70	5.50	5.01	5.02	5.07	5.14	5.22	5.35	5.46	5.47	5.46	5.53	5.48	5.82	5.70
Jul 16	5.57	5.51	5.03	5.04	5.09	5.17	5.24	5.38	5.46	5.49	5.48	5.56	5.50	5.83	5.72
Jul 17	5.42	5.50	5.01	5.04	5.09	5.14	5.24	5.37	5.46	5.48	5.49	5.57	5.51	5.85	5.75
Jul 20	5.65	5.50	5.00	5.05	5.09	5.09	5.26	5.37	5.46	5.47	5.47	5.53	5.48	5.83	5.71
Jul 21	5.51	5.51	4.96	5.05	5.09	5.09	5.25	5.37	5.46	5.47	5.46	5.52	5.45	5.78	5.67
Jul 22	5.48	5.51	4.94	5.04	5.09	5.07	5.24	5.37	5.48	5.48	5.47	5.52	5.46	5.79	5.68
Jul 23	5.55	5.52	4.96	5.04	5.07	5.09	5.24	5.35	5.46	5.47	5.46	5.52	5.45	5.77	5.66
Jul 24	5.53	5.51	4.95	5.04	5.08	5.08	5.24	5.36	5.48	5.47	5.48	5.52	5.45	5.79	5.68
Jul 27	5.68	5.51	4.96	5.04	5.08	5.06	5.22	5.36	5.48	5.47	5.49	5.54	5.47	5.81	5.70
Jul 28	5.50	5.52	4.94	5.00	5.07	5.07	5.20	5.35	5.46	5.47	5.49	5.56	5.50	5.84	5.74
Jul 29	5.49	5.52	4.94	5.01	5.09	5.07	5.21	5.37	5.49	5.49	5.52	5.59	5.52	5.87	5.77
Jul 30	5.61	5.52	4.94	5.01	5.10	5.07	5.21	5.38	5.49	5.49	5.52	5.56	5.50	5.82	5.73
Jul 31	5.63	5.53	4.97	5.01	5.10	5.10	5.21	5.38	5.49	5.48	5.52	5.56	5.50	5.81	5.72

* Market closed

FOOTNOTES

1. The daily effective federal funds rate is a weighted average of rates on trades through N.Y. brokers.
2. Weekly figures are averages of 7 calendar days ending on Wednesday of the current week; monthly figures include each calendar day in the month.
3. Annualized using a 360-day year or bank interest.
4. On a discount basis.
5. Interest rates interpolated from data on certain commercial paper trades settled by The Depository Trust Company. The trades represent sales of commercial paper by dealers or direct issuers to investors (that is, the offer side). See Board's Commercial Paper Web pages (http://www.federalreserve.gov/releases/cp) for more information.
6. The 1-, 2-, and 3-month rates are equivalent to the 30-, 60-, and 90-day dates reported on the Board's Commercial Paper Web page.
7. Representative closing yields for acceptances of the highest rated money center banks.
8. An average of dealer offering rates on nationally traded certificates of deposit.
9. Bid rates for Eurodollar deposits at 11 a.m. London time.
10. One of several base rates used by banks to price short-term business loans.
11. Rate for the Federal Reserve Bank of New York.
12. Auction date for daily data; weekly and monthly averages computed on an issue-date basis.
13. Yields on actively traded issues adjusted to constant maturities. Source: U.S. Treasury.
14. Unweighted average of rates on all outstanding bonds neither due nor callable in less than 10 years.
15. Estimate of the yield on a recently offered, A-rated utility bond with a maturity of 30 years and call protection of 5 years; Friday quotations.
16. Bond Buyer Index, general obligation, 20 years to maturity, mixed quality; Thursday quotations.
17. Contract interest rates on commitments for fixed-rate first mortgages. Source: FHLMC.

Note: Weekly and monthly figures are averages of business days unless otherwise noted.

DESCRIPTION OF THE TREASURY CONSTANT MATURITY SERIES

Yields on Treasury securities at "constant maturity" are interpolated by the U.S. Treasury from the daily yield curve. This curve, which relates the yield on a security to its time to maturity, is based on the closing market bid yields on actively traded Treasury securities in the over-the-counter market. These market yields are calculated from composites of quotations obtained by the Federal Reserve Bank of New York. The constant maturity yield values are read from the yield curve at fixed maturities, currently 3 and 6 months and 1, 2, 3, 5, 7, 10, 20, and 30 years. This method provides a yield for a 10-year maturity, for example, even if no outstanding security has exactly 10 years remaining to maturity. In estimating the 20-year constant maturity, the Treasury incorporates the prevailing market yield on an outstanding Treasury bond with approximately 20 years remaining to maturity.

Most of the yields relate to specific instruments, but the rates for coupon-bearing Treasury securities are somewhat different. The Treasury calculates what is called a *constant maturity yield*. In English, this means if the Treasury issued a specific maturity security *today*, the "Treasury constant maturities" section of the report tells what its yield would be. Each day, the determination of these yields, calculated for all the on-the-run or actively issued Treasury maturities, is done by *interpolating* yields for each maturity date from those currently observed on the Treasury yield curve. Interpolation is a statistical estimation of what the yield on a particular maturity will be, based on observed yields around this maturity. Among the number of ways to do this, the most popular methods are *linear estimation* and the *cubic spline method* (see Exhibit 2.7). The linear process essentially draws a straight line between two points on the yield curve and determines where the requested maturity would fall on that line. For example, if the yield to maturity on the 3-year Treasury note is 5.10%, and the 5-year Treasury note yield is 5.65%, a linear interpolation to the 4-year note would generate a yield of 5.375%, or midway between the 3- and 5-year maturities.

The cubic spline method uses a statistical or smoothing technique to interpolate a specific yield point. Maturity points above and below the yield to be calculated are studied, and a curve is drawn based on the relationships between those yields. This is the preferred technique for interpolating yield, and the method is used by the U.S. Treasury, but the difference in the results from linear interpolation is usually

EXHIBIT 2.7   Linear versus cubic spline interpolation

	INTERPOLATION		
Maturity	**Yield**		
4/30/00	5.000%		
5/15/01	5.100%	**Linear**	**Cubic Spline**
5/7/02		5.375%	5.356%
4/30/03	5.650%		
5/15/05	5.950%		

minor. Many Wall Street applications rely on a simple linear interpolation between two rates.

TOTAL DOLLAR RETURN

Total dollar return measures the total amount of money received from an investment. This includes change in principal (sale or maturity value – purchase cost), interest income, and interest on interest, or the reinvested returns. Exhibit 2.8 presents a simplified calculation of total dollar return.

COMPOUNDING FREQUENCIES

Return on investment is not only a function of purchase price, coupon, maturity, and reinvestment rate. Compounding frequency also plays a role in yield and overall returns. If a security pays interest on an annual basis, the investor can only reinvest any monies once a year. If the security pays interest semiannually, the investor receives the same total

EXHIBIT 2.8   Total dollar return calculation

On 5/15/98, purchase $1 million par value U.S. T-bonds 6.125% due 11/15/2027
Purchase price = 103
Accrued interest = 0

On 5/15/99, sell $1 million par value U.S. T-bonds 6.125% due 11/15/2027
Sale price = 104
Accrued interest = 0

Reinvestment rate for 11/15/98 coupon payment: Money Market Yield of 5.5%.

Total dollar return:

$$\text{Principal} = \$1,040,000 - \$1,030,000 = \$10,000.00$$
$$\text{Accrued interest} = 2 \text{ coupon payments} = \$61,250.00$$
$$\text{Interest on } 11/15/98 \text{ coupon payment} = \$30,625 \times 5.5\% \times (181 \text{ days}/360) = \$846.87$$

Principal	$10,000.00
Accrued interest	61,250.00
Interest on interest	846.87
Total dollar return	$72,096.87

EXHIBIT 2.9   Rates of return using different compounding frequencies

Coupon = 6.125%
Maturity = 11/15/2027
Settlement = 5/1/98
   Price = 102

Compounding Frequency	Annual	Semiannual	Quarterly	Monthly
Yield to maturity	5.9760%	5.9797%	5.9802%	5.9806%

The formula for converting yield in one compounding frequency to another is:

$$\left(1+\frac{y_2}{q_2}\right)^{f2} = \left(1+\frac{y_1}{q_1}\right)^{f1}$$

where: y_2 = yield to be solved,
   y_1 = yield calculated using current compounding periods,
   q_1 = number of periods used to quote given yield,°
   q_2 = number of periods used to quote yield to be solved,°
   f_1 = frequency of compounding of given yield in terms of number of times
         per year,
   f_2 = frequency of compounding of yield to be solved in terms of number of
         times per year.

° Usually $f_1 = q_1$ and $f_2 = q_2$.

amount of annual interest but gets to reinvest it twice a year. Presuming the same reinvestment rate for both payouts, the investor will earn a greater return with the more frequent interest payout. Exhibit 2.9 reflects the differences in rates of return when different compounding frequencies are used. It also outlines the formula for converting yield in one compounding frequency to another.

INTERNATIONAL FIXED-INCOME SECURITIES

The price quoting and calculation of yield to maturity on international fixed-income securities are essentially the same as on U.S. fixed-income securities. Some specific differences, however, are worth noting:

- Unlike U.S. securities, European bonds are quoted with a clean price and a dirty price. The difference is in the accrued interest.

As previously mentioned, a clean price is simply the purchase price of the security excluding accrued interest. The dirty price includes accrued interest.

- Some European bonds are quoted with a current yield as well as a yield to maturity. The investor must be careful to know which yield is being quoted.

- Some bonds have what is referred to as an "ex-dividend date." On this date, the security stops paying interest. In the United Kingdom, gilts are traded with accrued interest until 36 days prior to the interest payment date. The price of the issue is then reduced by the amount of the accrued interest until the payable date, when interest again begins to accrue.

- Some foreign government securities accrue interest on a 360-day year; others accrue on a 365-day year. Some bonds pay interest annually; others pay semiannually. There are also some bonds similar to the TIPS or inflation-indexed securities.

Investors need not be overly concerned about the idiosyncrasies of international government bonds. Real-time information services and a number of vendors of spreadsheet add-in applications take care of these issues, as discussed in Chapter 12. Nevertheless, it is important to be aware the issues exist. See Appendix A for the day-count basis on international securities. Appendix F lists some additional texts on international bonds.

SUMMARY

This chapter covered the concept of yield to maturity. It reviewed the positive and negative aspects of the calculation, and how to mitigate the constant reinvestment rate assumption. Constant maturity yields, total dollar return, and some of the idiosyncrasies of foreign debt yield calculations were also noted.

NOTES

1. Several different iterative techniques can be used to derive yield from price. The Newton-Raphson and Secant methods have proven to be the most efficient;

they usually require fewer than 10 iterations to derive the yield. For further information on these and other iterative techniques, see the Securities Industry Association's (SIA) Standard Industry Calculations, available from the SIA in New York City (120 Broadway, New York, NY, 10271-0080, 212-648-1500). See Appendix F.

2. Some iterative techniques use the coupon rate as a starting estimate to calculate yield.

3. Sidney Homer and Martin Liebowitz, *Inside the Yield Book* (Prentice Hall/ New York Institute of Finance, 1972).

4. Remember, the payments at maturity have no reinvestment period. Therefore, the yield to maturity can be used as the discount rate for all cash received on the maturity date.

5. The H.15 report reflects daily and weekly rates. The G.13 report reflects weekly and monthly rates.

3 YIELD SPREAD ANALYSIS

This chapter covers yield spread analysis, the core of value determination in fixed-income securities. Virtually all markets trade in a relationship to all other markets. More than 2 million domestically issued fixed-income securities are outstanding, and very few trade on a regular basis. How does the user determine value in these issues? The principles of yield spread analysis are discussed with respect to relative value calculations and market conventions on pricing. Readers learn the importance of using yields as a relative measuring tool. The concept and application of "rich/cheap" analysis are covered, with examples, and a quick-and-dirty, yet effective method of calculation is offered. Readers are also taken through yield comparisons in which the relationship between similar-maturity securities is evaluated using different yield calculation methods.

The valuation process for fixed-income securities is somewhat different from the process used for equities. As mentioned in Chapter 1, fixed-income pricing focuses on yield, which is a function of creditworthiness, maturity, and liquidity. Equity markets are more concerned with growth in earnings and dividend payments.

Valuation of an equity security is usually a little more subjective than valuation of fixed-income securities, but it is usually easier to locate a live market price for a particular stock. The combination of the various stock exchanges and NASDAQ (National Association of Securities Dealers Automated Quotations) provides relatively easy access to many stock quotations. Fixed-income securities, however, are a different story. There are approximately 2 *million* different domestic debt instruments, but the overwhelming majority are not actively traded. Transactions occur in an over-the-counter or negotiated marketplace. Additionally, no widespread quotation system similar to NASDAQ is actively used to post real-time fixed-income prices. As a result, investors must seek out securities dealers willing to make a market for a particular issue under consideration.

Pricing, or valuing, securities has the same source-based issues as the trading application. An investor can easily obtain a daily closing price for a particular stock, provided it is listed on NASDAQ or one of the exchanges. Getting daily quotes for a bond, particularly one that doesn't trade often (which is the majority of outstanding issues) is much harder. The degree of liquidity for most bonds is much lower than for stocks. As previously noted, in most cases, the life cycle of a bond is as follows: Born in an underwriting, the issue is sold by the issuer to one dealer or a group of securities dealers (sell side). The dealers reoffer the securities to the general public (buy side), first during an underwriting period, then in a secondary market through open market trading. During this period, some secondary market trading occurs among dealers and customers. Once the issue has been fully placed with the final investors, it generally remains in a buy-side portfolio, and the coupons are clipped (interest payments are received by the bondholder) until the maturity of the principal amount. Although the amount of secondary market trading in fixed-income securities has increased, trading activity on an issue-by-issue basis is relatively low compared to stocks.

TRADE EXECUTIONS

Dealer-to-Customer Trading

Where are prices for a fixed-income security quoted? Dealers make markets in these securities, but they need some method of determining value. This is where the terms *interdealer broker, relative value,* and *yield spread analysis* come into play. In the fixed-income markets, there are two ways in which the majority of trades get executed: (1) *between dealer and customer,* and (2) *through interdealer brokers.* The dealer–customer method accounts for over half of all debt trades. A customer calls up a designated sales representative at a securities dealer and asks the salesperson to bid or offer a certain amount of a particular security. The salesperson "requests" the bid or offer for the security (this could mean screaming across the trading room floor) from the trader who is making a market in that particular issue or class of issues. The trader communicates the price to the salesperson, who then relays it to the customer. If the price is acceptable to the customer, the trade is consummated.

Direct Interactive Dealer-to-Customer Trading

A number of primary dealers have begun offering trading services interactively through one or more real-time information services vendors. Some are even offering their services over the Internet. Indeed, this type of trading is going to grow in both size and sophistication as the technology and security surrounding interactive securities trading continue to evolve. An example of a primary dealer service that is currently available on multiple information services vendors, as well as the Internet, is Zions Bank U.S. Government trading. Known by multiple names, such as "The Odd-Lot Machine," this service provides competitive, live, executable markets in all U.S. Treasury cash market securities as well as principal and income Treasury STRIPS. A customer can simply call Zions to execute a trade, or interactively execute a trade through one of the information services providers of Zions interactive trading. To apply for trading privileges in any of the primary dealer services, an institutional customer must fill out an account form. Subject to credit approval, the customer will be provided with an account number and password. For further information on Zions, call 201–626-6700, or contact your salesperson at the primary dealer(s) where you do business. Ask whether the dealer has its own interactive trading service.

Interdealer Brokers

The second way a fixed-income trade is executed is through the *interdealer broker* market. An interdealer broker is an agent who deals exclusively with securities dealers. In the U.S. Government and federal agency securities markets, six major interdealer brokers execute trades for the 38 U.S. Government securities dealers recognized by the Federal Reserve.[1] Cantor Fitzgerald, the largest of the brokers, is the only interdealer broker that handles trades for both buy-side and sell-side market players. Page 500 on the Telerate real-time information network is among the most widely followed screens for actively traded U.S. Treasury issues. The firm has been doing this since it began brokering government securities more than 25 years ago. Exhibit 3.1 is a sample of Page 500.

The rest of the interdealer brokers have always dealt exclusively with the dealers.[2] The other interdealer brokers in U.S. Government securities are Liberty Brokerage Inc., Garban Securities, R.M.J. Securities (Richard M. Jackson), Hill Farber, and Tullett & Tokyo Securities.

In 1991, the U.S. Government "nudged" the primary dealer community to make pricing for U.S. Government securities more available to all the nonprimary dealer market participants. The result of the government's efforts was the creation of GovPX. This corporation, owned by the primary dealers and interdealer brokers, is responsible for creating a composite feed from all the interdealer brokers (except Cantor

EXHIBIT 3.1   A sample of the Telerate page 500

	Third Digit =	
N00 =	2 = $^{1}/_{4}$ of a 32nd	IL = Index Linked
November	+ = $^{1}/_{2}$ of a 32nd	(Treasury Inflation
2000	6 = $^{3}/_{4}$ of a 32nd	Protection Securities)

05/29	12:15 EDT	DJ TREASURY 500		(C)98 MDC	SOURCE: CANTOR FITZGERALD 500

CPN	MAT	PRICE	SIZE	YIELD	CPN	MAT	PRICE	SIZE	YIELD
5.500	200		X		IL3.625	702	98.26+-27+	1X1	3.935-927
5.500	300	99.29	1X	5.550	IL3.375	107	97.02+-04+	1X1	3.775-766
5.625	400	100.04/-04+	21X30	5.552-543	IL3.625	108	99.03+-	1X	3.736
> 5.500	500	99.30/+-306	12X15	5.525-521	IL3.625	428	99.15 -17+	1X1	3.654-650
5.750	N00	100.142-15	1X1	5.552-542	6.125	807		X	
5.375	201	99.176-18	1X4	5.551-548	5.500	208	99.126-14	1X1	5.580-575
> 5.625	501	100.082-08+	16X3	5.528-525	> 5.625	508	TAK 100.20+	X30TAK	5.540

[ISY 500 INDEX P499]									
FN5.625	301	99.23 /25+	1X1	5.700	FN5.750	208	99.00 /04	1X1	5.868
FN5.750	403	99.26 /30	1X2	5.762	MR5.750	408	99.00 /04	1X1	5.867
5.500	103	99.226	X1	5.569	FN6.000	508	100.29 /01	1X1	5.861
5.500	203	99.21 -23	1X1	5.581-566	BOND BASIS			X	
5.500	303	99.22 -236	1X1	5.573-560	6.625	227		X	
5.750	403	100.24+-256	1X1	5.568-559	6.375	827		X	
> 5.500	503*TAK	99.26	X5	TAK 5.543	> 6.125	N27	104.23+ HIT	2X	5.788 HIT

[3M TB	4.88	5X	]	[6M TB 5.12	5X	]	[1Y TB 5.13	5X	]

> Indicates Active (On-the-Run) Issues	FN = FNMA MR = FNLMC	Bond Basis = US T-Bond Basis for Active (Current) 30-yr T-Bond)	T-Bills

Fitzgerald, which distributes its prices to nonprimary dealer customers) and distributing it to the nonprimary dealer investing public. GovPX, with 30,000 screens in use during the first quarter of 1998, has become a popular vehicle for institutional customers to receive U.S. Government securities pricing. Exhibit 3.2 is a sample screen of GovPX pricing of U.S. Government securities.

If securities dealers have positions they want to buy from or sell to any other interested principal, they call one of the brokers and post their bid or offer. The brokers have installed computer screens in each dealer's trading room. Each time a bid or offer is received by the broker, it is posted on the screens. All the dealers watch these screens for two important reasons (among others): (1) they look for bids and offers on specific securities they need to purchase or sell, and (2) they get indications of where particular securities or groups of securities are trading.

EXHIBIT 3.2   GovPX pricing of U.S. Government securities

Third Digit Represents 1/8 of a 32nd   A "+" = 1/2 of a 32nd → BID /OFFER columns
Par Value (in Millions) → SIZE
Yields Bid Offer → YIELD
Last Trade → TRADE
Par Value (in Millions) → VOL
Total Volume for the Day or Last Day Issue Was Traded → A-VOL

GovPX MATURITY	COUPON	BID	/OFFER	SIZE	YIELD	L	TRADE	VOL	YIELD	PG 20 A-VOL
08/97	6 1/2	100.005	/005	31x65	5.446/446	T	00.005	17	5.542	08*05
08/97	8 5/8	100.02	/021	6x4	5.564/394	T	00.04	12	5.180	07*31
08/97	5 5/8	99.311	/312	1x1	5.902/643	H	99.315	4	5.661	08*05
08/97	6	99.316	/00	12x20	5.965/847	H	99.316	2	5.961	08*05
09/97	5 1/2	99.317	/317	5x11	5.422/422	H	99.317	15	5.422	25
09/97	5 3/4	100.011	/012	1x11	5.400/374	T	00.011	2	5.405	08*0
10/97	8 3/4	100.19	/19	2x1	5.421/421	H	00.191	9	5.400	5
10/97	5 5/8	100.005	/005	2x8	5.457/457	H	00.006	10	5.440	44
10/97	5 3/4	100.015	/016	1x1	5.443/426	H	00.016	100	5.430	08*05
11/97	7 3/8	100.141	/142	5x5	5.631/617	H	00.142	30	5.617	32
11/97	8 7/8	100.27	/272	2x1	5.609/581	T	00.272	3	5.612	08*05
11/97	5 3/8	99.297	/30	1x16	5.535/522	T	99.297	2	5.535	56
11/97	6	100.042	/04+	3x2	5.509/484	T	00.043	3	5.501	08*05
12/97	5 1/4	99.283	/28+	10x11	5.512/502	T	99.283	3	5.511	08*05
12/97	6	100.056	/06	1x8	5.503/483	H	00.06	1	5.483	1

TREASURY 2 YEAR

3M   5.14 /135   2Y   99.302/30+   3Y   99.302/302   2Y VOL 9,576
5Y   99.18 /18+   10Y 102.29+/30   30Y 101.27 /29   08/06 12:33 EDT

Active Issues for Each Maturity Sector

Total Volume for 2-yr Active Issue

Federal agency, STRIPS (U.S. Treasury zero coupon derivatives[3]), and cash/futures basis trades[4] also are handled by these interdealer brokers. There are brokers for other fixed-income market segments as well. In percentage of total trades, interdealer brokers are not as active in the corporate bond market as in the U.S. Government markets, although firms such as Cantor Fitzgerald are active brokers in corporate securities. The municipal market has several interdealer brokers with large brokering operations. Among these firms are J.J. Kenny, Titus and Donnelly, and Chapdelaine. Standard & Poor's Corporation has what is known as a "Blue List"—a daily report of municipal dealer offerings of securities (the hard-copy pages are blue in color). Mortgage-backed securities dealers also have their own interdealer brokerages, some of which are also U.S.Treasury interdealer brokers. Patriot Securities, Hill Farber, Cantor Fitzgerald, Garban Securities, and R.M.J. Securities all broker mortgage-backed securities. Despite these brokering operations, a large majority of fixed-income issues have little, if any, trading activity after initial placement. Nevertheless, for portfolio valuation and investment management strategies, investors need to know the prices of these issues. This is a good segue into how fixed-income securities get priced.

METHODS OF PRICE/YIELD QUOTATIONS

Securities are quoted in either a price or a yield format. Generally speaking, money market securities are quoted on some form of yield basis, and capital market securities are quoted on a price basis. An example of yield basis quoting would be 5.64%–5.62% where the bid side of the quote is higher than the offered side (remember, price and yield are inversely related).

A price quote can be denominated in one of several formats. As a rule of thumb, the more liquid and highly traded a security, the smaller the minimum price increment. As noted in Chapter 1, the high degree of liquidity in U.S. Treasury securities can make the spread between bid and ask as little as 1/256 of a point (this is equal to $39.06 per *million dollars* par value). Corporate bonds are not as liquid and are generally quoted in eighths of a point. Municipal bonds are generally quoted in two forms. Securities with one maturity date (not serial maturities) will be quoted as a dollar price and are called *dollar bonds.* Serial maturities (the majority of municipal issues) are quoted as a yield less some discount. For example, a New York State General Obligation security with a serial maturity in 2007 could be quoted as 5.95% – ¼. This means the security is being priced to yield 5.95% to maturity, with ¼ of a point deducted from the dollar price calculated from the yield.

In recent years, two different price-quoting methods have grown in popularity and are actively used on the interdealer broker screens, particularly in the securities markets related to governments. The two methods are *swaps* and *spreads.* For *spreads,* a dealer may be willing to purchase one security at a particular yield spread to another issue, usually the on-the-run security. For example, the dealer could quote the spread between the current 30-year Treasury bond and some off-the-run Treasury bond as 7–6½. This means the dealer will buy the off-the-run Treasury bond at a yield spread of 7 basis points *above* the yield of the current (on-the-run) 30-year Treasury bond. The dealer is also willing to sell the same U.S. Treasury bond at a yield of 6½ basis points above the yield on the current 30-year bond. From a dollar price perspective, the value of the two yields translates into a difference of approximately ²⁄₃₂ of a point, or $625 per million par or face value.

Swap quotes relate to the simultaneous purchase and sale of two different securities (as opposed to interest rate swaps, which will be discussed in Chapter 10). They work as follows. A dealer posts a quote of 3–2½ representing the yield spread differential between a particular off-the-run 10-year Treasury note and the current or on-the-run 10-year Treasury note. The dealer is willing to simultaneously buy the off-the-run Treasury note and sell the on-the-run Treasury note at a spread of 3 basis points. The dealer will buy the on-the-run and sell the off-the-run at a spread of 2½ basis points. The ½-basis-point difference represents about $325 in value per million par or face value, or slightly more than ¹⁄₃₂ of a price point on a 10-year note. The bid–offer quote is sometimes determined by what the dealer is doing with the off-the-run security.

Quoting for outstanding Treasury notes and bonds is done almost entirely on a price basis. Spread or swap quotes are used more actively in the federal agency and STRIPS markets. Most of these quotes are priced from an on-the-run U.S. Treasury issue. Exhibit 3.3

EXHIBIT 3.3   Spread and swap quotes on an interdealer broker screen

The Third Digits
Represent as Follows
2 = $^1/_4$ Basis Point
5 = $^1/_2$ Basis Point   Swaps for US Treasury STRIPS   Par Value
6 = $^3/_4$ Basis Point   Buy the Feb 2000 & Sell the Nov 1999   Swaps   (in Millions)
                                 STRIP at a Yield Spread of $^1/_2$ bp Lower

| | | Swaps | All Quotes in Basis Points | Buy the May 2007 STRIP at a Yield Spread of 19$^1/_2$ Basis Points over the Yield on the Active 10-yr T-Note. Sell it at 19$^1/_4$ Basis Points over the 10-yr Note. | Spreads for Treasury STRIPS |

P = Indicates Principal STRIP, All Others are Interest STRIPS

Source: Liberty Brokerage Inc.

shows how a particular security would be quoted in outright, spread, and swap formats.

YIELD SPREAD ANALYSIS: HOW TO DETERMINE VALUE

Given the lack of liquidity in many of the outstanding fixed-income is-sues, how are the values for these securities determined? The primary method is *yield spread analysis,* a relative value analysis in which the creditworthiness, maturity, and liquidity of an issue are compared to what is designated a benchmark for value determination. The difference between the two securities is expressed as a yield spread.

Spreading against a Benchmark

Once again, referring to the creditworthiness and maturity factors contributing to the determination of yield, each security fits into these two parameters in some manner. But against what benchmark are they measured? If an investor were offered a 10-year Treasury note with a yield of 8%, should the investor purchase the security? The answer is: It depends. If the active 5-year notes and 30-year bonds are yielding 13% (as they were in the 1980s), 8% looks pretty pathetic. On the other hand, if both 5-year and 30-year Treasury issues are yielding under 6%, as they were in August 1998, 8% looks like a real steal. What happens when this 8% yield is compared to a corporate bond with similar maturity? From a creditworthiness perspective, the 8% yield on the Treasury security can only be evaluated if the investor knows the yields on securities with different credit ratings but similar maturities. The point is: The market needs some benchmark measure from which it can value all other securities. That benchmark is the U.S. Treasury on-the-run securities.

The U.S. Treasury as a Benchmark

U.S. Treasury securities are used for a number of reasons. The most important reasons are:

- There is homogeneity of risk throughout all Treasury issues. They are all guaranteed by the full faith and credit of the U.S. Government.
- Treasury security maturities are issued in periodic intervals, some as frequently as weekly.[5]
- The size of a Treasury issue is huge, relative to non-Treasury issuers, thereby ensuring a high degree of liquidity in secondary market trading.[6]

During the fourth quarter of 1997, there were about 33 T-Bill and 215 T-note and bond issues outstanding. Out of all those securities, eight issues were considered current or on-the-run. As the most recently issued securities within each maturity sector, these issues were used to construct the U.S. Treasury yield curve. Exhibit 3.4 depicts the Treasury yield curve issues as of 5/12/98.

Most, if not all, fixed-income securities are priced either directly or indirectly off the U.S. Treasury yield curve. This pricing is done as a spread off the corresponding maturity Treasury issue. A 10-year corporate note would be spread against the 10-year Treasury Note. If a

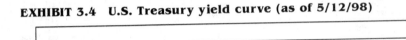

EXHIBIT 3.4   U.S. Treasury yield curve (as of 5/12/98)

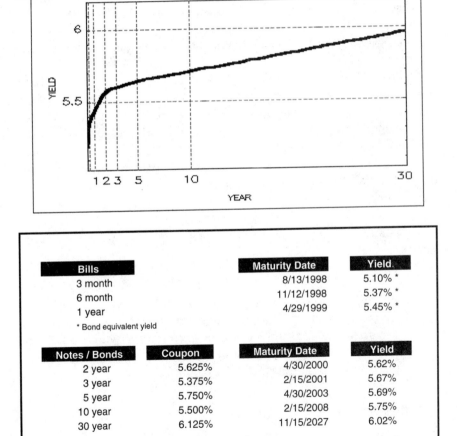

Bills	Maturity Date	Yield
3 month	8/13/1998	5.10% *
6 month	11/12/1998	5.37% *
1 year	4/29/1999	5.45% *

* Bond equivalent yield

Notes / Bonds	Coupon	Maturity Date	Yield
2 year	5.625%	4/30/2000	5.62%
3 year	5.375%	2/15/2001	5.67%
5 year	5.750%	4/30/2003	5.69%
10 year	5.500%	2/15/2008	5.75%
30 year	6.125%	11/15/2027	6.02%

security is callable and is trading to its call date, then the active Treasury issue with a maturity date nearest the corporate issues' call date would be used as the benchmark.

Yield Spreads by Credit Quality

Credit quality or *intermarket* spreads are a function of a number of market-related factors, including issue liquidity, whether an issue is callable, and new issue activity. On a more macro level, these yield spreads are a function of interest rates. Generally speaking, the higher the overall level of rates, the wider the spread *differential* between two credit-quality classes. The reason for this can be summarized in one word: *risk*. As interest rates rise, the cost of borrowing increases for everyone. The lower or weaker the credit rating of a particular issuer, the less likely it will be able to make interest and principal payments as interest rates rise.

The pricing of new taxable, fixed-income, non-Treasury debt is done as a spread to either an active Treasury issue or another active issue in the same market segment, which is ultimately tied to a Treasury security. Municipal issues are a little different because of income tax considerations, although the spread of the taxable equivalent yield against that of the corresponding Treasury maturity is closely monitored. Exhibit 3.5 reflects credit-quality yield spread relationships for long-term maturities in historically low, medium, and high interest rate environments.

Underlying causes for shifts in these types of spreads can be a function of:

- Changes in fundamental economic factors affecting the markets,
- Liquidity issues for one or more securities,
- Some exogenous factor such as political unrest, a war, or a credit crisis for a major bank, agency, or corporation, which causes investors to flee to the safety of short-term Treasury securities. This reaction is called the *flight to quality.*

Yield Spreads by Maturity

Another way of analyzing yield spreads is by maturity. These types of spreads are generally referred to as *intramarket* because the securities

EXHIBIT 3.5   Credit quality yield spreads for long-term maturities

Environment	Date	30-Yr Treasury	AAA Corp
Low	4/98	5.92%	77 bps
Medium	2/89	9.01%	63 bps
High	2/81	12.80%	55 bps

BAA Corp	AAA MUNI	AAA MUNI/TSY
141 bps	−69 bps	88%
160 bps	−178 bps	80%
257 bps	−334 bps	74%

Source: Federal Reserve Bank G.13.

being measured by this method have the same credit rating. They are most widely used in the U.S. Treasury market because of their credit-worthiness and liquidity. Given the Treasury's benchmarking role, it is important for investors to know whether a particular Treasury maturity is accurately priced relative to the other issues on the yield curve. If there is an apparent difference from the current relationship, it could have an effect on all the other non-Treasury securities priced off that particular maturity. Exhibit 3.6 reflects yield spread environments for U.S. Treasury issues in periods of low, medium, and high interest rates.

Off-the-Run versus On-the-Run

A third way securities are valued via yield spread—a way that is related to the maturity method—is as active versus *off-the-run* issues. As previously noted, in the U.S. Treasury market, off-the-runs are all the securities *not* considered as active or on-the-run issues. The on-the-runs in the Treasury market (and most recently issued securities in other

EXHIBIT 3.6   U.S. Treasury on-the-run yield spreads

Environment	Date	30-Yr Treasury	30-Yr, 3-Mo
Low	4/1998	5.92%	84 bps
Medium	2/1989	9.01%	48 bps
High	2/1981	12.80%	−278 bps*

30-Yr, 2-Yr	30-Yr, 5-Yr	30-Yr, 10-Yr
36 bps	31 bps	−8 bps
−36 bps	−26 bps	−16 bps
−112 bps	−61 bps	−39 bps

° Converted from discount to bond equivalent yield.
Source: Federal Reserve Bank G.13.

markets) are the most actively traded issues within their segments. All the other issues, which comprise the overwhelming majority of outstanding Treasury securities, are less actively traded and subject to more sporadic quote availability. From a trading perspective, shorter maturity issues in the Treasury market are more likely to have available quotes on broker screens than longer dated issues. The reason is the greater demand for shorter dated securities by more market players, particularly commercial banks, which are major players in the Treasury market.

The yields on off-the-run Treasury issues are derived from spreads to the active issues. In most cases, the yields fall in line with the slope of the yield curve created by the active issues. There are some exceptions, most of which are securities with maturities in excess of 10 years. When 30-year Treasury bonds came into existence in 1977, issues during the first 7 years came with 25-year call option features. Due to the current interest rate environment, all of the securities issued during that 7-year period carried coupons well in excess of the required yield to maturity for a 30-year bond over much of the past few years. As a result, each of these bonds trades to its call date, not its maturity date. Yields on these securities, however, are above the corresponding non-callable securities with the same maturity dates as the call dates. Another exception is the yield on old 30-year bonds with maturities between 16 and 29 years. The yields on nearly all of these securities are slightly higher than the yield on the on-the-run 30-year maturity. This can be attributed to lower issue liquidity and lower market interest in the off-the-runs.[7]

Traditionally, the trading of these types of spreads in the cash markets was confined mostly to dealers quoting on an "as requested" basis from the customer. A dealer would buy or sell a particular spread between two issues at some basis point differential, then purchase from and sell to the customer the securities in question. For example, a dealer "sells" the 2-year–10-year Treasury active issue yield spread at a differential of 30 basis points. In this case, the dealer is selling the 2-year to, and buying the 10-year from a counterparty. At this point, the dealer must deliver the 2-year note and purchase the 10-year note at a yield spread of 30 basis points (like the bond swap quote mechanism noted above), using the appropriate hedge ratio to mitigate interest rate risk (see Chapter 4 for an in-depth discussion of hedge ratios). The traded prices of both issues must translate into a yield spread differential of 30 basis points.

Inter- and intramarket yield spread trading is not confined to only the cash markets. The futures market traders have also implemented the spread trade concept in such trading relationships as the T-Bill/Eurodollar (TED) spread. We will discuss this further in Chapter 7, where we discuss on interest rate futures contracts.

It is important to remember the reasons for investment, when considering which particular security to buy. If the strategy for the investment is to hold until maturity, then creditworthiness, not liquidity, takes on increasing importance. The availability of an active market for any particular investment is only relevant if the investor wants to execute a trade. Otherwise, only price indications (via yield spread to the active issue) for valuation purposes are necessary. This holds true for any security. The question that needs to be answered is: What is the tradeoff between liquidity and return? In other words, how much is the investor giving up by purchasing a security with low liquidity versus one with high liquidity? The answers are a function of the specific strategy of each investor.

Yield Spreads on High-Yield Bonds

The yield spread relationship concept noted above generally holds for fixed-income securities that are considered investment grade. This constitutes the first four credit rating categories by the major ratings agencies.[8] For companies below these levels, yield spreads for *high-yield* or *junk bonds* are not as important; an increasing portion of the value of the issue is more subjective, and the companies are less prone to rely on credit issues as the primary determinant of value. This type of security is also referred to as a *story bond*. The value of these bonds is based on some event or series of events that is either currently ongoing or is expected to occur in the future. The securities could also get a large portion of their value from investors' confidence in the company's senior management team. Bid–offer spreads on these securities are usually wider than those for investment-grade issues.

Rich or Cheap?

After the yield spread between two securities has been determined, the next question is: How does the current spread compare to the historical relationship of the two securities? If the current spread between a 10-year and a 30-year Treasury security was 35 basis points, how does this match up to historical patterns between the two issues? The best way to determine this *relative value* is through rich/cheap analysis.

There are a number of ways to approach this analysis. A relatively simple way is to use the mean, or average, and standard deviation of the yield spread over some period of time (usually 1 to 3 months). The standard deviation is nothing more than a statistical measure of volatility over some period of time. The formula for standard deviation is:

$$\sqrt{\sum_{i=1}^{n} \frac{(X_i - \overline{X})}{N-1}}$$

where: $\overline{X}$ = the mean or average of X number of observations,

X_i = observation in time period i,

N = number of observations (use N − 1 for a population sample).

The rich/cheap formula is:

$$\frac{\text{Current spread} - \text{Mean (avg.) spread}}{\text{Standard deviation of the spread}}$$

If the current yield spread between the 10-year Treasury Note and the 30-year Treasury bond is 35 basis points, the average spread over the past 2 months is 41 basis points, and the standard deviation of the spread over the past 2 months is 3 basis points, then:

$$\frac{35 - 41}{3} = \frac{-6}{3} = -2 \text{ Standard deviations.}$$

This means the current spread is 2 standard deviations *below* the average for the past 2 months. Any statistical reference will indicate that approximately 95% of the yield spread observations over the past 2 months were *wider* than 35 basis points.[9]

This formula works better with two or more securities, when relative value or basis is being measured. Single-security analysis can be misleading, particularly when the market is trending in one direction or another. Using the above example, charges in a yield spread between two securities indicates: Either some fundamental change has occurred to cause the spread to narrow, or the spread is trading too narrow for its historical pattern. The latter reason could be interpreted as an opportunity for a trade. There is, however, some additional homework to be done. What mathematically caused the spread to narrow? Given a normal, or upward, sloped yield curve, did the 10-year note rise in yield did the 30-year bond fall in yield, or did a combination of both occur? Once this is determined, the investor needs to make a judgment based on either quantitative analysis (rich/cheap analysis) or qualitative analysis (change in fundamentals). If it is determined that one or more issues moved excessively in one direction for no apparent fundamental reason, the investor has an opportunity to buy the spread (buy the 10-year and sell the 30-year).

Changes in yield spread relationships could also have an exaggerated impact on the prices and yields of other securities pegged to these issues, thereby affecting the values of individual securities as well as portfolios.

BASIS TRADE: CAPTURING CHANGES IN RELATIVE VALUE

The most efficient way to execute a trade using relative value is through a basis trade. Many traders employ this strategy, which focuses on the yield spread between two or more securities. A generic basis trade can incorporate any two or more securities with similar or different risk, maturity, liquidity, or cash flow characteristics. The most popular basis trading relationships involve securities with (1) similar credit ratings but different maturities, or (2) similar maturities with different credit ratings. Their popularity is due to the direct tie, in many instances, into securities pricing relationships through yield spreads, as discussed earlier in this chapter.

Many market participants view a basis trade as the relationship between the U.S. Treasury's cash and futures markets. This is one type of basis trade, and it contains a number of considerations not germane to relationships between cash market securities. Cash–futures basis trades will be discussed in detail in Chapter 7.

Traders and portfolio managers examine basis relationships from a historical perspective. Where has the spread between security A and security B been recently? Why has it been there? Where is it now? The dynamics of the marketplace will precipitate yield spread changes, but any sustainable variation from some longer-term average most often results from a change in a fundamental factor such as credit ratings, the general level of interest rates, and economic conditions. Barring a change in one or more of these fundamental factors, logic tells us that a yield spread relationship should be adjusted back toward some longer-term equilibrium through the market process and that the securities will be purchased and sold to reach that end. Keep in mind that basis trades can also be implemented in anticipation of some change in an existing, longer-term yield spread relationship.

The differences between outright purchase or sale of one of the securities and the basis trade are: the degree of risk and the ultimate objective of the trade. Both situations are looking to earn a profit. In an outright purchase or sale, the investor wants to improve the yield on invested capital through comparatively higher rates of return. The risk in the trade is that the price of the security could fall (the yield would then rise). Basis, or relative-value, trades seek to extract a profit from a relationship between two or more securities where the yield on at least one of the issues will move closer to or farther away from the other issue(s) in the trade. The risk in the trade is that the yield spread may move in a direction that is opposite to the trader's expectation.

Parallel shifts in the yields on both securities should have only a negligible effect on profit or loss if the trade is weighted according to the price/yield sensitivity of each security. The amount of price movement in a fixed-income security relative to a change in its yield is a function of the security's coupon rate, time to maturity, and yield to maturity. For example, the price/yield sensitivity of a 2-year note is different from that of a 30-year bond. As a result, a one-basis-point change in yield on a 2-year note will have a much smaller effect on the change in its price as compared to the price change from a one-basis-point change in yield on a 30-year bond. The investor may need to purchase or sell several times the amount of one issue as compared to another in order to get the same absolute value change in both securities. The measurement concepts will be discussed in greater detail in Chapter 4.

Referring to the above example where the 10-year–30-year yield spread is −2 standard deviations below the mean, or average, a statistically narrow spread translates into buying the spread. (Buying the 10-year note and selling the 30-year bond; selling the spread is the reverse transaction.) The yield spread between this simultaneous purchase and sale is 35 basis points. The reason for buying the spread rather than buying or selling one of the issues outright represents the reason for doing the trade. The investor is focusing on the spread between the two and is less concerned about the actual rate levels of the two securities. Executing this type of trade basically eliminates the absolute interest rate risk and centers on *basis* or relative risk. The investor should be indifferent to absolute movement in the yields on both securities over some reasonably small range *as long as* the spread relationship doesn't change.

This trade seems (and basically is) reasonably straightforward, but some further calculations are needed before the trade can be executed.

EXHIBIT 3.7   U.S. Treasury issuers and yield spreads

The Top Half of the Grid Reflects the Number of Standard Deviations
Each Yield Spread Is above or below Its Three-Month Average

05/12	14:59 EDT	[DOW JONES TRADING ASSISTANT]							PG 25047
[14:45]		[US TREASURY ON-THE RUN RICH/CHEAP ANALYSIS]						[05/12]	
[R/C=#SD TO]	3M BL	6M BL	1Y BL	5.625	5.375	5.750	6.500	5.500	6.125
[3M SPRD AVG] 8/13	11/12	4/29	4/100	2/01	4/03	5/05	2/08	11/27	
3M BL 13-8	[R/C]	1.5	0.9	0.5	0.8	0.4	0.6	0.6	0.2
6M BL 12-11	24.8	[R/C]	-0.7	-0.8	-0.3	-0.9	-0.7	-0.6	-1.4
1Y BL 29-4	32.2	7.4	[R/C]	-0.7	0.4	-0.9	-0.5	-0.2	-1.7
5.625 APR-10	47.3	22.5	15.1	[R/C]	2.0	-0.6	0.1	0.4	-0.9
5.375 FEB-01	52.3	27.5	20.0	5.0	[R/C]	-2.1	-1.2	-0.8	-1.6
5.750 APR-03	52.1	27.3	19.8	4.8	-0.2	[R/C]	1.1	1.3	-0.8
6.500 MAY-05	62.6	37.8	30.3	15.3	10.3	10.5	[R/C]	0.8	-1.6
5.500 FEB-08	57.6	32.8	25.4	10.3	5.3	5.5	-5.0	[R/C]	-2.2
6.125 NOV-27	82.8	58.0	50.6	35.5	30.6	30.8	20.2	25.2	[R/C]

		[YIELD SPREADS]				[YIELD SPREADS]			
MATY	PRICE	YIELD	COUPON	MATY	PRICE	YIELD	COUPON	MATY	PRICE	YIELD
3M BL	4.99	5.134	5.625%	4/100	100.015	5.607	6.500%	5/05	104.09	5.760
6M BL	5.16	5.382	5.375%	2/01	99.10	5.656	5.500%	2/08	98.16	5.710
1Y BL	5.16	5.456	5.750%	4/03	100.14	5.654	6.125%	11/27	102.10	5.962

The Bottom Half of the Grid Reflects the Yield Spreads (in Basis Points) between Each of the Active Issues

One very important consideration is the amount or degree of parallel shifting up or down in the yield curve. These calculations will be discussed in Chapter 4.

Telerate (formerly Dow Jones) has a screen on its network where all the active U.S. Treasury issues are compared against each other in terms of yield spreads, in a rich/cheap analysis. Exhibit 3.7 is a sample of that screen.

SUMMARY

The overwhelming majority of fixed-income trades are executed over the counter. A fixed-income trade can be executed in several ways. Dealer-to-customer is the most popular way, but interdealer brokers provide an important degree of liquidity to the domestic bond markets. Fixed-income securities are quoted in either a price or a yield format. Yield is most often used for money market securities; price is used for longer-term securities.

Almost all fixed-income securities are priced at yield spreads over the U.S. Treasury market active issues. These spreads are created primarily from creditworthiness (for non-Treasury issues) or maturity and liquidity for nonactive or off-the-run Treasury securities. A good way to quickly determine the relative value of a security is to perform a rich/cheap analysis on the yield spread between the security in question and the active Treasury security used as the benchmark. Implementation of the rich/cheap analysis can be done by either purchasing or selling a specific security, or buying and selling both securities in what is called a basis trade.

NOTES

1. U.S. Government securities dealers recognized by the Federal Reserve maintain certain capitalization and securities distribution capabilities. For further information on dealer trading and operations, see *Fed Watching and Interest Rate Forecasts,* Third Edition, by David Jones, published by the New York Institute of Finance. Appendix J lists the current group of primary dealers.

2. The other interdealer brokers have, in recent years, allowed some or all of their screens into a few selected nonprimary dealers. This occurred because these nonprimary dealers were essentially performing the same functions as the primary dealers.

3. STRIPS = Separate Trading of Registered Interest and Principal on Securities. See Chapter 5 for a discussion of zero coupon securities.

4. See Chapter 7 for a discussion of cash–futures trading.

5. See Chapter 1 for auction schedules of Treasury securities.

6. Weekly Treasury Bill auctions averaged between \$14 billion and \$15 billion, and monthly and quarterly coupon issues (notes and bonds) ranged between \$10 billion and \$15 billion during the fourth quarter of 1997.

7. Daily closing prices and yields for outstanding U.S. Treasury securities are listed in most major newspapers.

8. The two major rating agencies are Moody's and Standard & Poor's. (See Appendix E for Moody's and S&P credit rating categories.) Fitch Investors Services and Duff and Phelps are also recognized credit rating agencies.

9. See Appendix I for the normal distribution function.

4 PRICE/YIELD SENSITIVITY

Virtually all individual fixed-income securities have a unique relationship to price/yield sensitivity. (How much does the price change, given a specific change in yield?) Determining these relationships represents the heart of risk management. What is the risk in owning this individual security or portfolio of securities? The discussion in this chapter includes the more popular techniques of price/yield sensitivity analysis (different measure of duration, and so on). The focus is on understanding why and how securities behave the way they do with regard to incremental changes in price/yield, coupons, maturity, and the different types of risk measured with these techniques. The definitions of and differences between interest rate risk and basis risk are explained. Exhibits cover the practical use of the various price/yield sensitivity measures in both individual and comparative yield analyses.

INTEREST RATE RISK AND BASIS RISK

Two generic types of market risk are associated with nonoption, embedded, fixed-income security yield spreads. As we mentioned in Chapter 3, *interest rate risk* represents the upward or downward movement of interest rates where the relationship or spread between rates doesn't change. This is a parallel shift, or a simultaneous movement of multiple rates along the yield curve. In other words, interest rate risk occurs with a parallel or similar change in yields of all maturities with a homogenous credit risk (intramarket risk), or in yields of several levels of credit risk with the same maturity (intermarket risk) moving the same amount and in the same direction. This can occur from changes in fundamental or technical factors that impact market prices and yields. Several measurements can be used to determine the level of interest rate risk and how to mitigate it. These will be discussed later in this chapter. Exhibit 4.1 reflects yield curve changes that generate interest rate risk.

In Chapter 3, we noted that many traders actively trade what is referred to as *basis risk*. Investment people tend to view this as the relationship between the U.S. Treasury cash and futures markets. Indeed, this is a popular *type* of basis trade (to be discussed in Chapter 7), but, as we observed, the concept of basis is not limited to one type of trade with two specific instruments.

Basis risk is a *relative* measure of risk. It reflects the difference between either the yield or the price of at least two securities. Yield is the most popular measurement for most basis relationships because the price of a fixed-income security doesn't directly reflect its value relative to other fixed-income instruments. Basis relationships can measure the movement of the yield differential between two or more securities with equal or entirely different risk parameters. It

EXHIBIT 4.1   Parallel yield curve shift

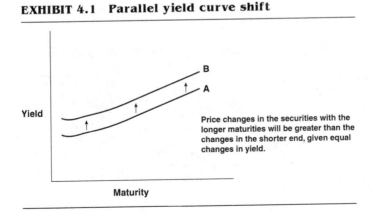

EXHIBIT 4.2   Nonparallel yield curve shift

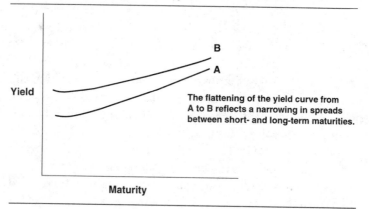

The flattening of the yield curve from A to B reflects a narrowing in spreads between short- and long-term maturities.

represents nonparallel shifts in multiple rates. This is where instances of *steepening* or *flattening* in the yield curve are observed. Exhibit 4.2 reflects a basis shift in a yield curve.

Basis risk is more difficult to hedge than interest rate risk. As a practical matter, the only way to absolutely ensure against loss from basis risk is through the use of over-the-counter options. This can be a very expensive process because the perfect hedge will most likely need to be structured with highly customized, illiquid options. The reduced level of market risk created by this strategy is similar to purchasing/selling a security and purchasing a put/call option on that security, creating what is known as a *synthetic call/put*. This will be discussed in more detail in Chapter 9.

Controlling and Measuring Interest Rate Risk

Mathematically, we can measure the amount of sensitivity or profit and loss (P/L) an investor will absorb because of smaller and larger swings in rates. These measurements work with both single and multiple securities transactions. The key to interest rate risk is knowing the *price/yield* sensitivity of each security being examined.

The sensitivity of a specific security's price/yield relationship is a function of:

- Time to maturity.
- Coupon.
- Yield to maturity.

For each element, there is an important rule to remember, as follows.

1. *The longer the time to maturity, the greater the change in price, given a set change in yield.* Any semiannual-paying 2-year note has four coupons and a principal payment. A semiannual-paying 10-year note has 20 coupons and a principal payment. As we discussed in Chapter 1, the price of a fixed-income security represents the present value of a future stream of cash flows associated with a specific security. When the yield to maturity on a security changes, the present value of each coupon and of the principal changes as well. Given that a 10-year note has five times the number of coupons as a 2-year note, the total of overall payments associated with the 10-year note is much greater than the total for the 2-year note. As a result, the sensitivity of a price change, given a set yield change, is much greater for the 10-year note than for the 2-year note. Using the modified duration price/yield sensitivity measure, the change in price is about four times larger for the 10-year note than for the 2-year note, given a similar change in yield. Later in the chapter, we will more thoroughly discuss and apply this concept.

2. *The higher the coupon, the lower the price/yield sensitivity of the security.* The total cash flow associated with a bond includes both principal and interest payments. As mentioned above, the faster the payment of these cash flows, the less sensitive the price/yield change will be. As the coupon of a security increases, a greater proportion of the total dollar return of that security will be represented by the coupon payments. As a result, the timing of the cash flow returns, on average, is reduced. For example, on a modified duration basis, a 6% 10-year note yielding 6% has a .5-year greater sensitivity (duration is longer) to a percentage change in price than a 10% 10-year note yielding 6%, given the same change in yield for both securities.

3. *The higher the yield to maturity, the lower the price/yield sensitivity of the issue.* It is important to conceptualize the dynamic relationship between changes in price and yield. Some readers might expect

these differences to be linear in nature, but they are not. Consider the following: An examination of the impact of principal and interest cash flows on price/yield sensitivity for a non-sinking-fund security indicates that the principal cash flow has a larger single effect on price/yield sensitivity than the individual coupon payments. As the yield to maturity changes, however, each cash flow takes on a different weight. Here is an easy way to visualize this concept:

$$2 - 1 = 1 \qquad 2/1 = 2$$
$$3 - 2 = 1 \qquad 3/2 = 1.5$$
$$4 - 3 = 1 \qquad 4/3 = 1.33$$
$$5 - 4 = 1 \qquad 5/4 = 1.25$$
$$101 - 100 = 1 \qquad 101/100 = 1.01$$

As you can see, the higher the numbers are in absolute size, the smaller the same one-unit difference becomes. Applying this analogy to fixed-income securities, price/yield sensitivity is impacted by the changing relative weights of the coupons and the principal payment as yield to maturity moves up and down. Assuming the maturity date and coupon rate are constant, as the yield rises, the coupons take on an increasingly larger portion of the present value dollar return because the principal is taking on a smaller and smaller portion of the total security value. Remember, the price of a coupon security is nothing more than the present value of all future cash flows associated with the security. Exhibit 4.3 reflects a security with the same coupon and maturity under different yield scenarios. A 1% change in yield to maturity (YTM) between the lower yields has a much larger price impact than a price change between the higher yield levels.

Hedge Ratio—The Equalizer in Interest Rate Risk

Differences in maturity date, coupon size, and yield to maturity all have an impact on the price/yield sensitivity of a security. We noted above that many traders enter into transactions where the yield spread between two or more issues, rather than the price relationship, is the focus. For example, a trader may feel the yield spread relationship between a

EXHIBIT 4.3   Impact of change in yield to maturity with respect to price

YTM	Price	Difference
3%	125.31	
4%	116.08	9.23
5%	107.67	8.41
6%	100.00	7.67
7%	92.98	7.02
8%	86.57	6.41

6% Coupon Maturity 3/1/08
Settlement 5/12/98

particular corporate bond and its corresponding maturity Treasury bond is out of line. Or, an unusually wide or narrow spread may be noted between an on-the-run Treasury issue of one maturity and another on-the-run issue of a different maturity. To mitigate interest rate risk in a multiple security trade, it is necessary to equate the dollar sensitivities of the security (securities) being purchased with those of the security (securities) being sold. This is where the concept of *hedge ratio* is applied.

A hedge ratio measures the difference between the price sensitivities of two issues, given a similar change in yield. The ratio allows the trader to calculate a multiple ratio between the securities, essentially stating: "Security A moves at [some amount] faster [or slower] than Security B." The calculation of a hedge ratio can be done using a few different price/yield sensitivity measures. These are discussed in the following sections.

BASIS POINT VALUE

Basis point value (BPV) reflects the dollar price change for a fixed-income security on a coupon date, given a one-basis-point change in its yield. In essence, BPV takes the price of a security a half-basis point above and below the stated yield to maturity and measures the difference between the two values. Exhibit 4.4 is a sample calculation of basis point value.

Using Basis Point Value to Trade Basis Risk

Exhibit 4.5 represents the use of basis point value to take advantage of a perceived anomaly in the slope of the yield curve. In this case, the trader is interested in the *spread* between the yields on two securities, not the absolute level of the yields. The expectation is for a widening of the yield spread between the two securities, and the trader wants to hedge against any upward or downward parallel movement in rates (see Exhibit 4.5a).

Given the trader's belief that the yield spread between the two securities is too *narrow*, the trader expects one of three things to happen: (1) the 3-year note will fall in yield, (2) the 10-year note will rise in yield, or (3) a combination of both will occur. Therefore, the trade is structured as shown in Exhibit 4.5b.

The yield spread between the two securities remained the same on day two. The profit-and-loss outcome, however, could be entirely different if the trader used the hedge ratio to structure the trade. Both situations are examined in Exhibit 4.5c.

Using the hedge ratio effectively eliminated the loss incurred with the nonhedged trade. The hedge didn't offset the exact difference

EXHIBIT 4.4   Basis point value

$6\frac{1}{8}$% T-bond due 11/15/2027
Yield 5.83%; settlement date 4/11/98
Price @ 5.825% yield to maturity = $ 104.2019
Price @ 5.835% yield to maturity = 104.0573

BPV per $100	$ .144662
BPV per $1 million	$1,446.62

EXHIBIT 4.5a   Mitigating interest rate risk by applying hedge ratios

Scenario, Day One
Settlement date: 3/2/98

	Current 3-Year Treasury Note		**Current 10-Year Treasury Note**
Coupon	$5\frac{3}{4}$		$6\frac{1}{8}$
Maturity	11/15/2000		8/15/2007
Price (in 32nds)	101		104
Yield	5.344%		5.575%
Spread (in basis points)		23.1 bps	
Basis point value (per $1 million)	$250.45		$745.28
Hedge ratio		2.976	

EXHIBIT 4.5b   Buy the 3-year note and sell the 10-year note

Scenario, Day Two: A 10-basis-point downward parallel shift in both yields

	3-Year Treasury Note		**10-Year Treasury Note**
Yield	5.244%		5.475%
Price	101.25035		104.74497
Price change ($ million)	$250.35		−$744.97
Spread (in basis points)		23.1 bps	

EXHIBIT 4.5c

Hedge Ratio Not Used

Buy $1 million par value 3-year notes; *sell* $1 million par value 10-year notes.
Profit/Loss *after* 10-basis-point downward parallel shift:
　　3-year note　　$2,503.54 Profit
　10-year note　　−7,449.70 Loss
　　　Net Loss　　−$4,946.16 Loss

Hedge Ratio Used

Buy $2.976 million par value 3-year notes; *sell* $1 million par value 10-year notes.
Profit/Loss Impact:
　　3-year note　　2.976 × 2,503.54 = $7,450.54　Profit
　10-year note　　　1 × 7,449.70 = $7,449.70　Loss
　　　Net Profit　　　　　　　$　　.84° Profit

°Excludes cost of carry considerations for purchase and sale of securities. The more days the trade is held, the more impact the cost of carry.

between the two securities because of rounding and the dynamic slope of the price/yield curve for both securities. We will come back to this shortly.

YIELD VALUE OF A 32ND

Another sensitivity measurement, similar to BPV, is called yield value of a 32nd. The measurement is the change in the yield to maturity, given a $\frac{1}{32}$ change in the price. We look at this particular price difference because $\frac{1}{32}$ of a point change is a common increment in the quoting of actively traded securities (on-the-run U.S. Treasury issues, for example).

To calculate the yield value of a 32nd, simply take the value of $\frac{1}{32}$ or .03125 ($312.50 per $1 million par value) and divide it by the basis point value of the security. Using the data in Exhibit 4.4, Exhibit 4.6 shows the conversion of basis point value to yield value of a 32nd. Both basis point value and yield value of $\frac{1}{32}$ are easily calculated by most spreadsheet add-in programs. (See Chapter 12.)

EVOLUTION OF RISK MEASUREMENT

All other things being equal, the longer it takes to recoup an investment, the greater the risk associated with getting the money back. In the business of risk measurement, a number of factors determine exactly when the money is returned to the investor. If a security is purchased with a *time to final maturity* of 10 years, is it reasonable to presume the

EXHIBIT 4.6   Deriving yield value of $\frac{1}{32}$ price change

Coupon: $6\frac{1}{8}\%$	Yield: 5%
Maturity date: 8/15/2027	Basis point value: $1,446.62
Settlement date: 4/11/1998	

$$\textbf{Yield Value of a 32nd} = \frac{\$312.50}{\$1,446.62} = .216 \text{ bps per } \frac{1}{32} \text{ change in price.}$$

Both basis point value and yield value of $\frac{1}{32}$ are easily calculated by most spreadsheet add-in programs. See Chapter 12.

investor will receive the money back in 10 years? Hardly. Perhaps a better measurement is *average maturity*. If principal payments are spread out like a sinking fund, an average of these payments, based on when they are received, will give us a better estimate of when the investor will get the money back. Better, yes. Correct, no. What if the principal payments are not equal? A *weighted average maturity* accounts for any uneven principal flows. Better, yes; but still not correct. We need to add in the coupon payments and calculate a *weighted average cash flow*. Almost there, but one factor is still missing. We are calculating the return of initial invested capital on *present value dollars*. We need to convert the weighted average cash flows into present value terms. Once this is done, the investor has a much more accurate measurement of when the initial investment will be returned. This measurement is called *duration*. Here is a summary of how duration evolves from time to final maturity:

Duration =

Time to maturity Principal only	→	Average maturity Principal only	→	Weighted average maturity Principal only	→	Weighted average cash flow Principal and interest

Initially developed in 1938 by Frederick Macaulay,[1] duration better quantifies the price/yield sensitivity measurement. It represents the time, measured in years, that it takes an investor to receive the *middle* dollar of an initial investment. (Remember, the purchase price of a bond is equal to the present value of the future stream of cash flows associated with the bond.) Exhibit 4.7 demonstrates the formula and calculation of duration.

Exhibit 4.7 tells us the investor will receive the middle dollar of the initial investment about 1.92 years from the date of purchase. Clearly, no money is received at exactly this time. It is important to remember that duration is a measure of maturity risk. The statistic is used to measure the risk generated by maturities of different securities. What makes duration more accurate than simply looking at time to maturity? The inclusion of all the cash flows, weighted by timing as well as present value, in the determination of return of investment.

Duration is a more accurate measure of maturity risk, but continuous compounding is assumed in the calculation. In other words, an

EXHIBIT 4.7   Formula and calculation of duration

On the coupon payment date:

$$\text{Duration (in years)} = \frac{1}{\text{PVTCF}} \sum_{t=1}^{n} \frac{C_t}{\left(1 + \dfrac{i}{P}\right)^t} \times \frac{t}{p}$$

where: C = nominal cash flow,
    P = number of coupons or compounding periods per year,
    t = time period in which cash flow is received,
    i = yield to maturity,
    PVTCF = present value of total cash flows (bond price).

Duration example:
    Price: $99.78
    Coupon: 5.75%
    Maturity date: 9/30/2000
    Settlement date: 9/30/98
    Yield: 5.868%

Years	Cash Flow	Present Value Factor	Present Value Cash Flow	Weighting	Present Value WTD Cash Flow
.5	28.75	.9715	$ 27.93	.5	$ 13.97
1.0	28.75	.9438	27.13	1.0	27.13
1.5	28.75	.9169	26.36	1.5	39.54
2.0	1,028.75	.8908	916.38	2.0	1,832.76
			$997.80		$1,913.40

Duration = 1.9134 years × 1/.9978 (price) = 1.9176 years

investor is expected to receive continuous returns over the life of the security. Unfortunately, this does not happen. Most fixed-income securities pay interest semiannually. John Hicks[2] altered the duration concept to adjust for different compounding frequencies. This method is called *modified duration*. The adjustment formula divides duration by (1 + yield to maturity, divided by the number of annual compounding periods). Exhibit 4.8 reflects the conversion of the duration calculation to modified duration. A more practical way to view modified duration is: *A 100-basis-point change in a securities yield will reflect a price change in percent approximately equal to the number of years measured by the modified duration statistic.* For example, a duration of 5

EXHIBIT 4.8   Converting Macaulay duration to modified duration

$$\text{Modified duration} = \frac{\text{Macaulay duration}}{\dfrac{(1 + \text{Yield to maturity})}{\text{Compounding frequency}}}$$

$$\text{Modified duration} = \frac{1.9176}{\left(1 + \left(\dfrac{.05868}{2}\right)\right)} = 1.86 \ \text{years}$$

years indicates an approximate 5% change in price, given a 100-bp change in yield to maturity in either direction.

DOLLAR DURATION

Dollar duration, another form of duration measurement, generates results similar to those of the basis point value statistic. It requires multiplying the modified duration of a security by the *full* or *dirty price* (principal + accrued interest). Modified duration represents a *percent* change in the price of a security, given a 100-bp change in its yield. Dollar duration—also known as *risk,* or ΔPΔY (change in price, given a change in yield)—adjusts the percentage change calculated by modified duration to an actual dollar change. For example, for the settlement date of November 24, 1997, the U.S. Treasury bond 11¼%, due 2/15/2015, traded at a price of 155⁷⁄₃₂ (decimal of fraction = .21875). The modified duration of the security is 9.2179 years, and its yield to maturity is 6.0448%. The dollar duration equals:

$$\overset{\substack{\text{Modified} \\ \text{duration}}}{9.2179} \times \Big[\big(\overset{\text{Price}}{155.21875} + \overset{\substack{\text{Accrued} \\ \text{interest}}}{3.0876} \big) / 100 \Big] = 14.5925 \ \text{Dollar duration}$$

The dollar price of the security will change $14.5925, or $1,459.25 per basis point per $1 million par value. Similarly, the basis point value is $1,459.25. The major differences between modified duration and dollar duration are: (1) modified duration measures *percent price* change, and dollar duration measures price change in *price points;* (2) dollar duration includes any accrued interest in its calculation whereas modified duration does not. (*Effective duration* is used to measure securities with stochastic, or uncertain, cash flows. We will discuss this concept in Chapter 6.)

CONVEXITY

Exhibit 4.8 outlined the measurement of modified duration, given a 100-basis-point change in yield, but the actual change in price is somewhat different from the projected change of the duration estimate because of the nonlinear relationship between price and yield. To adjust for this difference, a second moment of difference, or a *change in the change,* must be calculated. *Convexity* represents the change in the change of a price, given a change in yield. It is a measure of the curvature of the price/yield curve. Combining both duration and convexity essentially covers the entire actual change in price, from a specific change in yield. Exhibit 4.9 represents graphically the duration and convexity measurements. Exhibit 4.10a measures the portion of actual change in price, given a change in yield, that is explained by modified duration and convexity. As the change in yield gets larger versus the yield used to calculate modified

EXHIBIT 4.9 Graphic representation of duration and convexity

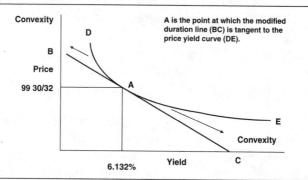

duration, the percent price change explained by duration gets smaller. Again, this is due to the curvilinear relationship between actual price and yield changes. The actual statistic calculated by the convexity formula in Exhibit 4.10a (65.5) measures the curvature of the price/yield curve at that point where the yield to maturity being

EXHIBIT 4.10a   Convexity measures the curvature of the price yield relationship (*change* in the change)

Coupon: 6.125%	Maturity: 8/15/2008
Settlement date: 10/21/98	Yield to maturity: 6.132%
Price: 99³⁰⁄₃₂	Modified duration: 7.218 years

Yield	Actual Price	Estimated Price from Modified Duration	Convexity (est.)
2.132	135.20	128.79	6.41
3.132	125.13	121.58	3.55
4.132	115.95	114.37	1.58
5.132	107.57	107.15	.42
6.132	99.94	99.94	0.00
7.132	92.96	92.72	.24
8.132	86.59	85.51	1.08
9.132	80.76	78.30	2.46
10.132	75.42	71.08	4.34

Convexity @ 6.132% = 65.5

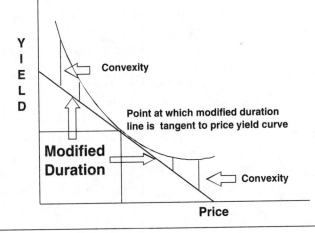

EXHIBIT 4.10b

Assume 200 bp *decline* in rates.
Percentage price change due to convexity is equal to:

$$.5 \times \text{Convexity} \times (\Delta \text{YTM})^2 \times 100$$
$$.5 \times 65.5 \times (.02)^2 \times 100 = \underline{1.31\%} \text{ price change from convexity}$$

Combining the modified duration and convexity impacts on price\yield sensitivities accounts for nearly all of the actual change in the securities price:

Duration change = 7.218% × 2 = 14.44%
Convexity change = 1.31%
Total (14.44 + 1.31) = 15.75%
Actual change = 16.02%   (Difference 0.27%)

---

examined is tangent to the price/yield curve (see Exhibit 4.9). To change this number to a percentage price change, a conversion formula is necessary. Exhibit 4.10b shows the conversion formula and calculates the total price difference accounted for by modified duration and convexity against an actual price/yield movement. As you can see, the actual price change is almost entirely accounted for by these two statistics.[3]

Positive and Negative Convexity

Positive convexity exists in noncallable bonds. Remember, the actual price/yield curve for these securities is *curved* (see Exhibit 4.9). *Negative convexity* could exist in callable bonds as the yield to maturity of the security moves between a call likelihood and a noncall likelihood. Under a normal, or upward sloping, yield curve, an increase in price above the stated call price will reduce the maturity of the security to the call date, thereby reducing the price accordingly (discussed in Chapter 6). This occurs largely as a function of changes in required market rates of return (yield to maturity) for the particular risk category and maturity represented by the security in question.

Using our security in Exhibit 4.10, let's assume it is callable on 8/15/2003 at a price of 100. Once the security trades above the 100 price level (below 6.125% yield to maturity), the market will price it with a maturity of 2003 rather than 2008. Substituting the 2003 maturity date into the change in actual prices reveals the following:

Yield to Maturity	Option-Adjusted Actual Price	Previous Price Estimate from Modified Duration	Difference
6.132	99.94	99.94	0
5.132	104.18	107.15	−2.97
4.132	108.62	114.37	−5.75
3.132	113.28	121.58	−8.30
2.132	118.19	128.79	−10.60

The higher the price rises, the larger is the negative gap between the modified duration estimate and the market price (creating negative convexity) adjusted to account for the call feature. Remember the actual price with yields below 6.125% assume a maturity date of 08/15/2003 (the call date).

Effective convexity, like effective duration, more commonly measures convexity in securities with uncertain cash flows. These types of securities will be examined in greater detail in Chapter 6.

SUMMARY

The two basic kinds of market risk associated with nonoption fixed-income securities are interest rate risk and basis risk. Interest rate risk measures price/yield sensitivity for parallel shifts in the yield curve. Basis risk measures risk with nonparallel shifts in the yield curve. Basis point value and yield value of a 32nd are two measures for valuing price/yield sensitivity. Duration and convexity are risk measurements used to evaluate relative risk in both individual securities and portfolios. The dollar duration calculation is similar to basis point value, although measured in years instead of dollars. Securities with stochastic or contingent cash flows are also susceptible to call or to early redemption risk, largely as a function of interest rate levels. This will be discussed in more detail in Chapter 6.

NOTES

1. Frederick Macaulay, "Some Theoretical Problems Suggested by the Movements of Interest Rates, Bond Yields, and Stock Prices in the United States since 1865" (New York: National Bureau of Economic Research, 1938).
2. John Hicks, *Value and Capital* (Oxford, England: Clarendon Press, 1939).
3. Mathematically, modified duration and convexity represent the first two moments of difference, or price/yield sensitivity, explained through the Taylor order series of the price function. For a more precise measurement of price differential, it is necessary to go to a third-order difference, or the *difference* in the *difference* in the *difference*. As a practical matter, the combination of duration and convexity explains nearly all price difference calculations.

5 TERM STRUCTURE OF INTEREST RATES

This chapter examines yield curves, the term structure of interest rates, and relevant applications to the U.S. Treasury market. The history, development, and valuation of Treasury STRIPS are described. Among the questions answered are: How is a STRIPS security priced? What is the difference between a STRIP'S fair value and its market value?

YIELD CURVES AND THE TERM STRUCTURE OF INTEREST RATES

In Chapter 3, we discussed the concept of pricing fixed-income securities based on yield spread relationships. The reasons for using U.S. Treasury securities in a benchmarking capacity include: the homogeneity of credit risk in all Treasury securities, the broad range of outstanding issues, and the liquidity of the market. The marketplace uses the yields on Treasury issues (rather than price) for benchmarking because yield represents return on investment. Price is simply the present value cost of purchasing that return. Investors' requirements for relative measures of return can't be properly evaluated by using price. If the marketplace required a 6% yield on a 5-year Treasury security, any

83

Treasury issues with a maturity of 5 years would need a yield of 6% to be competitively priced. Two issues with 5 years to maturity might have, respectively, a 4% and a 10% coupon. Both securities might be priced to yield 6% in 5 years, but, from a price perspective, they would be dramatically different. The issue with the 4% coupon would be priced at just under 91½, and the 10% issue would cost just over 117. This is why yield, rather than price, is used for benchmarking securities valuations.

The yield on any optionless[1] security is composed of four factors: (1) the risk-free rate determined by the U.S. Treasury security returns; (2) a risk premium associated with a security other than a Treasury issue (in most cases, the greater the risk the higher the required return); (3) liquidity considerations—the amount of a security outstanding and the length of time it has been outstanding both contribute to its valuation; and (4) the inflation premium. If both the rate of inflation and the yield to maturity of a security are the same, the investor is basically earning nothing on a real or inflation-adjusted basis. Add to this any income tax and transaction costs, and the real return becomes negative.

The relationship between the yield and the maturity of securities with equal credit risk can be graphically depicted through a yield curve. Changing inflation expectations, supply–demand conditions, and other liquidity considerations can all contribute to the structure or slope of a yield curve. Yield curves come in different shapes. The one most people are familiar with is known as a *coupon curve,* or *on-the-run curve,* where investors look at the U.S. Treasury markets. The maturities on this curve stretch from 3 months to 30 years. The first three maturities (13, 26, and 52 weeks) are single cash flow issues (T-Bills). The rest of the curve is made up of coupon-bearing issues. T-Bills, as discussed in Chapter 1, are quoted on a discount basis and must be converted to a bond equivalent yield in order to reflect consistency on this yield curve.

The yield on the coupon-bearing issues represents semiannual compounding of each interest payment at the same rate that was calculated at the time of purchase. It is therefore not what could be called an accurate representation of the market-required yield for a particular maturity, presuming that the security under analysis has only one cash flow on the maturity date. (Remember, the investor is getting cash flows at several times prior to the final maturity of the security.)

The zero coupon curve is the representation of single cash flow securities with maturity dates ranging out as far as the longest maturity coupon security. This curve could be either structured, with rates observed in the marketplace, or implied, based on similar maturity coupon-bearing securities. Zero coupon securities and yield curves are discussed later in this chapter.

1980: ROCK 'N' ROLL INTEREST RATES

Generally speaking, short-term rates move faster than long-term rates—in part, because investors are attempting to adjust shorter-term returns to economic conditions at the time. Longer-term rates tend to reflect an average of expected economic conditions over longer periods of time. A good example is the year 1980. Short-term interest rates and inflation for the year reached levels that were unprecedented in the United States in the twentieth century. The cause of these wild swings was a combination of Federal Reserve activities and the marketplace's perception of future rates of inflation. During the year, the market expectations for inflation shifted between relief and alarm as the growth in the money supply alternated between fast and slow.[2] As a result, the short end of the yield curve reflected the volatility, and the long end basically kept its fingers crossed that all this would pass. Fortunately, the long end was right. Inflation and interest rates eventually returned to more moderate levels.

A review of prime rate (used for short-term lending) and the 30-year Treasury bond movements during 1980 (see Exhibit 5.1) reflects the sharp difference in volatility between the two rates. Perhaps a reason for this was the market's expectation that double-digit inflation was only a temporary phenomenon.

EXHIBIT 5.1   1980 interest rate volatility

Date	Prime Rate	30-Year Treasury Bond
January	$15\frac{1}{4}$	10.60
April	20	10.83
June	$10\frac{3}{4}$	9.81
December	$21\frac{1}{2}$	12.40

The observed real, or inflation-adjusted, rates of return on long-term Treasury issues post-1981 never really reverted to the 2½%–3% average achieved between 1946 and 1981. Since 1981, the real rate of return on Treasury securities has almost always stayed north of the historical average. In 1982, inflation fell to the 6% range but long-term interest rates were largely unchanged. This created real, or inflation-adjusted, rates of return of 8%! The double-digit rates of inflation in the late 1970s and early 1980s seem to have left an indelible mark on investors' concerns over inflation and real rates of return. As of June 1998, inflation, as measured by the Consumer Price Index (CPI), was growing at an annual rate of 1.7% while 30-year Treasury bonds were yielding 6.4%—a spread of 4.7%. Appendix C reflects the structure of the yield curve for each year between 1970 and 1997.

DIFFERENT YIELD CURVE STRUCTURES

There are four basic types of yield curve structures: (1) upward sloping, (2) flat, (3) downward sloping, and (4) hump-backed. The reason an upward sloping curve, also referred to as a normal curve, is considered normal relates to the concept of investment liquidity. Investors, as a general rule, require a higher rate of return on a fixed-income investment as the maturity date of the security draws nearer. Intuitively, this makes sense; the further out in time one goes, the more opportunity external forces (e.g., inflation) and internal forces (e.g., changes in credit ratings) have to move the price and yield of a security from their current values. Exhibit 5.2 reflects a normally sloped yield curve.

Where there is a flat curve, the yield on all maturities is essentially the same. Investors may perceive a longer-term stability of inflation, with both short- and long-term rates having equal corresponding real rates of return. In August 1998, the U.S. Treasury yield curve structure had a spread of less than 75 basis points between the 3-month and 30-year issues. Historically, this represents a flat yield curve (see Exhibit 5.3).

In the third type of yield curve structure, a downward sloping or inverted curve, the shorter-term maturities have higher yields than the long-term issues. One possible reason for this structure is investors' expectations of declining inflation over time. A good example occurred

EXHIBIT 5.2   Normally sloped yield curve

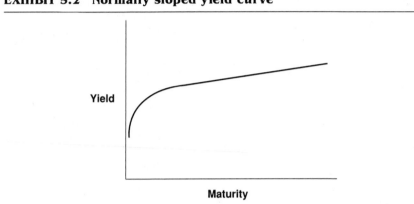

during the early part of 1981, the last in a series of three years in which the annual rate of inflation in the United States exceeded 10%. As mentioned above, the greater volatility observed in the shorter end of the yield curve reflects investors' expectations of, and ways of dealing with, conditions existing over the short term. The inverted yield curve could reflect investors' belief that currently high rates of inflation will not continue over time.[3] Exhibit 5.4 reflects an inverted yield curve.

EXHIBIT 5.3   Flat yield curve

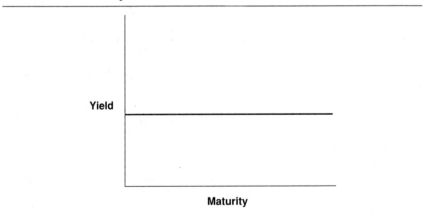

EXHIBIT 5.4   Inverted yield curve

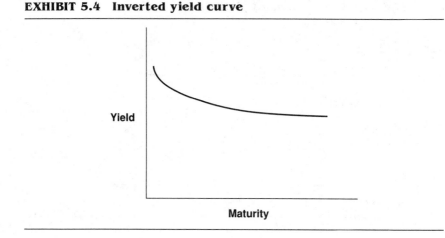

    The fourth type of curve is hump-backed. This occurs when one or more rates between the shortest and longest maturity on the curve are either lower than the previous shorter maturity or higher than the following longer maturity. Supply and demand considerations, inflation expectations, and liquidity issues can play a role in creating this structure. Over time, observed yield curves with a hump-backed structure are usually not overly pronounced in terms of the size of the hump, and they don't exist over extended periods of time. Exhibit 5.5 depicts a hump-backed yield curve.

THE SPOT, OR ZERO COUPON YIELD CURVE

Chapter 3 focused on the yield to maturity for the active or on-the-run U.S. Treasury securities as the benchmarking determinant for valuing other fixed-income securities. As we noted, yield to maturity presumes one rate of discount for all cash flows included in a security. It is this concept of periodic receipt of cash flows that we need to explore further for the valuation process.

    Any fixed-income security, no matter what its structure, is nothing more than a series of one or more cash flows. These payments, representing principal and/or interest, are received over the life of the

EXHIBIT 5.5   Hump-backed yield curve

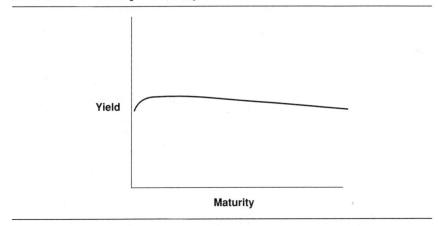

Yield

Maturity

security. Therefore, it stands to reason that the accurate price and yield of a security (package of cash flows) should be the sum of the present value of each cash flow, computed by discounting the future value or payment amount by the rate of interest that was applicable to the period of time between the purchase date and the receipt of payment. The marketplace has developed a method of valuing fixed-income securities that more closely resembles the actual discount rates associated with each cash flow in a security. This method uses what is known as the U.S. Treasury *spot* or *zero coupon* yield curve.

A LITTLE HISTORY

In the early 1980s, several large U.S. Government securities dealers purchased some longer-term Treasury issues, then separated or *stripped* the interest coupons away from the principal amount and sold each piece separately. At the time, no official government program was in place to handle these types of transactions. As a result, the dealers individually titled their new securities with homegrown names. The acronyms they chose for these securities tended to spell the names of members of the feline family. TIGRS (Treasury Income Growth Receipts) and CATS (Certificates of Treasury Accrual) were among the offerings to investors seeking what amounted to low prices for high-quality investments.

At the end of 1984, the Treasury joined the club when it initiated a program called STRIPS (Separate Trading of Registered Interest and Principal Securities). Under the STRIPS program, U.S. Government securities dealers could "strip" interest payments from the principal and trade them separately. Traders also could submit the principal and interest pieces necessary to recreate, or *reconstitute* a security (we will discuss this in greater detail shortly). At the outset, only securities with an initial maturity of 10 years or more were eligible for stripping,[4] but that rule was changed in September 1997. Now, all newly issued coupon-bearing Treasury securities (including the inflation-indexed issues) are eligible for the STRIPS program.

TRADING TREASURY STRIPS

The U.S. Treasury zero coupon market forms the basis for the most actively traded zero coupon securities. STRIPS are created by financial market traders who believe they can make the sum of the parts equal more than the whole. The actual size of the market is limited only to the underlying coupon-bearing securities that are issued by the Treasury. Individual investors for retirement accounts and college funds actively purchase STRIPS. They are also popular with institutional investors looking to more accurately match longer-term asset and liability maturities. For example, an insurance company would consider zero coupon securities as investments that will mature in conjunction with specific payment dates for an annuity.

STRIPS are quoted on a yield-to-maturity basis. The price/yield calculations can be done in the same format as a coupon-bearing security; the only difference is that the coupon value is equal to zero. STRIPS are traded in three formats. The first is on an *outright yield* basis. A customer looking to purchase a STRIP would be quoted a yield value for a particular maturity. For example, an interest STRIP due 5/15/2016 could be offered at a yield to maturity of 6.15%. The bid yield, like the T-Bill and other single cash flow securities, would be slightly higher—say, 6.17%. This is where the investor could sell the STRIP to the dealer. The offer yield, say 6.15%, is where the investor could purchase the STRIP from the dealer.

The second way a STRIP is quoted is in a *swap*. A dealer might say, "I will sell a 5/15/2016 interest STRIP and buy a 11/15/2016 interest STRIP at a spread of three basis points." This dealer is willing to sell the 5/15/2016 interest STRIP at a spread of three basis points below the yield the dealer is willing to pay the customer to purchase the 11/15/2016 interest STRIP. The actual yield on each security is not as important as the fact that the spread between the two yields is equal to three basis points. Swap quotes are primarily purchased and sold between U.S. Government securities dealers, who communicate via the interdealer broker screens. (See Exhibit 3.3 for a sample interdealer broker page that carries swap quotes on Treasury STRIPS.)

The third way a STRIP is quoted is on a *spread* basis. A dealer may be willing to sell the 5/15/2016 interest STRIP at a spread of 12 basis points over the yield to maturity of the on-the-run 30-year Treasury bond. The dealers' bid for this STRIP could be 14 basis points over the 30-year yield. Once again, the value of the spread between the STRIP and the 30-year bond is more important than the actual yield levels of both issues. Like the swaps, spread quotes are traded among the primary dealers.

Treasury STRIPS can also be *reconstituted*. Reconstitution occurs when a trader believes the component parts of a Treasury issue can be purchased at a cheaper price than their sale can realize. The pieces of the issue are deposited together at the Federal Reserve, and a whole security is issued. This process entails purchasing the correct amount of interest and principal payments with the correct maturity dates to reconstruct a previously existing issue. It is interesting to note that it is not necessary to purchase the exact issue interest STRIPS in the reconstitution process. As an example, a trader could purchase an interest payment from a Treasury bond issue for reconstitution into a 10-year Treasury note, provided the interest payment dates were the same for both securities. Principal STRIPS must be the same as the issue being reconstituted. Otherwise, it would be possible to create more of an issue than was actually sold at auction.

Treasury STRIPS come in principal and interest forms. There may be a price/yield difference between the principal and interest STRIP with the same maturity. This could be a result of liquidity and of supply-and-demand considerations. Keep in mind that the delivery on a purchase of an interest STRIP could contain coupon payments from any Treasury security with that particular maturity as part of its cash flow structure. A principal STRIP can come from only one particular security because there is only one principal payment date for any U.S. Treasury issue.[5]

The purchase or sale of Treasury STRIPS can be done through most of the primary dealers as well as other securities dealers who specialize in these securities. Ragen McKenzie is one of the largest U.S. Treasury zero coupon dealer-specialists in the country. This firm maintains inventories not only of securities created under the STRIPS program, but also of zero coupon securities created prior to the beginning of the STRIPS program.

A monthly report on all stripping and reconstitution activities is prepared by the Treasury and issued to the public. The report reflects all securities eligible for stripping, their opening nonstripped balance, stripping and reconstitution for the month, and a closing nonstripped balance. Investors find this information valuable when determining the availability of securities in either stripped or whole form.

STRIPS types of securities are also available from a number of federal agencies. Issuers such as FICO (Financing Corporation) and RefCorp (Resolution Funding Corporation) have issued long-term securities eligible for stripping. Some of these securities had maturities as long as 40 years.

PRICING AND VALUING A TREASURY STRIP

The theoretical or implied value of a STRIP can be calculated through what is best described as a break-even process. A popular form of this calculation is called the *bootstrapping* method. Exhibit 5.6 reflects the implied value determination of an 18-month zero coupon Treasury by calculating the break-even value required to make an investor indifferent to purchasing either an 18-month coupon-bearing security or a package of STRIPS with the equivalent cash flow dates. Note that the formula for calculating the 18-month STRIP value is the same format used to determine the price of an option-free security, detailed in Chapter 2. As shown in Exhibit 5.6, the combination of an 18-month STRIP yield of 6.017%, along with

EXHIBIT 5.6   Valuing a U.S. Treasury STRIP

Given: 6-month T-Bill bond equivalent yield = 5.30%
12-month T-Bill bond equivalent yield = 5.50%
18-month coupon-bearing security coupon rate and yield to maturity =
6% (price = 100)
$10,000 par value

$$\frac{300}{\left(1+\frac{.053}{2}\right)} + \frac{300}{\left(1+\frac{.055}{2}\right)^2} + \frac{10,300}{\left(1+\frac{X}{2}\right)^3} = 10,000$$

292.2552   284.1565

$$\left(1+\frac{X}{2}\right)^3 = \frac{10,300}{9,423.5883} \qquad X = 6.017\%$$

the observed 6- and 12-month bond equivalent yields for the two Treasury bills, equates to the value of the 18-month coupon-bearing security. The proof of the calculation is: The sum of the present values of the three STRIPS equals the price observed on the coupon-bearing security.

Exhibit 5.6 calculates an implied 18-month STRIP yield. To determine the 24-month STRIP implied value, use the 6- and 12-month T-Bill yields, the 18-month implied STRIP yield, and the yield on a 24-month coupon-bearing security. Perform the same calculation as for the 18-month security. By continuing this process throughout the yield curve, a series of implied or theoretical spot rates is derived. Exhibit 5.7 reflects an implied zero coupon curve derived semiannually out to 5 years, using a hypothetical U.S.Treasury coupon yield curve. The settlement date for each security's calculation was 5/16/1998. Assume: (1) each coupon-bearing security is priced at 100 (coupon and yield to maturity are equal) and (2) the 6- and 12-month coupon yields are Treasury Bills.

Each of the derived zero coupon yields represents the break-even value for that particular maturity, using the previously derived zero yields. For example, the 42-month zero yield (7.10%) was derived as follows. The 42-month coupon yield is 7%. What does the 42-month zero have to yield to make the investor indifferent to purchasing the 42-month coupon-bearing security with a yield of 7%, or the series of

EXHIBIT 5.7   Derivation of a zero coupon curve

Maturity	Coupon Yield to Maturity	Derived Zero Coupon Yield
6 months	5.280%	5.280%
12	5.360	5.360
18	5.500	5.505
24	6.000	6.027
30	6.250	6.289
36	6.750	6.830
42	7.000	7.100
48	7.500	7.667
54	7.750	7.950
60	8.000	8.242

implied zero coupon securities maturing from 6 months to 42 months? Using the bootstrap formula, we get the following:

$$
\begin{aligned}
&\text{6 months } 3.5/(1+.0528/2) & 3.41 \\
&\text{12 months} + 3.5/(1+.0536/2)^2 & 3.31 \\
&\text{18 months} + 3.5/(1+.05505/2)^3 & 3.23 \\
&\text{24 months} + 3.5/(1+.06027/2)^4 & 3.11 \\
&\text{30 months} + 3.5/(1+.06289)^5 & 3.00 \\
&\text{36 months} + 3.5/(1+.0683)^6 & 2.86 \\
&\text{42 months} + 103.5/(1+.071)^7 = & \underline{81.08} \\
& & 100.00
\end{aligned}
$$

(3.5 = ½ of 7% coupon for the 42-month maturity)

Here the derived 42-month zero coupon rate equals 7.10%. How do implied spot rates compare to market-quoted STRIPS rates or the coupon securities from which their values are derived? The answer is: If they were significantly different, traders would either make outright purchases of the more profitable alternative or arbitrage away the difference. If the implied STRIP yield (6.017%) in our 18-month example was measurably *lower* than the quoted STRIP rate, traders would be better off purchasing the three STRIPS. If the implied STRIP yield was measurably *higher* than the quoted STRIP yield, traders would be better off purchasing the 18-month coupon security. Given equal risk parameters for both the three STRIPS and the 18-month coupon-bearing security, market forces would bring the two alternative investments back into line, subject to specific supply/demand considerations for either alternative.

SUMMARY

This chapter took a brief look at the term structure of interest rates. The various yield curve shapes were examined, and the spot, or zero curve, was introduced. The history of the STRIPS market was covered, and a method for determining the implied value of a particular maturity STRIP was presented.

NOTES

1. The yield on securities with embedded options is also affected by the potential for early redemption via the call or put privilege. This will be discussed further in Chapter 6.

2. During the early 1980s, monetarism, or the impact of growth in the money supply on inflation, was widely followed in the financial markets. Monetarists feared that an excessively fast increase in the money supply would stir up inflation. The wild ride of monetary growth rates during 1980 precipitated the volatile interest rate swings in the same year.

3. The yield curve has traditionally humped between 10 and 30 years; currently, it is peaking in the 20–25-year range. This is largely a function of investor demand. Note that the size of the hump is relatively small; approximately 10 basis points separated the highest yielding security and the current 30-year Treasury bond early in the second quarter of 1998.

4. When the STRIPS program was created, one callable issue was included as eligible for delivery: the 11¾% due 11/15/2014. To date, this is the only callable issue that has been accepted for the STRIPS program. The government no longer issues callable securities.

5. Principal STRIPS with maturity dates can't be interchanged where more than one eligible coupon security is maturing. If a 3-year note and a 10-year note mature on the same date, delivery of a principal STRIP for the 3-year note must be made from the principal portion of that security, not from the 10-year note. The reason is: If commingling was allowed, the potential exists to create more of an issue than was actually issued.

6 SECURITIES WITH CONTINGENT CASH FLOWS

Thus far, we have been dealing with fixed-income securities with known, or defined, cash flows. We estimated value based on the certainty of the timing of these flows. In the world of fixed income, there are several different types of securities with stochastic or uncertain cash flows based on the occurrence of one or more events. The reasons for their conditional nature are usually centered on some form of a call or put option or on a convertibility feature associated with the security. For example, a security may have a final maturity of 10 years but may be callable at the option of the issuer after 3 years. It may also be putable back to the issuer, at the discretion of the investor and at some predetermined price, prior to final maturity. In either case, the potential change in maturity date can clearly have a material impact on the current or present value as well as on the yield to maturity of the security. Many books and articles have been written on the valuation and analysis of securities with uncertain or contingent cash flows. This chapter outlines three popular types of securities with uncertain cash flows. A description of each will be followed by an overview of the mathematics associated with valuing the security. Appendix F lists some of the many quantitative texts that readers can access for more definitive discussions of the valuation of securities with stochastic cash flows.

Who issues securities with contingent cash flows? During the 1960s, 1970s, and the first part of the 1980s, the U.S. Treasury issued securities with various call features. The most popular of these maturities were the 30-year bonds issued between 1977 and 1984. Each of these securities had a 25-year call feature attached; the Treasury at its discretion could call any of these issues at the 25-year mark at a call price of 100. During the 1980s, this security structure fell out of favor with investors. Ultimately, it was eliminated from the financing schedule in favor of a noncallable 30-year security structure. In recent years, the major issuers of fixed-income securities with conditional cash flows have been corporations and federal agencies, which issue both unsecured debt and debt backed by a pool of different classes of assets. The most popular of these asset-backed securities are related to the mortgage markets. These instruments, called *mortgage-backed securities,* will be discussed later in the chapter.

The main purpose of callable or putable securities is to give either the issuer (callable) or the investor (putable) the opportunity, at some point in the life of the issue, to rethink whether it should remain outstanding. As an example of callable securities, an issuer may issue a 10-year fixed-rate note with a 5-year call feature. This call could be discreet (callable only on the anniversary of the 5 years remaining to maturity), or continuous for the remaining 5-year life of the security. Alternatively, multiple call dates could be specified at different periods during the security's life. Different call prices can also be specified. In many cases, price levels above par, or 100% of face value, are set for earlier dates in the security's life, as an incentive for the investor to purchase the security. These higher prices, at least in theory, help to offset the potential of early retirement of the debt.

The logic behind issuing a callable security is simple. As interest rate environments change, issuers like to have enough flexibility to maintain the lowest possible overall financing cost. If, for example, a corporation issues a 10-year fixed-rate note with a 9% coupon, and, 5 years later, the same corporation can raise 5-year money at a 7% rate, the corporation would like the opportunity to refinance the 10-year note at the lower rate for the remaining 5-year period. A 5-year call feature would enable the corporation to redeem the old 9% notes and issue 7% 5-year notes in their place. Clearly, this saves the issuer a significant amount of interest expense over the next 5 years. From a break-even perspective, the present value of the saving on interest expense over the 5-year period after the call date represents the amount of money available for a premium over par value offered to the investor on the call date. As the security approaches its final maturity date, the premium will be reduced as the present value declines. Exhibit 6.1 reflects the interest cost savings between 9% and a refinancing at 7%. It also shows the sliding premium on the issue that can be offered over the remaining 5 years, based on the interest cost savings.

Any call price at the end of 5 years that is less than 100 + ($8,316,607/$1,000,000), or $108.316607, will result in cost savings to the corporation. For example, if the call price were 104, the corporation would be required to pay out $104,000,000 when the security was called. The additional $4,316,590 (less transaction costs) would represent the present value cost savings from refinancing. Exhibit 6.2 reflects the present value of the cost savings at the end

EXHIBIT 6.1   Calculation of interest cost savings on callable debt securities

ABC Corporation issues a $100 million, 10-year, 9% fixed-rate note that is callable annually beginning in year 5. If a projection is made for a 7% 5-year rate in 5 years, the interest cost savings would be:

$$\$100,000,000 \times (9\% - 7\%) \times 5 \text{ years} = \$10,000,000.$$

The present value of the $10,000,000 at the 5-year mark, discounted at the 7% 5-year rate is:

Coupon Payment	Period (Years)	Present Value Factor	Present Value
$1,000,000	.5	.966184	$ 966,184
1,000,000	1.0	.933511	933,511
1,000,000	1.5	.901943	901,943
1,000,000	2.0	.871442	871,442
1,000,000	2.5	.841973	841,973
1,000,000	3.0	.813501	813,501
1,000,000	3.5	.785991	785,991
1,000,000	4.0	.759412	759,412
1,000,000	4.5	.733731	733,731
1,000,000	5.0	.708919	708,919
Present value			$8,316,607

**EXHIBIT 6.2   Present value of cost savings, and
break-even call prices, using the
projected 7% five-year rate**

Year	Cost Savings	Break-Even Call Price (Rounded)
5	$8,316,607	$108.3166
6	6,873,965	106.8740
7	5,328,553	105.3286
8	3,673,079	103.6731
9	1,899,694	101.8997
10	0	100.0000

of each year (presuming refinancing at 7%) and the maximum, or breakeven, call price to the corporation. The lower the refinancing rate, the higher the break-even call price can be. Unfortunately, the reverse holds true if refinancing rates rise.

A putable issue is, in effect, a bonus for the investor. The put feature allows the securities to be sold back to the issuer at the discretion of the investor. Unlike callable securities, the put option will usually have an increasing put price over time. Once again, different interest rate environments represent the most likely reason for exercising this type of feature. For example, an investor purchases a 10-year fixed-rate security with a 6% coupon at 100% of face value, and a put feature at the end of 5 years, exercisable at a price of 98, or 98% of face value. In 5 years, interest rate levels in general have moved considerably higher; 9% returns are available on similar quality 5-year notes. Using the put feature, the investor could get more of the initial capital investment returned at a time when the current market value of the original 6% coupon security was significantly lower (about 88% of face value) than 98% of face value. Additionally, the redemption proceeds could be reinvested at a more favorable rate.

The marketplace generally prices a security with call or put option features based on the most likely redemption date of the issue. In the case of the U.S. Treasury bonds noted earlier, each of the issues auctioned between 1977 and 1984 carries coupon rates between 7⅝% and 14%. At the beginning of 1998, the level of required rates of return for Treasury securities maturing between 2007 and 2014 was less than half of some of the earlier coupon rates. In this interest rate environment, an investor holding any of these securities can logically expect the Treasury to call these issues as they reach their specified call dates, because the price of any of these securities will be over 100% of face value. As a result, the yield to maturity, price, and other price/yield sensitivity measures should be calculated using the call date of the Treasury bond, not its final maturity date.

The theoretical value of a security with an embedded option can be viewed as follows:

Security with a call option = Optionless security − Call option.

Security with a put option = Optionless security + Put option.

A call option reduces the value of a security to the investor by giving the issuer the right to redeem the security during its life at some predetermined price. The put option enhances the value of the security to the investor by placing a set future value on the security, regardless of market conditions at that time.

A PRACTICAL VIEW OF SECURITIES WITH EMBEDDED OPTIONS

From a practical perspective, there are several ways to view the value of an embedded option in a noncollateralized security. The following factors affect the value of the option:

1. Historical or estimated price volatility of the underlying security.
2. The amount of time until the option can be exercised.
3. The nature of the option—either discreet (can only be exercised at a specific point in time) or nondiscreet (can be continuously exercised from a particular point onward, either to another particular point or to final maturity).
4. The spot and forward interest rate curves.
5. Changes in the credit rating of an issuer.
6. The call price schedule of the security.

The first two factors are major components of an options time value, and will be discussed in detail in Chapter 9. Discreet or nondiscreet exercise is analogous to European or American style options. European options (discreet) can only be exercised at a specific point in time (an option expiration). American options (nondiscreet) can be exercised at any time, thereby adding value to an American option compared to a European option.

The spot or zero coupon curve, as discussed in Chapter 5, represents the yield to maturity of securities with no cash flows other than a payment at maturity. Investors use the spot curve as a tool in pricing coupon-bearing securities because spot rates represent a more exact investor return requirement for specific maturities. The forward interest rate curve reflects yield-to-maturity values for different maturity structures starting and ending sometime in the future. An example of this is the yield on a 3-year note issued in 2 years. The value of the 3-year note would be the break-even amount between purchasing a 2-year note today and reinvesting the redemption proceeds into a 3-year note, versus purchasing a 5-year note today. In other words, what does the yield on the 3-year note have to be to make the investor indifferent to purchasing the 2-year note and subsequently the 3-year note versus purchasing the 5-year note? The values for both the spot and forward curves are functions of the associated cash market coupon curves of securities with the same degree of risk.

A change in an issuer's credit rating will have an immediate impact on both optionless and embedded-option debt securities. Changes in credit rating can also have an impact on the probability that an issue will be called by the issuer or put by the investor. Higher credit ratings lower a company's cost of raising debt capital, thereby boosting the prices of any of its fixed-income securities that are currently outstanding.

Consider the following. A corporation issues a 10-year note with a call option exercisable after 5 years. At the time of issuance, the corporation has a Baa, or bottom-tier, investment-grade rating. The day before the call date, the rating on the corporation is raised one notch to A. As discussed in Chapter 3, most debt securities are priced at a yield spread to the corresponding U.S. Treasury security's maturity. If the yield spread in year 5 for a 5–7 year Baa issue is 80 basis points over the associated Treasury issue, and 30 basis points over an A-rated issue, the yield on the security could drop by 50 basis points on the rating change announcement. This would have a significant price impact on a noncallable security of similar quality and maturity. For a callable security, an unexpected price change of this magnitude may cause the security to rise high enough above the call price to warrant a much greater likelihood that the issuer will exercise the embedded call option at the 5-year mark. If the marketplace believes this will occur, the security would shift from a perceived 6-year maturity to a 1-year maturity. Depending on the slope of the yield curve, the actual price shift of the issue could be minimal or tremendous.

In our simplified example, assume the security has an 8½% coupon, a required market yield to maturity for a 5-year Baa-rated security of 8½%, and an 8% required yield to maturity for a 5-year A-rated issue. The call price on the security is par, or 100. When the rating change occurred, the price of our callable issue would not move, while the noncallable issue price would increase sharply.

8½% Coupon	Price
Five-year noncallable Baa-rated security with an 8½% yield to maturity	$100.000
Five-year noncallable A-rated security with an 8% yield to maturity	102.027
Call price of security:	100.000

In this case, the rating change gives holders of the noncallable issue an increase in market value of more than 2 points per $100 par value. The callable issue, however, remains unchanged in value. The cost of the call option to investors in this instance would be 2.027 points represented by the 5-year A-rated security price (102.027) less the call price of the security (100). In our example, if the call price was 101 and the issue was called, the call option would cost the investor 1.027 points (102.027 − 101).

It is also important to note that changes in market forces can activate option-related features in a security. If, for example, yields on Treasury issues suddenly dropped, there would be an impact on all the securities priced off of Treasury issues. Even without a rating change, the yield on our Baa security could fall enough to warrant calling the security.

The issuer call potential is the reasoning behind why callable issues usually come with attractive yields. These higher yields entice investors into buying a callable security over a similar noncallable issue, the yield offsetting the risk of having to sell the security below market value on the call date.

As you can see, the call or put exercise price of a security plays a very important role in the determination of option valuation. As a general rule, the higher the call price or the lower the put price, the lower the value of the option. This is similar to strike prices on options on securities, discussed in Chapter 9. The further away this exercise or strike price is from the market or trading price of the security, the less likely an option on the security will be exercised.

Many callable securities have multiple call dates and call prices. These various call dates and call prices can have an impact on the current price and yield of a security. If a security has an original maturity of 10 years and is callable at different prices each year beginning in the sixth year, the marketplace will note the current price and yield on the security to its final maturity date and will compare them to all the potential call dates and prices on the call schedule. The first call date that has a price less than the current price (the yield will be more) represents a potential time to call the security. If this is determined to be the likely scenario, the issue will begin trading to that call date, using the call price as the redemption value. The same concept applies to securities with embedded put options.

QUANTITATIVE PRICING OF SECURITIES WITH UNCERTAIN CASH FLOWS

Mathematicians and other financial engineers have created numerous approaches to valuing securities with contingent, or uncertain, cash flows. These models generally derive their results from a probabilistic look at potential rate outcomes or expectations—that is, they assign a projected price volatility estimate and some probability of occurrence to each outcome. An in-depth analysis of this type of securities valuation is beyond the scope of this book, but it is important to have at least a basic understanding of the underlying logic that makes these models work.

Binomial Tree

One popular model, uses a binomial tree. This "tree" model, can be used to value both optionless and embedded-option securities. The following series of relationships comprises the structure of the tree. Each concept has been enumerated as a separate step, to make it easier to follow the overall process.

Step 1. The basic structuring of a binomial tree stems from assigning an equal probability of occurrence to two one-period rates starting one period in the future from each principal or interest payment date (including the dated date of the issue) contained in the security.

Step 2. The number of branches in the tree is a function of the number of compounding or payment periods in the security. If the security is a one-year security with two interest coupons, the structure would be as shown in Exhibit 6.3.

Each rate alternative or node (H and L) within each payment period equals a present value of the security at that point. In the case of a two-period security, T_{2HH}, (or T_{2LH}), and T_{2LL} all have the same principal or issue value and coupon rate. This is the period in which the security matures, and, consequently, the investor receives a return of the principal value plus the final interest payment. Because they are all the same value, the principal portion of both T_{1L} and T_{1H}, multiplied by their respective one-period rates, will equal the redemption price plus the last interest payment. Again, the compounding or interest factors for the two principal values in T_1 (T_1 is the first time period, or coupon period, after T_0.) are the estimated one-period rates (noted in Step 1) that will equate them with the sum of the redemption price plus the interest payment for the last period. The present value of T_{1H} will be lower than the present value of T_{1L} because the compounding factor (estimated one-period forward rate) is higher for T_{1H}.

Step 3. The difference between the two estimated rates generated from each previous payment period is defined by a user-specified interest rate volatility. The greater the volatility, the wider the difference between the rates. The formula for determining R_H (the higher

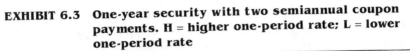

EXHIBIT 6.3   One-year security with two semiannual coupon payments. H = higher one-period rate; L = lower one-period rate

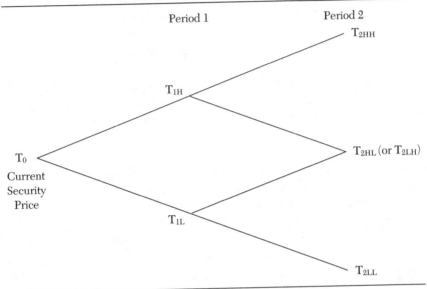

rate) is R_L (the lower rate) multiplied by $e^{2\sigma 1}$. For example, if the user-implied volatility is 10% and the lower one-period rate is 5%, the higher rate is .05 × 2.71828$^{2°.1}$ or 6.107%. As the tree widens, the difference between each pair of interest rate estimates, from the lowest to the highest, will be $e^{2\sigma}$. For example, a security with three payments or cash flow periods will have three interest rate estimates for period T_2. The difference from the lower to the middle rate, and from the middle rate to the upper rate estimates will be $e^{2\sigma}$. The lower-to-upper-rate difference will be $e^{4\sigma}$. The difference between the lowest and highest rate estimates in a four-branch period prior to the maturity date will be $e^{6\sigma}$, and so on.

Step 4. The value of the security for each alternative on each payment date, when multiplied by its one-period spot rate, is equal to the numerical average of the two projected principal values associated with that current value, plus their coupon payments. It is an average because at any alternative or node within the binomial tree, there is a presumed equal probability of occurrence for either the higher or lower one-period spot rate. The coupon payments—simply the annual rate of interest on the security being analyzed, divided by the number of payments per year—are used throughout the calculation. As noted earlier, the values at the final period (maturity date) must be the same. This condition makes it necessary for the computer to begin performing this process from the last period (where every value alternative equals the redemption price plus the final coupon interest payment) and work backward to reach the final pricing solution. Exhibit 6.4 outlines the generation of two estimated one-period forward rates.

Using annual-pay securities for simplicity, Exhibit 6.5 reflects the two estimated one-year spot rates (given an assigned volatility estimate), one year forward, for a two-year security priced at par, or 100% of face value. An average of the two prices generated from these two rates and their interest payments equals the market price in the previous period (T_0) times the estimated one-year spot rate in that previous period. Remember, the estimated one-year spot rate in period T_0 is the current one-year spot rate. Either of the two T_1 prices, multiplied by the respective one-year spot rates (as determined by the initial volatility estimate), equals the average price plus interest payment in the next payment period of the two possible outcomes—in this instance, the redemption price plus interest payment for the last period. In Exhibit 6.5, the observed market rate for the one-year spot rate is 5%, the two-year 6% coupon security has a yield to maturity of 6%, and the estimated

EXHIBIT 6.4   A generic analysis of the generation of two estimated one-period rates using the spot rates estimated in step 1

Today (T_0)

Security price ×
(1 + Current one-period rate) = AVG
(Price A + interest coupon) +
(Price B + interest coupon)

Contents of Rate Alternatives
One Period in the Future (T_1)

B: Security price, coupon rate, and one-period rate derived from user-specified price volatility:

$$(B \text{ rate} = A * e^{2\sigma})$$

A: Security price, coupon rate, and one-period rate (est. thru iteration)

EXHIBIT 6.5   Binomial tree for two-year optionless security

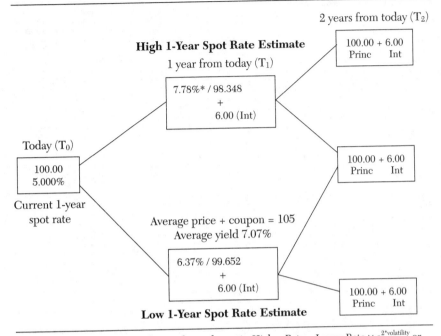

2 years from today (T₂)

High 1-Year Spot Rate Estimate
1 year from today (T₁)

| 100.00 + 6.00 |
| Princ   Int |

| 7.78%* / 98.348 |
| + |
| 6.00 (Int) |

Today (T₀)

| 100.00 |
| 5.000% |

| 100.00 + 6.00 |
| Princ   Int |

Current 1-year
spot rate

Average price + coupon = 105
Average yield 7.07%

| 6.37% / 99.652 |
| + |
| 6.00 (Int) |

| 100.00 + 6.00 |
| Princ   Int |

Low 1-Year Spot Rate Estimate

* The relationship between the two forward rates is: Higher Rate = Lower Rate $\times e^{2 * \text{volatility}}$ or
$7.7806\% = 6.3702\% \times 2.71828^{2 \times 10}$ (e is the natural logarithm base).
$(98.348 + 99.652 + (2 \times 6)) / 2 = 105$ (100 + the 5% earned over the first year)
$99.652 \times 1.0637 = 106$ $98.348 \times 1.0778 = 106$

price volatility is 10%. The outcome will be the redemption price (100) plus the interest payment (6) to be received in year 2. Because of the virtually infinite number of comparisons of rates to choose from, an iteration technique similar to that discussed in Chapter 2 is used to determine the lower of the two one-year rates one year forward.

In determining the rate estimates for each period or compounding period, only the lowest rate is determined by iteration. The rest of the rates are some multiple of $e^{2\sigma}$.

It is also important to remember that the value of a nonembedded option security calculated using this method produces the same results using spot rates, the one-year forward rates, and standard yield to maturity. Exhibit 6.6 reflects these relationships.

EXHIBIT 6.6 Value calculation using spot rates, forward rates, and yield to maturity

		Coupon Rate	Spot Rate	One-Year Forward Rate
Given:	One year	5 %	5 %	5 %
Maturity:	Two years	6	6.03	7.071
	Three years	6½	6.5556	7.614

Coupon calculation: 6½% coupon, 6½% yield to maturity, price = 100

Spot rate price calculation:

$$\frac{6.5}{(1.05)} + \frac{6.5}{(1.0603)^2} + \frac{(100+6.5)}{(1.065556)^3} = 100$$

Forward rate price calculation:

$$\frac{6.5}{1.05} + \frac{6.5}{(1.05)(1.07071)} + \frac{(106+.05)}{(1+.05)(1.07071)(1.07614)} = 100$$

Using the binomial method to value callable or putable securities works the same way as optionless securities, with one exception. Let's assume our 6% 2-year noncallable security has a current market price of 101 (yield to maturity = 5.59%). Let's then assume it is callable at the end of one year at 100. The two estimated one-year rates one year forward, based on a 10% volatility estimate, are 5.357% and 6.5434% for both the callable and noncallable issues. If the security was non-callable, the corresponding prices for the two estimated yields would be 100.6103 (5.357%) and 99.49 (6.5434%). Given a call price of 100 at the end of one year, the higher price (lower yield) estimate becomes 100. This is done because the issuer could potentially call the outstanding security and reissue a new security at a yield lower than 6%. Using the same current one-year spot rate of 5% and substituting 100 for 100.6103, the option-adjusted price of the 2-year security becomes 100.7095. This represents a difference of .2905, which is the value of the embedded option:

101	−	100.7095	=	.2905
Option-free security		Callable security		Value of embedded call option

Exhibit 6.7 outlines the price differences between the callable and noncallable securities.

In Exhibit 6.7, the highest price (lowest yield) the callable security could have at the end of one year is 100. Any price higher than that would induce the issuer to call the securities. Putable securities are calculated in essentially the same manner, although the price cap will be on the downside, not the upside as with a callable security.

The determination of implied one-year forward rates (or whatever the payment frequency of the security happens to be) beyond two periods (or years, in this case) is calculated in the same format as noted above. For a three-year 6½% annual-pay, noncallable security priced at par, with a 10% volatility estimate, the one-year forward rates in year 2 must satisfy the following conditions:

1. The difference between the lower and middle rate estimates, and between the middle and upper rate estimates must each be $e^{2\sigma}$, or e raised to 2 times the volatility estimate (the difference between the middle and upper rate estimates is also $e^{2\sigma}$), as outlined in the structure of the model.

EXHIBIT 6.7   Valuation difference between 2-period callable vs. noncallable securities

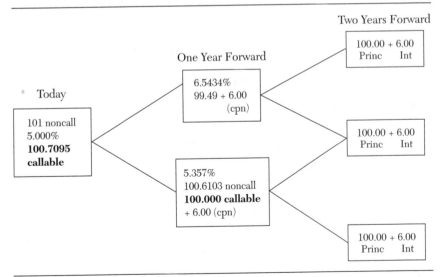

2. The value of the security in year 3 must equal 106.5 (100 redemption value plus 6.5 coupon payment), regardless of the estimated one-year forward rates in year 2.

3. The averages of the lower and middle security values and the middle and upper security values (principal plus coupon payment) in year 2 must equal the lower and upper, respectively, values at the end of year 1 multiplied by 1+ the estimated one-year forward rates in year 1.

Exhibit 6.8 reflects the binomial tree with all appropriate values for the three-year 6½% security.

There are several considerations to keep in mind with the preceding exhibits:

1. We used a coupon payment date (in this case, the security's dated date, or the date the security first begins accruing interest) to do

EXHIBIT 6.8   Binomial tree structure for 3-year annual pay, noncallable 6¹⁄₂% bond priced at par (100)

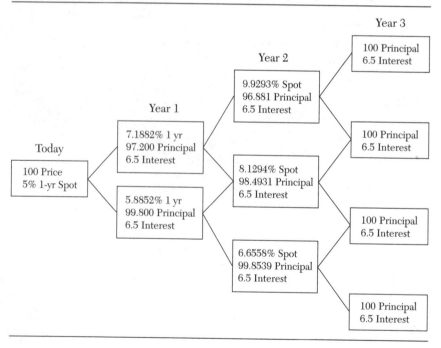

our calculations. In practice, this type of fair-value analysis is done between coupon periods, and partial coupon periods must be taken into consideration.

2. Taxes and transaction costs could have an impact on whether an issuer will call a security.

3. The larger the volatility assumption, the wider the spread between the lower and higher rate.

4. At each decision point, or node, we are presuming an equal likelihood of either of the two outcomes in the one-year rate, one year forward. This can be adjusted with different weightings and different volatility assumptions.

Monte Carlo Simulation

Another popular method of determining price and yield on a security with contingent cash flows is the *Monte Carlo Simulation* (named after the famous gambling mecca). In this technique, a large number of random paths for interest rate movements are computer-generated. These paths are generally consistent with historical rate patterns and the spot curve. A present value determination is made for the sum of the cash flows of each of these paths. The average of these paths is estimated to be the fair value of the security being analyzed. For further information on this method, see Appendix F.

Mean Reversion in a Monte Carlo Simulation: Keeping the Players in the Ballpark

Theoretically, interest rates could move from zero to infinity[1]. Realistically, neither of these extremes is likely. As a result, interest rate modelers sometimes implement a statistical technique that, in effect, reduces the potential volatility of interest rate movements by introducing factors to redirect interest rate paths toward longer-term forward rates implied by the term structure or spot curve, or toward some longer-term historical average, or mean rate. This technique is called *mean reversion.* The use of mean reversion can be implemented with varying degrees of severity. The stronger the mean reversion factor, the quicker in time the sample of paths is moved closer to the designated longer-term spot rate or average rate. The bottom-line effect is to reduce the volatility of the estimated sample, and ultimately the value of the call, or (in the case of mortgage-backed securities) the prepayment feature of the security. Determination of the degree of severity to use is a function of the modeler's view on interest rate projections.

A number of other valuation methods are used to varying degrees in the securities industry. As we mentioned earlier, this book is not the correct venue for comparing and contrasting all of these methods. Appendix F presents alternative texts for the more serious student of the quantitative side of understanding investment mathematics. Remember, if you are not planning to either create or program a pricing model, it is only necessary to understand the concepts used in creating the models as an intuitive guideline for more sophisticated applications.

MORTGAGE-BACKED SECURITIES: A FURTHER TWIST IN THE VALUATION OF SECURITIES WITH EMBEDDED OPTIONS

The securities types we discussed above apply to essentially straight or unsecured debt. The world of collateralized debt is not only huge (over $1 trillion domestically) but requires a set of more specialized considerations in the valuation process. Again, this is not the place to begin a quantitative explanation of collateralized securities pricing, but it is important to understand the basic structure of these instruments, and to recognize the factors that go into the pricing algorithms, where they come from, and why they are important. Once again, texts with more of an eye toward quantitative applications are noted in Appendix F.

The collateralized debt markets are essentially divided into two sectors: (1) mortgage-backed securities (MBS) and (2) asset-backed securities (ABS). The latter category covers various types of loans, acceptances, and other receivables. We will spend time with the MBS markets because they continue to represent the dominant share of this market segment. The valuation principles for ABS are similar.

The mortgage-backed securities (MBS) markets grew out of a need to replenish the capital of primary mortgage lenders such as commercial banks and savings and loan institutions. Lenders provide homeowners with the mortgage funds necessary to purchase their homes. If these lenders had to hold every mortgage they granted until its maturity or a sale by the homeowner, the lenders would be limited to their own available resources in granting loans. The MBS market provides a conduit for these primary lenders to sell the mortgage assets to investors in the marketplace, thereby recuperating their investment and enabling them to grant additional loans.

Three main government-sponsored agencies were created to facilitate, or *securitize* mortgage loans: (1) Government National Mortgage Association (GNMA, "Ginnie Mae"), (2) Federal National Mortgage Association (FNMA, "Fannie Mae"), and (3) Federal Home Loan Mortgage Corporation (FHLMC, "Freddie Mac"). Each of these entities converts or *securitizes* groups or *pools* of mortgages created by primary lenders. These securities are then bought by the sellers of To Be Announced ("TBA"; see next paragraph) mortgage securities in what is referred to as the TBA market. The money from the sale is returned to the initial mortgage lenders for possible recycling to other prospective homeowners.

The MBS "TBA" Market

The TBA market for MBS is a type of primary forward market where investors can buy and sell commitments to purchase mortgage pools to be issued in the future. The product for delivery (specified mortgage pools) is created by GNMA, FNMA, and FHLMC (see above definitions) and sold once a month, at the then-prevailing market rates, to the TBA sellers noted above[2]. The seller hopes to profit from the spread between the original TBA sale (at a higher price) and the purchase cost paid to the federal agency. Both 15- and 30-year fixed-rate mortgages and various degrees of floating rate mortgages are traded in the TBA market. Quotes for these securities are denominated in 32nds of a point, like Treasury securities. TBA securities are traded to the monthly settlement (or delivery) date of the securities from the federal agencies. Interest begins to accrue on the first calendar day of the month and is accrued on a $30/360$ basis. No interest is paid for the 31st day of a month.

The coupon rate on an MBS pool is usually ½%, or 50 basis points below the interest rate on the underlying mortgage loans. The reason for this is the funding of monthly securitization and servicing fees. The securitization fee goes to the issuing federal agency, and the servicing fee represents the cost of collecting and processing the mortgage payments from the homeowners, passing the principal and interest payments through to the investors, and managing each homeowner's escrow account. This is where the term *MBS pass-through* is derived. The 50 basis points are broken down (in percentages) about 90–10. The servicer (in many instances, the original mortgage lender) receives about 44 bps, and the federal agency gets 6 bps. The actual fees paid each month to the servicer and the agency are based on the remaining outstanding principal balances of the mortgages.

TBA mortgage securities trade for delivery on a monthly basis, up to several months into the future. In March, for example, TBAs are traded for April, May, and June deliveries. Valuing the difference between similarly structured TBA mortgage securities with different delivery dates, or as compared to the cash market (these instruments are termed *specified mortgage pools*), is in theory nothing more than a "carry" market. In effect, an investor in a TBA is purchasing an interest-bearing asset for no money. At the same time, the investor will not earn any interest on the security until settlement. The dollar difference between what the investor would earn in interest income and what it would cost to carry finance market securities between the trade date and forward settlement date is called the *net carry*. Exhibit 6.9 is a summary of this type of valuation.

The pricing relationships are "in theory" because the price differences, or *rolls* between the months, do not, in many cases, mirror a

EXHIBIT 6.9   Valuation of the spread between MBS cash and a TBA, or forward mortgage-backed security, or between two forward periods

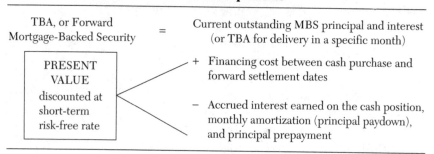

break-even relationship. The reason for this boils down to liquidity issues of supply and demand. Remember that the available supply of new mortgages is a function of whatever the primary lenders have created. Changing demand dynamics could make a specific TBA particularly expensive, relative to other delivery dates. In many instances, this occurs with a "current" coupon TBA. This security contains a coupon interest rate (after adjustment for the 50-bps payout to the mortgage servicer and the securitizing agency) closest to the currently prevailing required yield to maturity for the particular class of TBA securities.

Calculating the yield on an MBS is somewhat more complicated, compared to a Treasury or corporate bond. Some additional parameters must be considered in the calculation. Initially, an MBS pays principal and interest on a monthly basis. Virtually all non-MBSs pay semiannually. As a result, when comparing yields on MBS versus non-MBS issues, it is important to convert one calculation to the other in order to accurately compare returns. Because a mortgage yield is compounded monthly while most bonds are compounded semiannually, the equivalent mortgage yield will be slightly lower, due to a higher number of compounding periods. For example, a 7.5% bond yield compounded semiannually translates into a 7.385% mortgage yield. [Remember, the monthly compounding allows the interest on a mortgage security (compounded 12 times per year) to grow faster than a semiannually compounded security.]

Mortgage-backed securities are essentially fixed-income securities that contain an embedded American-style, or nondiscreet call option with no officially predefined call price. A homeowner would liquidate a mortgage (1) because the home is being sold or (2) because interest rates have experienced a sharp enough decline to make it worthwhile for the homeowner to refinance the mortgage at the lower rate. While the likelihood of the first reason is left to demographic, economic, and statistical tables, but the refinancing issue is largely a function of interest rate levels. Clearly, a homeowner saddled with a 12½% fixed-rate mortgage would have a big incentive to refinance the mortgage if the current rate for a similarly structured mortgage was 7%. The exact threshold for each homeowner is, again, an issue for statisticians. One thing, however, is certain. The lower mortgage rates fall, the more likely the prepayment speed is to increase. Remember that the yield to maturity on a mortgage, as on any other fixed-income instrument, assumes some maturity date. If that date is pushed up because of a statistically unexpected sale or refinancing, the investor's money is returned faster and either the effective holding period yield drops and/or the reinvestment rate is less favorable. Exhibit 6.10 tabulates monthly mortgage payments and changes in those payments, given a change in interest rates for 15- and 30-year fixed-rate loans.

Prepayment Speed

The big difference between calculating yield on a fixed-income security with an embedded option and a mortgage-backed security is the additional uncertainty surrounding the repayment date of the mortgage. Standard corporate or federal agency securities have call provisions with specific dates. Some indeterminate portion of an MBS could be called at any time during its life. This is compounded with the particular stated delay in receiving the first principal and interest payment on each particular or specified pool.[3] As a result, predicting investment yields becomes not unlike shooting at a variable-speed moving target.

The financial community has dealt with these problems by creating a statistical concept known as *prepayment speed*—a measure of the amount of additional principal in a mortgage pool that can be expected to be prepaid during each month of the life of a mortgage. Several different measurements are used to calculate prepayment speeds. Two of the most popular ones are Constant Prepayment Rate (CPR) and Public

EXHIBIT 6.10   Monthly payments on 15- and 30-year fixed-rate mortgages

Given: $200,000 mortgage

Mortgage Period	6%	7%	8%	9%	10%	11%
15 years	1,687.71	1,797.66	1,911.30	2,028.53	2,149.21	2,273.19
30 years	1,199.10	1,330.60	1,467.53	1,609.25	1,755.14	1,904.65
Difference	488.61	467.06	443.77	419.28	394.07	368.54

Securities Association (PSA; now called the Bond Market Association). CPR reflects the projected constant annual percentage of a mortgage pool's principal that is being prepaid over the life of the mortgage. The Single Monthly Mortality (SMM) is the monthly prepayment speed equivalent. The relationship between CPR and SMM is:

$$SMM = 1 - (1 - CPR)^{1/12}$$

If the CPR on a particular mortgage pool is 7%, the SMM would equal $1 - (1 - .07)^{1/12}$, or .6029%. The SMM is not exactly $\frac{1}{12}$ of 7, or .58333%, because the calculation is done on a continuously declining principal balance.

In calculating the dollar change in a mortgage pool's principal balance, if a mortgage pool has a principal balance of $1,000,000, an SMM of 1%, and a scheduled principal reduction of $2,000, the principal balance at the end of the month will be:

$$
\underset{\substack{\text{Opening pool}\\\text{balance}}}{\$1,000,000} - \underset{\substack{\text{Scheduled principal}\\\text{reduction}}}{\$2,000} = \underset{\substack{\text{Scheduled remaining}\\\text{principal balance}}}{\$998,000}
$$

$$
\$998,000 - \underset{\substack{\text{1\% Prepayment}}}{\overset{\$9,980}{(1\% \text{ of } 998,000)}} = \underset{\substack{\text{balance}}}{\overset{\$988,020}{\text{Remaining principal}}}
$$

The PSA prepayment speed, quoted in terms of percentages, is used as a benchmark. A 100% PSA translates into a prepayment rate beginning with .2% in the first month of a pool, increasing in .2% increments for the first 30 months, and leveling off at 6% for the remainder of the mortgage. If, for example, the PSA is quoted at 200% in month 3 of the pool, there will be a 1.2% prepayment over the scheduled principal reduction (the third month at 100% PSA would be .6% prepayment). A 200% rate requires the user to multiply the benchmark rate for that month by 2. The subsequent monthly prepayments would also double, ending in a rate of 12% at the end of 60 months of the mortgage's life.

How does one project CPR or PSA rates on mortgages? As mentioned above, many factors are associated with this estimate. Indeed, interest-rate levels are important. Historical trends, economic conditions, and demographic changes can also play important roles in the payment speed on any individual pool. The U.S. Department of Housing and Urban Development compiles a series of survivorship data for Federal Housing Authority (FHA) guaranteed mortgages from which prepayment rates are extrapolated. A number of services provide modeled CPR/PSA rates to the investing public; many come from the dealer community and are usually restricted to customers of the dealers. Other services, such as the Advanced Factor Service (AFS) from Telerate, are sold widespread on an interactive basis. Subscribers get several future monthly prepayment estimates for various MBS coupon securities, as well as market commentary.

The prepayment estimates are used to develop the cash flow structure of the mortgage pool. Once the amount and timing of the cash flows are input, a yield can be calculated. Additionally, the various price yield sensitivity measures, such as duration and convexity, can also be estimated. Each mortgage pool has what is termed a *pool factor*—the percent of principal left from the initial issuance. Investors use these historical factors to estimate future prepayment rates as well as to structure the current absolute size of certain price/yield statistics such as basis point value. Pool factors are available from some of the U.S. Government primary dealers as well as from external services such as the Asset-Backed Securities Group of Thomson Financial Services Inc.

Other Important MBS Pool Characteristics

The *weighted average coupon* (WAC) represents the average coupon of a mortgage pool. It is calculated by weighing the coupon rate by the outstanding principal balance of the mortgage at the end of each month. Ginnie Mae pools all have the same gross coupon; Fannie Mae and Freddie Mac pools can contain different coupon rates.

The *weighted average maturity* is the maturity of the mortgage pool weighted by the par value outstanding of each mortgage within the pool.

The *maturity date* is the latest maturing mortgage in the pool.

The *MBS pool issue date* is the date of issuance of the mortgage pass-through security.

Price and Yield Calculation on a Mortgage-Backed Security

To calculate yield on a mortgage-backed security, the following additional variables, beyond the standard or straight debt price and yield calculations, are required:

- Prepayment speed: outlined on page 118.
- Initial mortgage period: the total number of months in the original term of the mortgage.
- Remaining term: number of months until the mortgage is fully paid off.
- Gross and net coupons: the gross coupon is the interest rate charged to the mortgagee. The net coupon is the rate of interest paid to the investor. The difference is split between the mortgage servicer and the federal agency that securitized the whole loan or mortgage.
- Payment delay: The first payment on a mortgage is due at the beginning of the second month after origination. The mortgage servicer doesn't send the mortgage payment through to the servicer until some number of days after receipt of the payment. After the first payment is made, each succeeding payment is received one month after the previous payment.

The two basic mortgage formulae given below are for the monthly payment and for the principal amount remaining at the end of a particular period.

$$\text{Monthly payment} = \text{Original balance} \times \frac{(i \times (1+i)^n}{(1+i)^n - 1}$$

where: i = annual mortgage interest rate divided by 12,
        n = number of months in mortgage.

If i = .5%, the mortgage balance = $200,000 and the term = 360 months.

$$\text{Monthly payment} = \$200,000 \times \frac{(.005 \times (1 + .005)^{360}}{(1 + .005)^{360} - 1}$$

$$= \$1,199.10$$

$$\text{Balance at the end of the 90th month} = \text{Original balance} \times \frac{(1 + .005)^{360} - (1 + .005)^{90}}{(1 + .005)^{360} - 1}$$

$$= \$177,439.67$$

OPTION-ADJUSTED SPREAD

In our discussion of securities with embedded call or put options, we referred to the binomial model as a reasonable estimator of fair-value yield and price for these types of securities. Because mortgage-backed securities are more involved in terms of estimating mortgage life and cash flows, modelers prefer to use the Monte Carlo simulation for determining value for this type of security. It is important to remember that the results of either of these valuation techniques represent an educated quantitative guess at value. The actual market value for a security can clearly be different from its fair value. Additionally, differences in the observed interest rate path versus the estimated path in a model will also change the rate of return on the security.

The one-period forward rates used in the binomial method and the average yield generated from the Monte Carlo method are ultimately created from the U.S. Treasury yield curve. When securities have greater risk than Treasuries, the actual or observed market price for the securities being analyzed will most likely be lower than the value generated from either of the models. The price measure of this additional risk is the difference between the model-generated value and the observed market price and is derived through a technique that creates what is known as an *option-adjusted spread*, or simply OAS.

The basic idea in an OAS is to create one yield spread over every U.S. Treasury one-period forward rate or spot rate initially used to price the security. When this spread is added to the spot rates for the cash flows associated with the security, it creates a present value equal to the observed market price of the security.

The process used to create this spread has four steps:

1. The tree or average interest rate path for the security is created.

2. The call, put, or prepayment assumptions are factored into the interest rate path. (Exhibit 6.7 reflected the call potential for the security by substituting a value of 100 for 100.6103, generated from the tree.)

3. The cash flows and derived security price are generated from the discount rates and contingency assumptions in the model.

4. The derived security price is replaced by the observed market price and, through an iterative process, the OAS is calculated as the yield spread above the value initially derived from the model.

Some OAS Caveats

It is important to remember that the best OAS modelers in the business warn that the actual returns earned on an MBS will not necessarily mirror the results of an OAS analysis. Any model for estimating actual returns can only incorporate historical and current data as absolute or observed. The statistical techniques noted here as being applied to the data are "street"-accepted value estimators. Nevertheless, fundamental, technical, liquidity, and exogenous factors such as weather, war, political turmoil, and tax code alterations all have the potential to significantly change a security's estimated cash flow structure or the term structure of interest-rates in ways that may broadly affect the returns on that security.

A second consideration involves the use of a single volatility estimate for an entire model. Many modelers have changing views on interest-rate volatility over longer periods of time. While mean reversion is one way to alter volatility estimates, some models input specific volatility levels at particular times, reflecting their individual estimates on changes in the term structure.

Third, the OAS that is reported on a mortgage-backed security is usually quoted on a semiannual basis. The calculations in the model are done on a monthly basis, because mortgages are paid off monthly. The MBS yield, therefore, must be converted from a monthly to a semiannual basis for calculation consistency.

The valuation methods we have been discussing in this chapter are not limited to securities with stochastic, or uncertain, cash flows. As noted, any fixed-income issue can be valued through the binomial lattice or Monte Carlo techniques. The difference in execution of either model would be an absence of the need to adjust future cash flows based on some contingent event, such as a call feature or prepayment estimate.

Aside from specified pools of fixed-rate mortgages, there are a number of different types of mortgage-backed securities, such as adjustable rate mortgages (ARM), graduated payment mortgages (GPM), and balloon payment mortgages (BPM). Among a host of MBS derivatives are: interest only (I/O) and principal only (P/O) mortgage zero coupons (similar in concept to U.S. Treasury STRIPS), and collateralized mortgage obligations (CMOs), which are also portions of traditional mortgage structures. Analyses of these types of securities, although similar in certain respects to our discussions in this chapter, are beyond the scope of this book. Refer to Appendix F for additional texts covering these securities.

EFFECTIVE DURATION AND EFFECTIVE CONVEXITY

In Chapter 4. we reviewed the concepts of modified duration and convexity as measures of price/yield sensitivity for fixed-income securities. Debt with embedded options is more involved and requires some additional consideration with regard to how these sensitivities are calculated.

Duration and convexity on callable or putable securities are conceptually utilized the same way, in terms of valuing small changes in yield to maturity for duration and larger changes for convexity. The major difference between optioned and nonoptioned cash flow securities is how the yield change is structured. In straight debt, the yield to maturity used to discount all cash flows within the security is moved up and down. In contingent cash flow issues, the entire term structure of spot and forward rates, along with the OAS used to derive the price/yield structure, is moved up or down by a similar number of basis points, and a price revaluation is done.

The impact of changes in prepayment estimates on MBS issues will have corresponding effects on the duration and convexity statistics. It is important to remember that both duration and convexity calculations are functions of (1) the amount of all cash flows associated with any security and (2) the timing of receipt of those cash flows. The quicker an investment flows back to the investor, the shorter the duration, and the steeper (larger) the convexity. This movement is analogous to an increase in the prepayment speed.

COLLATERALIZED MORTGAGE OBLIGATIONS: A TWIST TO MBS PASS-THROUGHS

The growth of the MBS industry spun off a derivative of the generic mortgage pass-through security: the collateralized mortgage obligation or CMO, for short (ed note: it's interesting to note that most financial instruments and terms are shortened to acronyms. Perhaps this is one of the reasons the average person gets lost in the jargon used by many Wall streeters). Initiated in the early 1980s by Freddie Mac, CMOs were developed to facilitate new and more innovative ways to sell collateralized debt to the investing public. Basically, they divide up underlying collateral—usually, mortgage pass-through securities issued by federal agencies, or whole loan mortgages issued by nonagency entities—into several asset groups or classes. The securities are placed in a trust, which administers the principal and interest payments to the different asset classes, or in tranches created from the collateral. The purpose of the CMO is to create different types of asset structures that more closely fit potential investors' needs. By structuring in this method, the securities have more value, and, ultimately, higher prices than they would if they were not divided up. One of these created structures is the *planned amortization class* (PAC) bond, which contains protection from prepayment volatility. This protection is provided through supporting classes called *companions*. The companions absorb the excess PAC principal paydown in periods when the prepayment speeds (designated as the *PAC bands*) outlined in the PAC bond, are faster than anticipated, and they amortize more slowly during periods of slower-than-anticipated prepayments.

Stripped MBS pass-throughs are also created. Like Treasury STRIPS, the MBS equivalents are purchased at a discount and redeemed at their face value. As previously noted, investors can purchase claims on either principal or interest payments from one security or a pool of mortgage securities. *Principal only* (P/O) *STRIPS* are used to hedge against falling interest rates (faster prepayment rates reduce the time the investor must wait to get a return of capital). *Interest only* (I/O) *STRIPS* hedge against rising interest rates. (The higher the interest rate, the slower the prepayment speeds.)

There are a number of generic factors for CMO structures with which the investor should become familiar. These include types of collateral used, assumed prepayment rates, and the principal and interest guarantee process. Appendix F lists additional texts that offer further information on CMOs.

In calculating yields on CMOs, the process is similar to other fixed-income securities. The investor must, however, identify the amount, timing, and certainty of all cash flows associated with a security before price yield and other price/yield sensitivity measures can be determined.

CONVERTIBLE BONDS

For many years, corporations have issued debt securities with what can be termed an "equity kicker." The bondholder is granted the right to convert the bond into the common stock of the company at some predefined conversion rate. Many convertible issues are also callable, thereby reducing the potential value of the security. Additionally, some issues contain put features that allow the investor to sell the security back to the issuer. Convertibles come in many forms, including fixed coupon rate, zero coupon, or step coupons. Conversion privileges can include specific dates, ranges of dates, and fixed or variable conversion prices. This section will discuss some of the more important characteristics of convertible debt, highlight some basic relationships, and present an overview of a more quantitative approach for valuation.

Convertible bonds contain some basic characteristics that distinguish them from nonconvertible debt. In its simplest form, a convertible bond is the combination of a nonconvertible fixed-income security and a call option on the common stock of the company. Some convertible bonds have one or two embedded options: the issuer has a right to call the securities at its discretion, and/or the investor has the right to put the securities back to the issuer. In valuing these types of issues, each component must be analyzed separately to arrive at a combined value.

Three basic formulae are associated with convertible bonds. The *parity* represents the current market price for the common stock times the conversion ratio. If the current market price of ABC common stock is $45 per share and the conversion ratio is 20 shares per $1,000 par value, parity is $900. Generally speaking, the value of the convertible bond should be equal to the greater of an equivalent nonconvertible, fixed-income security or parity.

The second formula is *premium over parity*. This statistic, calculated as a percentage, measures the degree to which the price of the convertible bond exceeds parity. It is calculated as [(convertible price/parity) − 1] × 100. If a convertible's price is 110 and parity equals 100, the premium over parity equals 10%.

The third formula is referred to as the *payback period*. This statistic, measured in years, calculates how long it will take for the investor to recoup the premium paid for the convertible bond, as measured against the dividend income received by paying the parity price for the common stock. For example, if a $1,000 bond with a 5% coupon can be converted into 20 shares of common stock paying a cash dividend of $1.25 per share, and currently selling for $45 per share, the following cash flows would be compared:

Convertible bond: $1,000 cost with $50 annual interest income.

Common stock: 20 shares × $45 = $900 with $25 annual income.

The initial cost difference is $100 ($1,000 − $900). The income differential is $25 ($50 − $25).

Based on this analysis, it will take 4 years to recoup the price difference between the two investments:

$$\text{Payback period} = \frac{\text{Cost of convertible bond} - \text{Cost of common stock at parity}}{\text{Annual interest on convertible bond} - \text{Annual dividend on number of parity shares}}$$

$$= \frac{\$1,000 - \$900}{\$50 - \$25}$$

$$= \frac{\$100}{\$25} = 4 \text{ years}$$

This formula, while simple, neglects the concept of present value. The payback period measured in present value dollars is slightly longer than

4 years. Additionally, this analysis doesn't take into account potential changes in the cash dividend rate. Nevertheless, the shorter the payback period, the more attractive the convertible bond.

The coupon rates on convertible issues are almost always significantly lower than rates on the same issuers' nonconvertible debt. This is the tradeoff an investor makes. A lower fixed rate of return is accepted in anticipation of a higher common stock price.

Quantitatively, the value of a convertible bond is divided into two sections: (1) the straight debt portion of the security and (2) the conversion provision. The straight debt portion is easy to calculate using standard yield-to-maturity formulae. The conversion and any other option-related features are considerably more rigorous and require the use of option pricing models, which we discuss in greater detail in Chapter 9. The cost of the convertible bond will be the straight debt value plus the net value of the conversion and any other option features. Intuitively, the higher the underlying stock price, the more valuable the conversion feature.

SUMMARY

This chapter looked at the world of securities with stochastic or contingent cash flows. One way to price callable bonds, such as corporate and federal agency securities, is based on a series of implied one-period forward rates, using an estimated volatility for determining the rate distribution. The option value of the security is the difference between the optionless security and the security with the option. Mortgage-backed securities add the uncertainties of continuous principal reduction and the prepayment potential throughout the entire maturity period of the security. OAS analysis calculates a spread in basis points that, when added to each one-period forward rate, will equate the present value of the security to its market price. Effective duration and effective convexity are specialized forms of these price/yield sensitivity statistics that more accurately calculate duration and convexity for securities with embedded options. Convertible bonds offer the investor the safety of a fixed-income security with the potential to cash in on price appreciation in the issuer's common stock.

NOTES

1. e^{2sigma} is equal to the value of e(2.71828) raised to the power of 2 times sigma, or a volatility estimate.

2. Delivery of TBA securities is completed on a monthly basis. The exact delivery date for each coupon level and maturity is determined by the issuing agency.

3. Stated delay varies by agency and type of security. Generally, it runs between 45 and 75 days. Stated delays are different from real delays in that the stated delay measures the time lag between the issue date of the pass-through and the first payment date to the investor. After that, the timing of the payouts to the investor and the payments made by the mortgagees are both monthly. The real delay measures the time between when the mortgage payment is due each month and when it is actually distributed to the investor. The following table reflects the actual versus stated delays for different types of mortgage pass-through securities.

	Real Delay	**Stated Delay**
GNMA-1	14	45
GNMA-2	19	50
FNMA	24	55
FHLMC-Gold	14	45
FHLMC	44	75

7 INTEREST RATE FUTURES CONTRACTS

This is the first chapter on derivative securities. We begin with a general discussion of derivative definitions and structure. We then turn to interest rate derivatives, where the study is divided into two sections. *Short-term* interest rate derivatives focus on futures contracts and forward rate agreements written on money market instruments—most specifically, the 3-month Eurodollar time deposit. *Longer-term* futures contracts focus on the U.S. Treasury-related group of contracts. Valuation of the contracts and some basic speculation and hedging strategies are also discussed.

Many traders and investors, particularly those on the buy side, have taken one of two views of derivative securities:

1. Their use is "hazardous to your financial health."
2. They represent a nefarious black hole of uncertainty, thereby definitely making them hazardous to your financial health.

Derivatives have been given this very undeserved reputation for one of three reasons:

1. The accusers have no basic knowledge of the derivatives markets and how they operate. In essence, they are afraid of what they don't understand.

2. The accusers have taken a hit on their bottom line because they entered into a derivatives transaction without truly understanding the associated market risks.

3. The accusers have taken a hit on their bottom line because they entered into a derivatives transaction, understood the risks, lost money, and blamed the loss on the fact that they really didn't understand the risks.

A quick review of the several derivatives-related horror stories that have occurred over the past few years appears to indicate that all three of the above reasons have in some way played a part. Additionally, it is impossible to exonerate every salesperson and trader associated with the sale of a derivative product. In short, the main culprit appears to be a lack of understanding of the products, how they operate, and their associated risks.

Indeed, a host of different types of derivative securities are outstanding. To compound the situation, new variations on existing themes seem to be appearing at a rapid rate. According to industry studies, the total notional amount of outstanding derivative securities traded over the counter exceeded $28 *trillion* in value at the end of 1997! That's right, *trillion*. And that doesn't include exchange-traded futures and options. Granted, a relatively small amount of securities dealers account for a large portion of the derivatives transactions, but tens and perhaps hundreds of thousands of institutional investors have successfully incorporated these instruments into their investment and/or funding strategies. The simple reality is: Derivative securities can be a very important part of maintaining and even improving your financial health *if* you understand what you are getting yourself involved in.

The basic definition of a derivative instrument is *a security created in the image of another security*. Simply put, when the underlying security changes value, so does the derivative. An investor could be attempting to understand a salespersons offering of an index-amortizing, inverse-floating, four-speed, positraction, frost-free, blah, blah, blah, blah, blah, security based on the Malaya rubber index and traded on the Jakarta exchange, but with only $5 million left in inventory, you had better grab it now! This may seem confusing on the surface, but all derivatives seem to boil down to one or two basic objectives:

1. The derivative security places a future rate or price value on a financial transaction to take place in the future. This may be expressed as a price or yield on an asset or liability either currently existing or to be created sometime in the future.

and

2. The derivative security reflects the likelihood that some asset or liability either currently existing or to be created in the future will achieve a specified rate or price level.

If market participants use this as a baseline for beginning the search for value and they break down the complexities of any type of structured derivative product into one or both of the components listed above, the value search becomes much easier to understand and perhaps easier to complete.

FINANCIAL FUTURES

We start our discussion of the derivative markets with *financial futures*. These instruments fall under objective 1 in the preceding section. A financial futures contract, as opposed to a "soft" commodity or agricultural futures contract, represents the potential obligation to make or take delivery of a particular amount of a financial instrument at a particular price at some point in the future. The important word here is *potential*. If the seller of the futures contract elects to make delivery of the underlying security, the buyer is obligated to take delivery under the terms of the contract. The exchange where the futures contract is traded is responsible for matching up longs and shorts in the delivery process. This becomes particularly important, given the relatively wide delivery window for some futures contracts. For example, the securities underlying Treasury futures can be physically delivered on almost any business day during the entire expiration month of the contract.

This definition leaves little to guesswork in terms of delivery responsibilities, but, in reality, less than 1% of financial futures contracts with physical delivery requirements are actually settled with a physical delivery. Either the positions are liquidated prior to contract expiration, or the contract specifications require settlement via what is termed a *cash settlement*. We will discuss this in greater detail later in the chapter.

Futures contracts are, for all intents and purposes, without credit risk. When a buyer and seller execute a trade, the counterparty to both the buyer and the seller is the exchange. Every trade is guaranteed by the exchange. This guarantee, combined with the rigid rules and regulations surrounding futures trading, brings a high degree of credit security to each transaction.

The price of a futures contract, like the prices of most other derivatives, is largely a function of the underlying security on which it is written. There are four categories of underlying securities for financial futures: (1) short-term interest rates, (2) long-term interest rates, (3) currencies, and (4) equities indexes. The major financial advantage—or disadvantage, depending on which side of the trade you are on—is the leverage available with futures. Purchasing or selling a contract gives control over a large amount of securities for a very small cost. Investors need put up only a small deposit, known as *initial margin*, to gain control of these securities. This is allowed because the investors are not physically purchasing the underlying security. Nevertheless, they are participating in market movements. Futures are simply claims on or against the securities for some period of time.

The amount of initial margin required to buy or sell short a futures contract is established by the exchange on which it is traded (all futures trade on an organized exchange). Generally speaking, the more volatile the price swings on a contract, the higher the required margin. Nevertheless, the margin amount as a percent of the underlying contract value remains very small. Exhibit 7.1 lists examples of initial margin requirements for several of the more popular financial futures contracts.

The implied value of a futures contract can be viewed as a breakeven situation in the case of fixed income and foreign exchange. Short-term interest rate and foreign exchange contracts are valued off of the associated cash market yield curves. Longer-term interest rate contracts look more at the effects of financing costs and accrued interest on the underlying cash market instruments. We will review each of these in more detail.

EXHIBIT 7.1   Margin requirements for some actively traded financial futures contracts (as of 5/28/98)

Contract	Initial Margin	Maintenance Margin
3-month Eurodollar	500	375
Treasury bond	2,700	2,000
10-year Treasury note	1,350	1,000
S&P 500	12,563	10,050
Deutsche mark	1,215	900

SHORT-TERM INTEREST RATE FUTURES CONTRACTS

In 1976, the Chicago Mercantile Exchange ("the Merc") began trading in the first short-term interest rate futures contract still in existence, based on the 3-month Treasury Bill. The idea of the contract was to provide what amounted to a forward market for T-Bills, where investors and traders could either hedge or—to use the dreaded "S" word—speculate, on future movements of T-Bill rates. This contract was preceded by futures contracts on several foreign currencies, which were introduced at the Merc in 1972.

Over the next 5 years, other short-term interest rate contracts were introduced, but not until 1981 was the next major contract milestone created. Based on a 3-month time deposit, Eurodollar futures contracts became (and remain) the most actively traded interest rate contracts in the world. There are three very good reasons why this occurred. First, Eurodollar time deposits are major cash market vehicles for investment and funding in money-center banks.

Second, a major portion of bank lending on a cost-of-funds basis is pegged off either 3- or 6-month LIBOR (**L**ondon **I**nter-**B**ank **O**ffered **R**ate). This is the official rate setting for the offered side of the Eurodollar market.[1] It is no surprise that the commercial bank investment and funding rates have the same maturity scheme as the bank lending rates. Banks look to *tenor-match,* or maturity-match, their assets and liabilities to eliminate market and liquidity risks and focus on the creditworthiness issues.

The third reason represents more of a convenience than anything else. Eurodollar futures contracts do not have a delivery option at expiration. They are *cash settled*. On the last trading day, the contract simply expires. No fuss, no muss. This represents a great benefit to futures traders because they don't have to worry about delivering or accepting a cash market security. Eurodollar futures were the first cash-settled contracts traded in Chicago. Since their introduction, other financial futures contracts, particularly in the deposit and equity arenas, have adopted the same cash-settled process.

As a general rule, money market securities are quoted in money market yield or discount yield. Money market futures trade $100 \times (100 - \text{Yield})$. For example, a 3-month Eurodollar futures contract trading at a money market yield of 5.15% would be quoted as $[100 \times (100 - 5.15)]$ or 9485. A ½-basis-point move up in the yield translates into a one-"tick" move down in the futures price. Tick is the generic name for the minimum price movement in a futures contract. Each futures contract has its own minimum, or tick, value. In our example, if yield moves to 5.155%, the futures contract is then quoted at 9484.5. Exhibit 7.2 shows the calculation of tick value for the 3-month Eurodollar futures contract. Appendix G contains a chart of contract specifications for the more popular financial futures contracts.

Every futures position is marked to market on a daily basis. The prices used in this process are official closing or *settlement* prices

---

EXHIBIT 7.2   Three-month Eurodollar tick value

Each "tick" is worth ½ basis point°:

$$\frac{\$1,000,000 \ (\text{Contract size})}{10,000} = \$100, \text{ or } 1 \text{ bp.} \qquad \frac{\$100}{2} = \$50, \text{ or } \frac{1}{2} \text{ bp.}$$

If an investor earned ½ basis point on $1,000,000 for 1 year, the return would be $50. A 3-month Eurodollar contract is ¼ of a year:

$$\frac{\$50}{4} = \textbf{\$12.50 per basis point.}$$

° Tick value for Eurodollar futures is $12.50 or half a basis point for the first four contract expirations in the March-June-September-December cycle, as well as the two serial month expirations.

traded at the end of each day session on the Chicago exchange.[3] The clearing corporation for each exchange compares the closing prices between the previous and current trading days, calculates the difference in ticks, and multiplies the tick value × change in ticks × number of contracts outstanding in each position. Because the total number of outstanding long contract positions must, by definition, equal the total number of short positions, the clearing corporation will debit the accounts whose positions lost money and credit the accounts that increased in value. Margin rules dictate that a minimum level of equity, or maintenance margin, must be on deposit for each outstanding futures position (see Exhibit 7.1). Investors don't need to add any cash to their accounts unless the accumulated net debits to the account drop the margin balance below the minimum required level. When this occurs, the investors are required to replenish the margin value to the amount initially deposited.

Exhibit 7.3 shows the use of Eurodollar futures in a simple hedging example. On 9/15/97, a bank had a commitment to provide 3 months of $10 million in Eurodollar financing, beginning in 3 months. The bank was concerned that interest rates might rise between 9/15 and 12/15. To protect against having to pay a higher cost of funds, the bank sold 10 December 1997 Eurodollar contracts at a price of 9450, or

---

EXHIBIT 7.3   Eurodollar futures borrowing house

On 9/15/97:

Sell 10 Dec '97 Eurodollar contracts at 9450.

On 12/15/97:

Buy 10 Dec '97 contracts at 9420.

Profit/loss: 60 ticks (30 bps) × $12.50 × 10 = $7,500 profit

The 7,500 profit will be used by the bank to reduce the higher cost of borrowing (7.80%) by 30 bps. If interest rates moved in the other direction and the 3-month Eurodollar cash deposit fell to 5.20%, the contract price would have risen to 9480. The loss on the Eurodollar futures, however, would be offset by a decline in borrowing cost due to the decline in cash market rates. In other words, the Eurodollar position taken on 9/15 locked the bank into a borrowing cost of 5.50%.

5.50%. On December 15, the 3-month Eurodollar rate had risen to 5.80%, with a corresponding fall in price to 9420. The bank mitigated the rising cost of borrowing in the 3-month Eurodollar cash market by shorting the futures contracts.

Inter- and Intramarket Spreads

Aside from buying and selling futures contracts outright, traders also trade the contracts as spreads in what could be viewed as a basis relationship. Intermarket spreads, like their cash counterparts, are the simultaneous purchase and sale of either similar maturities with different creditworthiness or different maturities with similar creditworthiness. For those spreads with different creditworthiness, the higher the general level of rates, the normally wider these spreads will be. This is due to the risk perception of differences in potential principal and interest payment ability by the different credit quality issuers. In short-term interest rate futures, a traded intermarket spread is the 3-month Treasury Bill against the 3-month Eurodollar time deposit. This is referred to as the *TED spread*. Purchasing the TED means buying the T-Bill contract and selling the Eurodollar contract. The trade will be profitable if the spread widens. Exhibit 7.4 reflects a trade in the TED spread.

EXHIBIT 7.4   Buying the TED spread

On 4/1/98:

Buy 10 June '98 U.S. T-Bill futures at 9465, or a discount of 5.35% (100 − 94.65).

Sell 10 June '98 Eurodollar futures at 9435, or a money market yield of 5.65% (100 − 94.35).

The spread is 30 bps (9465 − 9435).

In 30 days, the TED has widened to 40 bps.
On 5/1/98: The long position is liquidated.
Sell 10 June '98 U.S. T-Bill futures at 9490, or a discount of 5.10%.
Buy 10 June '98 Eurodollar futures at 9450, or a money market yield of 5.50%.

Profit/loss on the trade is 10 basis points (40 − 30). Each basis point equals $25 per $1 million ($1,000,000/10,000/4). Remember that a basis point is 1% of 1%.

$$10 \text{ bps} \times \$25 \times 10 \text{ contracts} = \$2,500$$

Intramarket spreads compare the same futures contracts with different maturities. In short-term interest rate futures, this is referred to as a *calendar spread*. The reason is the forward rate nature of the futures contract. For example, in March, a trader buys the June Eurodollar futures contract and simultaneously sells a September Eurodollar futures contract. This is called buying the intramarket spread. The trader is buying a 3-month deposit beginning in June and selling a 3-month deposit beginning in September. This could be executed as a speculation; the trader may believe that the spread between the two contracts will widen. The September contract represents the second half of a six-month deposit beginning in June. If the spread widens, the trader makes money. If the reverse occurs, the trader loses money. Exhibit 7.5 reflects a calendar spread trade in the Eurodollar contract.

Calculating Yield and Returns on a Eurodollar STRIP

Traders, investors, and corporate financial managers need to lock in future borrowing and lending rates for periods spanning multiple years. In March 1998, a corporation funding a $1 million one-year loan beginning in one year at 3-month LIBOR with quarterly resets may find the

EXHIBIT 7.5   Trading a calendar spread

On 3/16/98:

Buy 10 June Eurodollar futures contract at 9435.

Sell 10 September Eurodollar futures contract at 9425.

Spread = 10 bps (9435 − 9425)

On 3/23/98:

Sell 10 June contract at 9433

Buy 10 September contract at 9420

Spread = 13bps

Profit/loss on the trade equals 3 bps × 10 contracts × $25 per bp = $750.

current cost structure for that period to be attractive, based on interest rate projections for the coming year. To lock in today's view of interest rates for that period, the corporation sells a *STRIP* of the March 1999–December 1999 Eurodollar futures contracts. To determine the actual borrowing cost, the following calculations are made:

Eurodollar Contract	Price	Yield	Interest Cost
March 1999	9453	5.47%	$13,675°
June 1999	9447	5.53	13,875
September 1999	9442	5.58	13,950
December 1999	9433	5.67	14,175
Total cost			$55,675

° These are approximate. Interest calculations on cash Eurodeposits are on an actual/360 basis. Given the similar settlement convention for each Eurodollar futures contract, the actual number of days in each deposit period will vary.

As time marches on, interest rates begin a steady climb. By March 1999, interest rates have begun to move higher. The March 1999 contract is 100 basis points lower in price than it was in March 1998. As the year progresses, the June, September, and December contracts also fall 100 points in price from the March 1998 levels. At each quarterly reset, the corporation has had to pay 100 bps more in yield. This additional cost, however, has been offset by the corporation's gain in the futures market.

Eurodollar Contract	3/98 Price	Price at Contract Expiration
March 1999	9453	9353
June 1999	9447	9347
September 1999	9442	9342
December 1999	9433	9333

The value of 1 bp on the Eurodollar contract = $25 ($1,000,000/$10,000/4). Therefore, each contract earned 100 × $25 = $2,500. The total income from all four contracts equals $10,000, which offsets the additional borrowing cost created by the rise in interest rates. The actual borrowing cost for the period, generated from the futures position, will be adjusted by the actual number of days in the deposit period and by the reinvestment of the futures revenue from the daily credits and charges arising from initial margin and daily mark-to-market adjustments. The faster the contracts generated positive cash flow (as yield went up and price went down), the greater the opportunity for incremental revenue from reinvestment.

Let's now look at this trade from an investment perspective. The investor who purchased these four contracts (for every short position, there must be a long position) could have been concerned about a fall in interest rates over the same period, which would have reduced potential investment income. As we observed, however, rates rose and future investment prospects became more lucrative. That's the good news. The bad news is that our investor was long (owned) the contracts. Over the period between futures purchase and contract expiration, the investor's account was charged a total of $10,000 in mark-to-market adjustments as the contract values declined. As a result, the investment income earned between March 1999 and March 2000 will be partially offset by the cost of financing the $10,000 in negative cash flow from the mark-to-market adjustments.

Had interest rates fallen the same 100 bps, the investor would have benefited in three ways:

1. The drop in rates would have generated the futures revenue through variation margin.
2. This revenue could have been reinvested during the March 1998–December 1999 period.
3. The quarterly compounding effect of the four investment rates would have generated an annualized yield of 6.726% over the March 1999–March 2000 period.

As a practical matter, the only logical way to invest the variation margin revenue is on an overnight basis, because daily price declines would require the investor to return some of the gains to the CME clearing corporation for distribution to the investors with short positions.

The quarterly compounding effect of the four 3-month investment rates between March 1999 and March 2000* is:

Contract Expires	Price	Yield
March 1999	9353	6.47%
June 1999	9347	6.53
September 1999	9342	6.58
December 1999	9336	6.67

$$\left[1+\left(.0647\times\left(\frac{91}{360}\right)\right)\right]\times\left[1+\left(.0653\times\left(\frac{91}{360}\right)\right)\right]\times\left[1+\left(.0658\times\left(\frac{91}{360}\right)\right)\right]\times$$

$$\left[1+\left(.0667\times\left(\frac{91}{360}\right)\right)-1\right]=6.80\%\ \ \text{annualized yield}$$

° Approximate, due to actual day count differences in each period.

Many other types of trading and hedging strategies can be created using short-term interest rate futures. Much of this information is available free of charge via mail or e-mail from the Chicago Mercantile Exchange. (See Chapter 12 for Internet contact information.)

FRA: Over-the-Counter Cousin of the Eurodollar Futures Contract

An FRA, or forward rate agreement, is the over-the-counter equivalent of the Eurodollar futures contract. Essentially, it represents the same kind of forward interest rate as the futures contract. There are, however, some significant differences, as highlighted in Exhibit 7.6.

As you can see, the FRA is much more flexible, and the Eurodollar futures contract is more liquid with less credit risk. In practice, this intuitively translates into more speculative applications for futures contracts and more hedging applications for the FRA. Futures contracts, however, are also widely used for hedging because of their high degree of liquidity. Additionally, futures contracts represent virtually no credit risk while FRAs have counterparty risk.[4]

FRAs are quoted on a money market yield basis (actual/360) in the following manner:

$$1\times 4\qquad 5.13-5.15$$

EXHIBIT 7.6   Comparison of Eurodollar futures contract versus forward rate agreement (FRA)

Parameters	Eurodollar Futures	FRA
Expiration	Quarterly (March, June, September, December) with two serial months	Can be any date
Length of deposit	Three months	Can be any length; 3 and 6 months most popular
Contract size	$1 million	Can be any amount
Margin requirements	Yes	No
Credit risk	Virtually none	Yes (counterparty)
Liquidity	High liquidity	Held to expiration

This means that, 1 month from now, a 3-month time deposit maturing 4 months from now is bid by a potential borrower at 5.13%, and a potential lender is willing to invest money during this period at 5.15%.

The buyer of an FRA is said to benefit from a rise in interest rates; the seller will benefit from a decline in interest rates.

Payment for an FRA interest rate differential is determined by multiplying the par value of the contract by the present value of the

EXHIBIT 7.7

Par value = $1,000,000
FRA Contract rate = 6.5%
Settlement rate = 6%
Number of days = 90
Basis = 360

$$\$1,000,000 \times \frac{(.065-.060) \times \left(\dfrac{90}{360}\right)}{\left[1+\left(.06 \times \left(\dfrac{90}{360}\right)\right)\right]} = \$1,231.53$$

In this case, the buyer of the FRA must pay the seller because the settlement rate is lower than the contract rate.

difference between the contract rate and the actual or settlement rate at the expiration of the FRA contract, times the number of days in the FRA contract period divided by the day count basis (usually, 360).[5] The formula is (see Exhibit 7.7):

$$\text{Par value} \times \frac{(\text{Contract rate} - \text{Settlement rate}) \times (\text{Number of Days / Basis})}{1 + \text{Settlement rate} \times (\text{Number of Days / Basis})}$$

Pricing Eurodollar Futures Contracts and FRAs

Short-term interest rate futures and FRAs are all priced off of the associated Eurodollar cash market yield curve. The process used is one of break-even analysis:

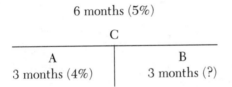

$$
\begin{array}{c}
6 \text{ months } (5\%) \\
\hline
\text{C}
\end{array}
$$

A	B
3 months (4%)	3 months (?)

If the cash market rate for a 3-month Eurodollar deposit (A) is 4% and the 6-month rate (C) is 5%, what rate does the second 3-month period (B) have to be to make the investor (1) indifferent to buying a 3-month deposit and a 3-month forward or futures contract or (2) purchase the 6-month deposit? The formula for the break-even forward rate is:

$$R_b = \left[\frac{[1 + R_c \times (T_c / 360)]}{[1 + R_a \times (T_a / 360)]} - 1 \right] \times \frac{360}{T_b}$$

where: R_a = rate for period A, T_a = time period A,
        R_b = rate for period B, T_b = time period B,
        R_c = rate for period C, T_c = time period C.

$$R_b = \left[\frac{[1 + .05 \times (180/360)]}{[1 + .04 \times (90/360\ )]} - 1 \right] \times \frac{360}{90}$$

$$R_b = 5.94\%$$

Proof: $.05 \times \dfrac{180}{360} \times \$1,000,000 = \$25,000$

$$.04 \times \frac{90}{360} \times \$1,000,000 = \$10,000$$

$$.0594 \times \frac{90}{360} \times \$1,010,000 = \$15,000 \text{ (rounded)}$$

$$\$10,000 + \$15,000 = \$25,000$$

Remember, the interest earned on the first 3-month deposit is presumed to be reinvested into the second 3-month deposit. If this weren't the case, the break-even forward or futures price would be 6%.

The same concept applies to all short-term futures contact and FRA valuations. As the diagram on page 141 reflects, the easiest way to think about a futures contract is as a later piece of a longer-term cash market instrument. As a practical matter, 3- and 6-month FRA quote liquidity stretches out to 2 years. Eurodollar futures contracts currently mature every 3 months, out as far as 10 years. For those unavailable cash market rates, street convention is to use linear interpolation to derive cash market rates between available cash quotes. Linear interpolation divides the difference between two rates into equal pieces. For example, if the 18-month cash rate is 5.5% and the 24-month cash rate is 5.7%, the linear interpolation for a 21-month cash rate would be 5.6%.

LONGER-TERM INTEREST RATE FUTURES: U.S. TREASURY MARKET

Chicago has two major futures exchanges: the Chicago Mercantile Exchange and the Chicago Board of Trade. "The Merc" handles FX futures and the bulk of short-term interest rates. "The Board" handles the longer-term interest rate futures contracts. When we say longer-term, we mean the maturity of the underlying cash market instrument, not the length of the contract.

Treasury futures contracts come in four maturities: (1) a 2-year note contract, (2) a 5-year note, (3) a 10-year note, and (4) a bond contract. In each case, the stated coupon of the deliverable security is 8%. (Appendix G lists the specifications for all four of these contracts.) The bond contract, the first coupon-bearing Treasury futures contract, was introduced in 1977. It was followed by the 10-year note contract in 1981, the 5-year note contract in 1987, and the 2-year note contract in 1990.

The Treasury complex of futures contracts is highly popular and actively traded. These instruments provide viable opportunities in hedging and speculative transactions to traders and to longer-term investors. Like short-term interest rate futures, a multitude of speculative and hedging strategies can be used for Treasury futures contracts. All this information is available free of charge through the Chicago Board of Trade. (See Chapter 12 for telephone and Internet contact information.) We will focus on different forms of value analysis. The rest of the examples in this chapter will use the Treasury bond futures contract, but the logic and applications apply to all of the Board of Trade Treasury contracts.

Pricing a Treasury Futures Contract

The price of a Treasury futures contract is a function of several factors. It is important to remember exactly what you are buying or selling when you take a position in any of the Treasury contracts. Unlike the Eurodollar contract, Treasuries settle with a physical delivery of securities. The liquidity of the Treasury futures market, however, allows the investor to quickly and easily liquidate a position of contracts prior to the delivery period. When purchasing or selling short a futures contract, an investor is contracting to take or make physical delivery of a security sometime in the future. In effect, the Treasury bond is being bought or sold in the forward market. Before we further examine a futures price valuation, let's look at the implied forward price of a straight cash market security. It is the difference between the accrued interest and the financing (funding) cost of the security for the holding period:

$$P_f = P_{pr} - AI\$ + FC\$$$

where: P_f = forward price,
        P_{pr} = present cash price,
        AI = accrued interest for the holding period,
        FC = the funding cost for the holding period.

$1,000,000 par value of a 7% Treasury bond, due 4/1/2020, priced at 100 for settlement in the cash market on 4/1/98, was purchased for payment 5/1/98 (with accrued interest). The annualized funding cost is 6%. The implied, or break-even forward value of the bond would be:

$$P_f = \$1,000,000 - \$5,737.71 + \$5,000.00 = \$999,262.29$$

Subtracting the net positive carry amount of $737.71 ($5,737.71 − $5,000; accrued interest is greater than the financing cost) from the cash market price makes the investor indifferent to purchasing the security for cash or on a forward basis. (Remember, when the security is purchased, the buyer pays principal plus accrued interest.[6]) A simplified valuation concept for Treasury futures similarly examines the relationship among the price of a cash market security today, the accrued interest earned on that security between today and the delivery date into the futures contract, and the cost of funding the cash security over the same period:

Futures price = Cash price − Accrued interest + Funding cost

For example, if today's price of a deliverable cash T-bond is 105, accrued interest between today and the delivery date of the futures contract is 4, and funding the purchase of the cash bond for the same period is 2, the implied futures price equals 105 − 4 + 2 = 103.

If there was only one deliverable security into the T-Bond futures contact and it exactly matched the underlying cash market security outlined in the contract specifications, the above relationship would hold. This is, however, not the case. The concept of break-even analysis does play a role, but it is not as easily quantifiable as in the shorter-term interest rate contracts.

Like the Eurodollar contract, Treasury futures are priced from an underlying security. The T-Bond contract is based on a security with an 8% coupon and a minimum maturity of 15 years to either call date or final maturity. In August 1998, more than 30 different Treasury issues satisfied the September 1998 contract delivery requirement. Given a choice of issues to deliver, the short position in the September 1998 contract facing delivery needed to have at least one of the eligible securities in inventory at the time of delivery. It stands to reason that the seller would want to deliver the relatively *cheapest* available Treasury bond into the futures contract. The calculation for determining this *cheapest-to-deliver* security will be explained later in the chapter. For the time being, suffice it to say that, in theory, the futures contract should track, in part, the cheapest-to-deliver Treasury bond. We say "in part" because another factor is contributing to the value of the contract. Treasury futures contracts are designed to give the seller certain choices in the delivery process that are not available to the buyer. These will also be discussed later in the chapter.

As we mentioned, many Treasury bonds are deliverable into the futures contract. Nearly all of the deliverable securities, including the cheapest-to-deliver, not only don't have an 8% coupon, but also mature in more than 15 years. It is unlikely that $100,000 par value of a $6\frac{1}{8}$% coupon security due in 30 years will have the same value as $100,000 par value of a 10% bond due in 15 years. To resolve this value difference, the Chicago Board of Trade developed a system to equate the price of the futures contract with any of the deliverable cash bonds. *Conversion factors* represent a mathematical calculation which, when multiplied by the market price of the futures contract, generates a price that equates to an 8% yield to maturity for each deliverable bond. Another way to look at a conversion factor is that it is the price (divided by 100) of any deliverable security priced to an 8% yield to maturity. For example, the September 1998 conversion factor for the $7\frac{1}{4}$% T-bond, due 5/15/2016, equals .9300. When input into a yield-to-maturity formula for this security, a price of 93.00 equates to, approximately, an 8% yield.

Conversion factors for all the Treasury futures contracts are available from the Chicago Board of Trade. Appendix H is a chart of conversion factors for 1998–1999 T-Bond futures contracts.

Another way to look at this calculation is from the perspective of the futures contract. By multiplying the price of the contract by the conversion factor, the futures contract becomes based on the specific cash market bond. This converted market price is called the *adjusted futures price*.

Once this conversion to the futures contract price is made, a more logical comparison can be made to each cash market bond. Exhibit 7.8 reflects the conversion of the September 1998 futures price to an adjusted futures price. Using the $11\frac{1}{4}\%$ Treasury bond, due 2/15/2015, it also shows the difference between the cash market price of the bond and the adjusted futures price. This difference is called the *gross basis*, or simply the *basis*. For trading purposes, the basis is quoted in 32nds of a point. If, for example, the gross basis was bid at 63 and offered at 64, this means $^{63}\!/_{32}$ or $1^{31}\!/_{32}$ bid and $^{64}\!/_{32}$ or 2 offered. Exhibit 7.9, a sample screen from Liberty Brokerage Inc., an interdealer broker, shows how the basis on many of the deliverable Treasury bonds is quoted. As you can see, the futures price for the contracts where basis is being quoted is also posted on the page. These data are important to cash market traders because some "off-the-run" T-bonds are not quoted on brokers' screens in outright price. By multiplying the futures price by the corresponding conversion factor for each deliverable bond and adding the basis quotes, cash market traders have a good indication of where each deliverable cash Treasury bond is currently valued. If this weren't the case, and a particular cash T-bond was trading over or under its implied value from the basis quote, arbitrage forces would bring the relationship back into equilibrium.

EXHIBIT 7.8   Calculation of gross basis

Treasury Bond: $11\frac{1}{4}\%$, due 2/15/2015
Price: $158^6\!/_{32}$ (158.1875 in decimal form)
March Futures Price: 121-22 (121.6875)

121.6875	×	1.2968	=	157.8043, or $157^{26}\!/_{32}$
Futures Price		Conversion Factor		Adjusted Futures Price
$158^6\!/_{32}$	−	$157^{26}\!/_{32}$	=	$^{12}\!/_{32}$
Cash Bond		Adj. Futures		Basis

EXHIBIT 7.9   Cash/futures basis quotes for treasury bonds deliverable into the September T-bond futures contract

Deliverable Securities into the Bond Contract	On-the-Run Treasurys	Par Value (in Millions)		Par Value (in Millions)

All Basis Quotes in 32nds of a Point

Represents bid and ask prices for Treasury issues swapped for the current 30-year T-Bond. For example, an offer is posted to buy the 30-year T-Bond at 104-29/32 and sell the 7$^1/_4$% T-Bond due 5/16 at 115-21/32. The offer size is 5 mln par value.
"Weighted" means the bond swap is adjusted for interest rate risk. The basis point values of the purchased and sold securities are made equal. Therefore, the actual par amount of 30-year T-Bonds bought or sold against any of the securities noted will be slightly different for each security.

Futures Invoice Price

When delivery on a futures contract is made, the long (purchaser) of the cash market T-bond pays the short (seller) of the cash bond the futures' official closing or *settlement* price on the delivery date, times the conversion factor of the T-bond being delivered, plus any accrued interest on that bond since its last coupon payment date. Remember, any profit or loss on the futures contract between the settlement date on the purchase of the basis and the delivery date into the contract has

**EXHIBIT 7.10   Calculation of futures invoice price for 11 ¼%
Treasury bond, due 2/15/2015**

121.6875 Futures Price	×	1.2968 Conversion Factor	+	1.367403 Accrued Interest	=	159.171703 per $100 pv or $159,171.70 Invoice Price per $100,00 Contract

already been accounted for in the variation margin from the daily mark-to-market of futures positions. Exhibit 7.10 uses the 11¼% T-bonds due 2/15/2015 to deliver into the September 1998 futures contract. If the carry is positive (daily accrued interest > funding cost), delivery is assumed to be on the last business day of the delivery month because the seller is likely to hold the cash position and earn carry for as long as possible.

Popularity of the Nearby Contract

Securities traders, particularly those at the Primary Dealer shops, trade the basis on many, if not all, of the deliverable bond, 10-year, 5-year, and 2-year securities. The most popular contract used for basis trading is the current or *nearby* expiration (the futures contract with the nearest expiration date). As a general rule, the nearby contract has the most trading volume and open interest (the amount of contracts outstanding at the end of the trading day). For liquidity and delivery reasons, the volume and open interest shift to the next contract expiration sometime before the last trading day of the current contract. (With cash-settled contracts, the buyer and seller are comfortable holding their positions until the contract expiration date.) The short positions run the risk of being required to deliver at any time during the expiration month. To avoid the possibility of delivery, the contract positions are either closed out by purchasing an offsetting amount or are "rolled" into the next contract expiration. A trader looking to maintain a long or short position in a contract would sell/buy back the existing long/short position and reestablish a new short/long position before the next expiration date. During this process, the next contract becomes the current, or most active, contract. Because of the Treasury futures contract delivery rules, the switchover occurs prior to the beginning of the expiration month. The 2-year,

5-year, 10-year, and bond contracts all trade on a quarterly expiration cycle (March, June, September, and December).

"Cheapness" in Futures Prices (The Implied Put Option)

The cash market price of the T-bond being analyzed, plus or minus the net carry (accrued interest – funding cost) for the holding period between the settlement date of the cash bond purchase and the delivery date of the futures contract, equals the theoretical price of the futures contract. The fact is, however, futures contracts have historically been cheaper—in some cases, much cheaper—than the theoretical price. Why does this occur? There is no standardized formula to derive the exact traded futures contract market price. Here is where we bring in another factor that affects the pricing of the futures contract: the *optionality* of the *implied put option,* or perceived value for the futures seller in a choice of bond selection and delivery date selection. Consider the following: Over 30 T-Bonds are deliverable into the September 1998 futures contract. The futures seller can choose to deliver any one of these issues. According to the Treasury futures contract specifications, delivery can occur on any business day during the expiration month. The extra, implied value of these options is offset by the relative cheapness in the contract price.

Wildcard Delivery

Because of the available choices from among the many deliverable issues, and the structure of the delivery rules established by the Chicago Board of Trade, the "short" futures position has the additional option of potentially capitalizing on movements in the cash market after the close of futures trading. One strategy is the *wildcard delivery option.* Wildcard delivery can occur on any futures trading day up to, but not including, the last trading day of the contract. The short position doesn't need to declare intent to deliver nor specify which security will be delivered until 8:00 P.M. Central time on the day of delivery. The invoice price to the buyer (long futures position) will be the futures settlement price (2:00 P.M. Central time) *on that day,* multiplied by the conversion factor for the representative bonds, plus any accrued interest. If the market receives bearish news after the close of futures, cash market prices fall. The short could purchase the deliverable cash market securities at the reduced value and deliver them against an invoice price pegged to the futures settlement price posted earlier in the day. This may seem like a "no-brainer"; in reality, this condition doesn't arise very often. Nevertheless, it represents a potentially profitable strategy.

Under the right circumstances, other incremental-profit strategies can also be implemented, using the structure of the delivery process. For additional information on this and the concept and applications of U.S. Treasury cash-futures basis trading as a whole, see Appendix F.

CALCULATING HEDGE RATIOS WITH TREASURY FUTURES CONTRACTS

We discussed conversion factors and how they apply to equating the futures contract price with the cash market price of a particular bond. We use the same concept to develop hedge ratios. Given a parallel shift in interest rates for all maturities, the adjusted futures price should move in line with each of the deliverable cash market securities.

To calculate the hedge ratio for a particular deliverable Treasury security, find the basis point value (BPV) of the futures contract. This is done by dividing the BPV of the cheapest-to-deliver cash security by its conversion factor. For example, at the end of February 1998, the 11¼% T-bond due 2/15/2015 was the cheapest-to-deliver security into the March 1998 T-bond futures contract. It has a basis point value of $1,466.64 per $100,000 par value, and a conversion factor of 1.2968 for the March 1998 futures contract expiration. Dividing 1.2968 into $1,466.64 generates a March 1998 T-bond futures BPV of $113.10. This value is now used to calculate hedge ratios with the BPVs of the other deliverable securities into the bond contract.

The Cheapest-to-Deliver Concept

We have been using the cheapest-to-deliver concept in our calculations of value. How is this concept computed? Once again, we turn to the concept of *break-even analysis* for the answer. When a trader is "long" the basis (owns the cash security and is short the futures contract) and intends to deliver the cash bond into the futures contract on the delivery date, there are three separate cash flows to consider. The first is the gross basis. The price difference between the purchased cash market bond and the adjusted price of the futures contract represents either an immediate unrealized gain or loss. In Exhibit 7.7, the cash market bond price was $\frac{12}{32}$ *higher* than the adjusted futures price. If the trader could immediately deliver the cash bond into the futures contract at the adjusted futures price, there would be a loss of $\frac{12}{32}$ points, or $375 per $100,000 par value contract. If the adjusted futures price was higher than the cash market price, the trader could make an immediate profit by buying the basis and delivering on the first available business day of the delivery month. Basis, therefore, is virtually always a cash outflow.

The second cash flow to consider is accrued interest on the cash Treasury bond. The owner of the cash security will accrue interest on the cash security from the time of the settlement date on the cash security purchase until the delivery date into the futures contract. This is a cash inflow.

The third cash flow is the cost of funding the cash market security between the settlement date of the purchase and the delivery date into the futures contract. Both principal and interest need to be included in the amount to be funded. This is a cash outflow.

The difference between the accrued interest (inflow) and the basis (outflow) equals the amount of money that can be used to finance the cash market position. The logic is simple. If a trader can fund the cash position for exactly the difference between the accrued interest and the basis, that trader will be economically indifferent to doing the trade. As a result, the following equation holds in a break-even situation:

$$\text{Accrued interest} - \text{Gross basis} - \text{Financing cost} = 0$$

If the values input into this equation generate a net result of 0, the financing cost is the break-even level of money that must be generated. By dividing this amount by the amount to be financed (principal + interest of the cash bond) and multiplying by 360/number of days of required financing, the annualized financing rate is derived. This rate is referred to as the *implied* or *break-even repo rate*. It is called a repo rate because the financing of the cash T-bond is

EXHIBIT 7.11 Calculation of the break-even repo rate

Given: $100,000 par value 11¼% T-bond due 2/15/2015
Settlement date: 2/3/98
Price: 158%₃₂
March futures price: 121²²⁄₃₂
Conversion factor: 1.2968
Accrued interest: 8/15/97–2/3/98 = $5,258.15
Number of days settlement to delivery: 3/31/98–2/3/98 = 56
Accrued interest: 2/3/98 – 3/31/98 = $1,784.25
Basis: ¹²⁄₃₂ = $375.00
Funding (repo) rates: 5.5%

$$\text{B / E repo rate} = \frac{\left(\text{Accrued interest} - \text{Basis}\right)}{\left(\text{Cash T - bond principal} + \text{Interest}\right)} \times \frac{360}{\text{Number of days between cash settlement \& delivery date}}$$

$$\text{B / E repo rate} = \frac{\$1,784.25 - \$375.00}{\$158,187.50 + \$5,258.15} \times \frac{360}{56}$$

$$\text{B / E repo rate} = \frac{\$1,409.25}{\$163,445.70} \times \frac{360}{56}$$

$$\text{B / E repo rate} = 5.543\%$$

conducted in the repurchase agreement, or repo, market. Exhibit 7.11 details the calculation of the break-even (B/E) repo rate.

If a trader can finance the cash T-bond position for less than 5.543%, that trader can lock in a profit for the transaction period with virtually no risk. That's the good news. The bad news is if that condition existed, arbitrageurs would eliminate this profitable relationship. As a result, a break-even repo rate above available financing costs rarely exists for any period of time without being arbitraged away.

To determine the cheapest-to-deliver security, the break-even repo rate is calculated for each of the deliverable T-bonds. The bond with the *highest* break-even repo rate is deemed the cheapest to deliver because the higher the break-even repo rate, the easier to find repo financing.

Traders, salespeople, and portfolio managers need a quick-and-dirty way to determine the richness or cheapness of each security that is deliverable into a corresponding futures contract. Information services vendors provide this type of information to subscribers who require continuous access to real-time information. Bloomberg Financial Markets,[7] with its in-depth, interactive, analytical applications for all the cash and derivatives markets, is the industry benchmark of real-time information services vendors. The break-even repo rate for all the deliverable cash Treasury bonds into the current T-Bond futures contract is highlighted in the Bloomberg application reproduced in Exhibit 7.12.

EXHIBIT 7.12 Cheapest-to-deliver scenario analysis by Bloomberg financial markets

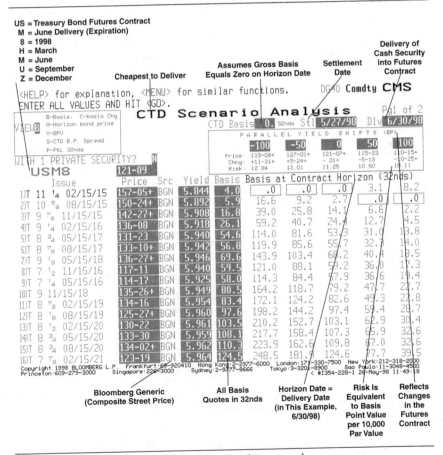

Source: Base Chart © 1997 Bloomberg L.P. All rights reserved.

Relationship between Duration and Cheapest to Deliver

As mentioned above, the conversion factor for each deliverable Treasury issue adjusts the market price of the issue to the equivalent price with an 8% coupon. An examination of the duration of every deliverable issue reveals an interesting, and mathematically logical, relationship. When the general level of interest rates for deliverable issues is above 8%, the security with the longest duration is usually the cheapest to deliver. When the general level of rates is lower than 8%, the security with the shortest duration is usually the cheapest to deliver. Why does this happen?

Let's quickly review the concept of duration. Chapter 4 states that a 100-basis-point (bp) change in a security's yield to maturity translates into a percent change in price equal to the modified duration statistic. If the duration of a security is 5 years, a 100-bp yield-to-maturity change, either up or down, will result in a price change of about 5%. The higher the duration, the more sensitive the price change will be to a given change in yield:

- When the general level of interest rates for the deliverable securities into, for example, the T-bond contract, is above 8%, the security with the highest duration will have lost the largest percent of its value between 8% and the current yield-to-maturity level.

- When the general level of interest rates for the deliverable T-bonds is less than 8%, the security with the lowest duration will have gained the smallest percent value below 8%, among all the deliverable issues. During the first quarter of 1998, the approximately 6% market-required yield to maturity on Treasury bonds deliverable into the September 1998 contract made the 11¼% T-bonds due 2/15/2015 the cheapest to deliver through virtually the entire quarter. This particular issue had the lowest duration level of any of the deliverable bonds.

SUMMARY

This chapter covered short- and long-term interest rate futures contracts. Our discussion included general definitions, trading parameters, and valuation techniques. Short-term interest rate futures are used by large financial institutions to hedge asset and liability positions. The most popular of the short-term contracts is the 3-month Eurodollar. The longer-term contracts use U.S. Treasury securities as the underlying cash market instruments. The value of these securities is a function of both break-even analysis and the optionality of the contract in the form of the seller's choices of deliverable security and delivery date. Chapter 8 covers the forward foreign exchange market, FX futures, and the concept of covered interest arbitrage.

NOTES

1. The bid side of the official Eurodollar quote and the average between the bid and the offer are also quoted as LIBID and LIMEAN, respectively.
2. The end of day for Eurodollar and T-Bill contracts on the Chicago Mercantile Exchange, as well as the Treasury futures on the Chicago Board of Trade is 3:00 P.M. Eastern time.
3. The credit risk in FRAs is minimal in the interdealer broker markets because all participants are recognized dealers. See Chapter 10 for more information on the interdealer broker markets.
4. Present value is used because payment is made at the beginning of the FRA period. At this point, the differential has not yet been earned.
5. The forward price + accrued interest ($999,262.29 + $5,737.71) equals the current price + funding cost ($1,000,000 + $5,000). In either case, this is what the investor has laid out as of the 5/1/98 settlement date. At the next coupon date, the investor will receive the full coupon payment in either case.
6. For further information on Bloomberg and other real-time information services providers, see Chapter 12.

8 FOREIGN EXCHANGE

Value in the foreign currency markets is a function of economic risk, country risk, and interest rate risk. An in-depth discussion of the first two risks is well beyond the scope of this book and its author. This chapter covers the relationships existing between foreign currency values and interest rates, and how changes in interest rates directly impact foreign exchange (FX) rates. We will also look at the FX futures markets and the valuation of contracts that represent the major foreign currencies.

CROSSRATES

A foreign exchange price is represented as a relationship between two currencies. Simply put, it is the value of one currency expressed in terms of another. When a traveler goes overseas, an exchange into the currency of the visited country is usually needed. The FX rate reflects the amount of foreign currency to be received for each unit of the currency being exchanged. The relationship of one currency to another is called a *crossrate*. The U.S. dollar is the major currency of international business and is actively traded against many of the currencies of other

156

EXHIBIT 8.1   Derivation of a crossrate

Currency A = .5 DEM
Currency B = .25 USD
USD/DEM = 1.8000, or 1.8 DEM per USD
Currency A = .5 DEM/1.8 or .2778 USD
Currency B = .25 USD
Crossrate A/B = .25/.2778 = .8999 (.9 rounded) currency A units for each currency
                         B unit

industrialized countries. In the United States, the relationship of one nondollar currency to another nondollar currency is called a crossrate.

There are many actively traded crossrates. To obtain a value for a crossrate that is not actively quoted, one must extrapolate from the available rates. For example, currency A is quoted against the Deutschemark but not against the U.S. dollar. Currency B is quoted against the U.S. dollar but not against the Deutschemark. To get a crossrate using currencies A and B, divide the currency A quote by the rate of USD/DEM.[1] This generates currency A's value against the U.S. dollar. Next, divide currency A by currency B to get the cross-rate. Exhibit 8.1 is a numerical example of this process.

SPOT RATES

Foreign currencies are quoted in what is termed a *spot* or *forward* rate format. The spot, or current exchange rate, reflects what one currency is worth in terms of another *for value* two business days from the trade date. This is the normal settlement period for business spot transactions. If the trade date is today, settlement or payment occurs in two business days. Like all other markets, the size of the transaction can have an effect on the quoted price. Generally speaking, the *smaller* the transaction size, the *wider* the spread between bid and ask prices.

FORWARD RATES

A forward rate reflects the value of a foreign currency to be delivered sometime in the future. Forward rates are used by both commercial and financial customers to lock in exchange rates tied to some hedging or speculative transaction. All financial markets are either directly or indirectly related to all other financial markets in terms of impact on pricing. Nowhere is this more evident than in the foreign exchange/interest rate arena. The value of foreign exchange in the forward markets is a function of interaction with the money markets. The calculation of a currency's forward rates is directly related to the interest rates of the currency being quoted and the reference, or base currency. The basic concept applied in such FX valuations is known as *covered interest arbitrage*. The forward FX price is a function of the difference in the Eurodeposit rates between the currency being quoted and the base currency. (Eurocurrency deposit rates are used because of their high degree of market liquidity.)

Given a spot rate for the U.S. dollar versus the Deutschemark, how is a forward exchange rate determined? If an investor could convert between one currency and another at the same rates in both the spot and forward markets, any difference in the deposit rates of these currencies could generate an immediate locked-in gain between the spot and forward dates. Unfortunately, this isn't the way it works.

CALCULATING BREAK-EVEN RATES THROUGH COVERED INTEREST ARBITRAGE

The concept of covered interest arbitrage looks at (1) the relationship between spot and forward rates as calculated between two currencies, and (2) the deposit interest rates of the two currencies associated with the time span between deliveries in the spot and forward markets. The difference in the spot versus forward relationship should equal the difference when the deposit rates are adjusted for the number of days between spot and forward. Many traders and investors examine these relationships closely, looking for inconsistencies. Solving for the break-even rate for each of the following four input factors (given the other three) discovers these inconsistencies. The input factors are:

1. Spot Rate (S),
2. Forward Rate (F),
3. Base currency deposit rate,
4. Secondary currency deposit rate.

The formulae for deriving the break-even values for each of the four inputs are listed below:

Let S = Spot Rate
F = Forward Rate

The examples for each of the break-even formulae below use these terms and values:

C_r = interest rate for the reference or base currency,
C_f = interest rate for the foreign or secondary currency,
T_{sm} = number of days to forward date,
Reference currency = U.S. dollar (USD),
Foreign/Secondary currency = Deutschemark (DEM),
Spot rate = 1.8000 DEM per USD,
Forward rate = 1.7911 DEM,
Number of days to forward date = 90,
3-month USD rate = 5%,
3-month DEM rate = 3%.

1. *Spot Rate:*

$$S = \frac{F \times \left[1 + (C_r(1 + T_{sm}/360°))\right]}{\left[1 + C_f(1 + T_{sm}/360°))\right]}$$

$$1.800 = \frac{1.7911 \times \left[1 + (.05(90/360))\right]}{\left[1 + (.03(90/360))\right]}$$

2. *Forward Rate:*

$$F = \frac{S \times \left[1 + (C_f(T_{sm}/360°))\right]}{\left[1 + (C_r(T_{sm}/360°))\right]}$$

$$1.7911 = \frac{1.800 \times \left[1 + (.03(90/360))\right]}{\left[1 + (.05(90/360))\right]}$$

° Or 365, depending on the day count convention for the currency.

3. *Base Currency Deposit Rate:*

$$C_r = \frac{S \times \left[1 + (C_f(T_{sm}/360^\circ))\right]}{F}$$

$$.05 = \frac{1.800 \times \left[1 + (.03 \times (90/360))\right]}{1.7911}$$
$$\frac{}{90/360}$$

4. *Secondary Currency Deposit Rate:*

$$C_f = \frac{F \times \left[1 + (C_r(1 + T_{sm}/360))\right] - 1}{F}$$

$$.03 = \frac{1.7911 \times \left[1 + (.05 \times (90/360))\right] - 1}{1.800}$$
$$\frac{}{90/360}$$

Generally speaking, financial markets are very efficient. Any opportunity for arbitrage-type profits similar to the above 3% locked-in profit would be adjusted through price action in trading activity. If the deposit rates were reversed, with the 3-month Eurodollar rate at 3% and the Euromark rate at 5%, the forward USD/DEM rate would reflect a cheaper DEM, to offset the additional revenue generated from the deposit spread.

Setting the 3-month Euromark rate at 5% and the 3-month Eurodollar at 3%, the 3-month implied forward rate is:

$$\text{FWD rate} = \frac{1.800 \times \left[1 + (.05(90/360))\right]}{\left[1 + (.03(90/360))\right]} = 1.8089$$

As we have demonstrated, each of the four price input factors to the covered interest arbitrage can be calculated in a break-even

---

$^\circ$ Or 365, depending on the day count convention for the currency.

method. In performing these calculations, the following considerations
should be kept in mind.

1. Most but not all returns on deposit rates are calculated on a 360-
   day basis. As we noted earlier, the currencies from the United
   Kingdom are calculated on a 365-day basis. When two currencies
   have different day-count bases, it is necessary to convert one to
   the other to ensure homogeneous comparisons in a break-even
   analysis. In the conversion formula, the 360-day return is multiplied by 365/360.

2. All deposits and currency rates are quoted with bid and ask
   prices. It is important to use the correct side of the quote to determine accurate break-even values. Exhibit 8.2 identifies the
   four variables used to calculate break-even values in a covered interest arbitrage transaction. The dependent variable (i.e., the
   variable being calculated) is listed under column A. Columns B
   through E represent the independent variables used to calculate
   the dependent variable. The assumption for using the noted side
   of each independent variable quote listed is that the user will buy
   on the offer side and sell on the bid side of each quote.

**EXHIBIT 8.2   Analysis of bid/offer factors pricing in covered
interest arbitrage transaction**

Dependent Variable	Independent Variables			
A	B	C	D	E
To Calculate	Spot	Forward	Base Deposit	Secondary Deposit
Spot Bid	—	ASK	ASK	BID
Spot Ask	—	BID	BID	ASK
Forward Bid	ASK	—	BID	ASK
Forward Ask	BID	—	ASK	BID
Euro Depo				
Base Bid	ASK	BID	—	ASK
Base Ask	BID	ASK	—	BID
Secondary Bid	BID	ASK	ASK	—
Secondary Ask	ASK	BID	BID	—

SECURITIES FUNDING IMPLICATIONS FROM THE FX MARKET

Given more favorable borrowing rates in a foreign currency, an investor may consider borrowing in a foreign currency, converting the currency to U.S. dollars, and purchasing U.S. dollar denominated securities. In this case, the profit/loss on the transaction will include the gain or loss on the security, and foreign exchange exposure on the original borrowed amount plus any loss on the securities transaction.

FORWARD POINTS

The quoting of forward currency rates can be done in one of two ways: (1) using the actual rate (i.e., 1.7911 marks per dollar for our 3-month USD/DEM), or (2) using the differential between the spot and forward rate. This difference, the more popular of the two quoting formats, is quoted in what are known as *forward points*. These points can be quoted in either a positive or a negative state. Exhibit 8.3 reflects the various conditions as they relate to currency deposit rates.

Forward points are usually expressed as the difference between the spot and forward rates, multiplied by 10,000. The reason for this is that most currencies trade in $\frac{1}{10,000}$ of a point, also called a *pip*. Two notable exceptions are the Japanese Yen (JPY) and the Italian Lira (ITL); both are quoted in $\frac{1}{100}$ of a unit. This is due to the large number of currency units needed to equal one U.S. dollar.

EXHIBIT 8.3   Forward points sign based on quotation terms: U.S. dollar market

	Forward Points Sign
For quotes in units per $ (European terms)	
Foreign deposit rate > USD deposit rate	+
USD deposit rate > Foreign deposit rate	−
For quotes in $ per unit (U.S. terms)	
Foreign deposit rate > USD deposit rate	−
USD deposit rate > Foreign deposit rate	+

Using our USD/DEM example, the spot rate is 1.8000 and the 3-month forward rate is 1.7911. The difference between the two rates is .0089, which, multiplied by 10,000, equals 89 forward points. A forward point quote may center around an implied value. Using our USD/DEM example, the 3-month forward quote could be formatted as 88–90. Here, the bid represents 1.8000 − .0088, or 1.7912, and the offer represents 1.8000 − .0090, or 1.7910.

A shortcut to approximating forward points is:

$$\text{Forward points} = \text{Spot} \times (E_f - E_\$) \times (\text{Days}/360 \text{ or } 365) \times 100$$

where: E_f = foreign currency Euro deposit rate,

$E_\$$ = Eurodollar deposit rate,

Days = number of days to settlement, or value, date.

Using our example above:

$$\text{Forward points} = 1.8 \times (3 - 5) \times (90/360) \times 100 = -90 \text{ points or } .0090$$

$$1.8 - .0090 = 1.791 \text{ (forward rate)}.$$

This is a good estimator, but keep in mind that it doesn't account for day count differences (for example, forward point calculations between the U.S. dollar and the British pound have different day count bases).

TRADING PRACTICES IN THE FX SPOT AND FORWARD MARKETS

The FX markets, like the securities markets, transact most business either between dealer and customer, or through a FX broker. Trading is done via telephone and interactively through services such as Reuters Dealing 2000, where dealers use computer screens to transmit bids and offers. Many FX dealers have, on their desks, "squawk boxes" that are linked to FX brokers. All day, bids and offers are screeched back and forth via these boxes.

Normal settlement on a commercial FX transaction is two business days following the trade date. The standard transaction unit amount for commercial transactions is 1 million.

EXHIBIT 8.4   Forward periods actively quoted in the FX market

Spot: Trade today, settle in two business days
Tom-Next: Trade as of next business day, settle the following business day
Spot-Next: Trade as of two business days from today, settle the following business day
One–Three weeks
One–Six months
Nine months
Twelve months

The forward FX market is very liquid out to one year. No compounding in Eurocurrency deposit rates is considered out to this period. Exhibit 8.4 highlights the standard forward periods quoted by FX dealers for the major traded currencies.

Reuters has been the leader in real-time foreign exchange spot and forward pricing. Exhibit 8.5 represents a sample Reuters screen for USD/DEM, available to all brokers and commercial customers over the Reuters network.

FOREIGN EXCHANGE FUTURES CONTRACTS

A good analogy to use in describing the structure of foreign exchange futures contracts is: FX futures contracts are to FX forward rates what Eurodollar futures contracts are to forward rate agreements (FRAs). The concept of futures and forwards is essentially the same—purchase a currency today for delivery sometime in the future. The value of the futures contract will be a forward rate calculation based on the delivery date of the contract.

As in the Eurodollar futures–FRA comparison, the differences revolve around credit and liquidity issues. Buyers and sellers of futures contracts trade with the futures exchange, virtually eliminating credit risk. FRAs are agreements between a buyer and seller where credit is an issue. Actively traded forward rates span a much wider range than currency futures contracts and can be customized to virtually any time period for any amount. Currency futures contracts, like Eurodollar futures, have specific expiration dates each year, and set contract amounts.

EXHIBIT 8.5   Sample real-time FX trading screen

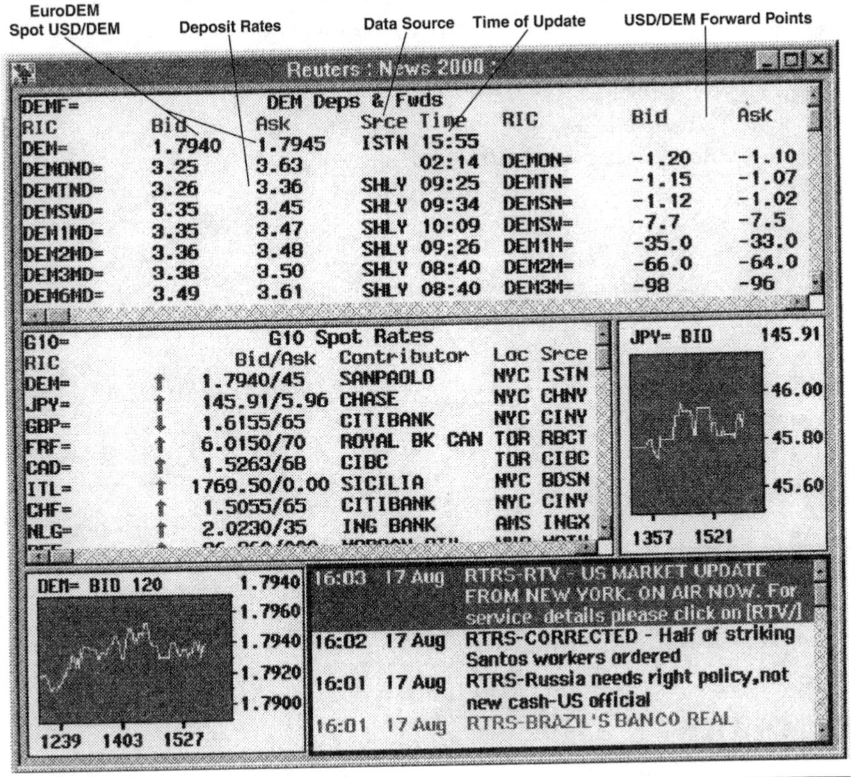

Futures contracts are better speculative vehicles because of their high degree of liquidity and minimal credit risk. Forward contracts can be customized to give the user an exact hedge for a future FX asset or liability position. Keep in mind, however, that customization translates into an additional expense and lower liquidity. You get what you pay for. Futures contracts can be valuable in the hedging process when position flexibility is important. Exhibit 8.6 shows a calculation of the fair value of a foreign exchange futures contract.

The Chicago Mercantile Exchange (CME) trades the largest amount of FX futures contracts in the United States. As of February 5, 1998, there were eleven currencies with listed futures on options on futures contracts. Appendix G lists the specifications of some of the more

EXHIBIT 8.6   Fair value futures price calculation

On 6/1/98, find the fair value of the September 1998 DEM futures contract.

Given: The value date for the September delivery of the Deutschemarks is 9/17/98.

9/17/98–6/1/98 = 108 days

1.78 = spot USD/DEM

5.64% = linear interpolated midpoint estimate of USD for 9/17/98 value date

3.55% = linear interpolated midpoint estimate of DEM for 9/17/98 value date

Using the forward rate formula (see page 000)

$$\text{Fair value futures price} = \frac{1.78 \times \left[1 + \left(.0355 \times \left(\frac{108}{360} \right) \right) \right]}{\left(1 + .0564 \times \left(\frac{108}{360} \right) \right)} = \textbf{1.7690 DEM per USD}$$

$$\left(\frac{1}{1.7690} \right) = \textbf{.5653} \text{ estimated September 1998 futures price}$$

popular contracts. For further information, contact the CME. Chapter 12 lists the Internet address.

SUMMARY

This chapter covered the valuation of spot and forward rates in the foreign exchange markets. The concept of covered interest arbitrage was introduced as the process used to determine fair value for spot and forward rates as well as for the associated deposit rates. Forward points were defined as the difference in value between the spot and forward rates. Futures contracts for FX were also reviewed, and the differences between futures and forwards were noted.

NOTE

1. USD and DEM are the SWIFT codes for the U.S. dollar and the Deutschemark. SWIFT stands for the Society for Worldwide Interbank Financial Transactions. Each currency has its own SWIFT code.

9 OPTIONS

At the start of Chapter 7, we identified the two types of derivative forms. The first type reflects the value of a security at some time in the future. This chapter discusses the second type of derivative instrument. Its value represents the *likelihood* that a security will have a particular value at some time in the future. Instruments of this type are known as *options*.

An option represents the *right* to make or take delivery of a particular amount of a financial instrument or nonfinancial commodity at a specified price on one date or within a range of dates in the future. This is in contrast to a futures contract, where the *right* becomes an *obligation*. Owners of, or holders of a "long" position in, an option can decide to exercise the option whenever their best interests are served. Sellers of, or those with a "short" position in, an option are at the mercy of the option owners. This may sound harsh, but both parties should be aware, or be made aware, of the risks of being long or short an option position. From a profit-and-loss (P/L) perspective, an option *owner's* maximum liability is the cost of the option. If it expires worthless, the option owner loses only the cost of the option. An option *seller's* maximum P/L liability is virtually unlimited in the case of a call option. The seller of a put option can lose only the value of the underlying security because prices can't go below zero. Nevertheless, the actual loss can be so large that, realistically, it can be viewed as almost unlimited.

There are two types of options. A *call* option represents the right to call from, or *buy,* an underlying security. A *put* option represents the right to put to, or *sell,* an underlying security. As the price of the underlying security rises, the call option also gains value. The put option increases in value as the price of the underlying security falls in value. The cost of purchasing an option is called its *premium.*

INTRINSIC VALUE

The price at which the underlying security may be purchased or sold through an option is called the *strike* price or *exercise* price. This price is usually established at the time the option is created (exotic options can be somewhat different; see Chapter 10). In almost all cases, the price doesn't change over the life of the option. The relationship between the strike price and the price of the underlying security determines whether an option is *in the money, at the money,* or *out of the money.* An in-the-money option has what is termed *intrinsic value:* if the option were exercised today, the owner of the option would reap some immediate economic benefit. For a call option, the strike price would be *lower than* the underlying security's market price. The option owner could exercise the option at the lower strike price and immediately sell the underlying securities at the higher market price. For an in-the-money put option, the strike price would be *higher than* the underlying security's market price. In both cases, the intrinsic value is represented by the difference between the strike price and the underlying security price. Exhibits 9.1 and 9.2 reflect the change in an options price, given a change in the underlying security's price or the strike price. Exhibit 9.3 shows the calculation of intrinsic value for in-the-money put and call options.

An at-the-money option occurs when the strike price of the option is *equal* to the underlying security's market price. In this case, there is no intrinsic value because an exercise by the option owner would not result in an immediate gain. An out-of-the-money option occurs when the strike price of a call option is *higher than* the underlying security's market price, or the strike price of a put option is *lower than* the underlying security's price. Like the at-the-money option, there is no intrinsic value

EXHIBIT 9.1   Option factor valuation: Underlying market price

- *Call Option:* The Higher the Price, the Higher the Option Value.
- *Put Option:* The Lower the Price, the Higher the Option Value.
- This Is Used in Measuring Intrinsic Value.

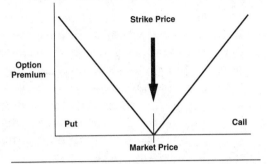

EXHIBIT 9.2   Option factor valuation: Option strike price

- *Call Option:* The Lower the Strike Price, the Higher the Option Value.
- *Put Option:* The Higher the Strike Price, the Higher the Option Value.
- This Is Used in Measuring Intrinsic Value.

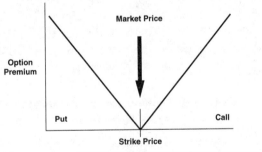

EXHIBIT 9.3   Calculation of intrinsic value

ABC Stock: Market price = $50 per share.
Call option on ABC = $45 strike price.
Put option on ABC = $55 strike price.

Call intrinsic value = Underlying market price − Option strike price
$5   = $50   − $45
Put intrinsic value =   Strike price   − Underlying market price
$5   = $55   − $50

because the option owner would have an immediately realized loss by exercising the option and buying or selling the underlying security.

TIME VALUE

An option is said to be trading *at parity* when the option price equals the intrinsic value. If intrinsic value were the only type of value associated with an option, only in-the-money options would have value. This, however, is not the case. Because an option's value represents the likelihood that a certain value or price level will be achieved in the underlying security, investors and traders place some worth on the likelihood that this will occur. This worth is referred to as *time value*. The amount of time value attached to an option is a function of several factors: number of days to option expiration, price volatility in the underlying security, and level of short-term, risk-free interest rates. The changes in the price of an option that are effected by these variables are presented in Exhibits 9.4 through 9.6. As with the intrinsic value charts, it is assumed that all variables other than the one under study remain constant.

The calculation of time value was first viewed from a quantitative perspective in the early 1970s. We will discuss the time value factors and the more quantitative options valuation approaches in greater

EXHIBIT 9.4   Option factor valuation:
Time to expiration

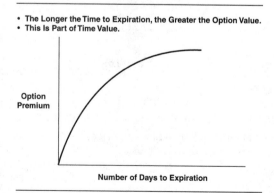

- The Longer the Time to Expiration, the Greater the Option Value.
- This Is Part of Time Value.

Option
Premium

Number of Days to Expiration

**EXHIBIT 9.5   Option factor
valuation: Volatility**

- The Greater the Implied or Historical Volatility of the Underlying Security, the Greater the Option Value.
- This Is Part of Time Value.

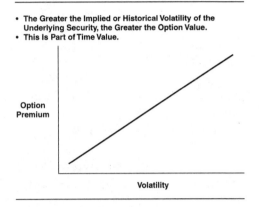

**EXHIBIT 9.6   Option factor volatility:
Risk-free rate**

- The Greater the Risk-Free Rate, the Greater the Option Value.
- This Is Part of Time Value.

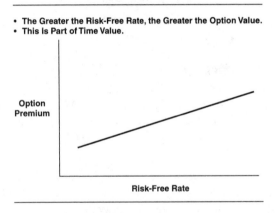

EXHIBIT 9.7   Calculation of time value

ABC Stock: Market price = $50 per share.
Call option on ABC: $45 strike price, $6.50 market price.
Put option on ABC: $55 strike price, $6.25 market price.
For ABC option: Market price = Intrinsic value + Time value.

	Market Price	=	Intrinsic Value	+	Time Value
Call option	$6.50	=	$5	+	$1.50
Put option	$6.25	=	$5	+	$1.25

detail later, in the section on option pricing. Exhibit 9.7 reflects the time value component in an option's price.

EUROPEAN-STYLE VERSUS AMERICAN-STYLE EXERCISE

The exercise of an option can be accomplished in one of two ways: (1) a *European-style* exercise provides for only one day (the expiration date) when the option can be exercised; (2) an *American-style* option can be exercised at any time from the purchase date through the expiration date. Intuitively, a European-style option written on the same underlying security, with the same strike price and expiration date as an American-style option exercise specification, will create a lower option price than the American-style option exercise. This incremental value represents the perceived worth derived from the additional flexibility of the American-style exercise alternative. As we will see, however, this difference is not as significant as one might think.

OVER-THE-COUNTER VERSUS EXCHANGE-TRADED OPTIONS

In the previous two chapters, we looked at the differences between over-the-counter forward rate agreements and forward FX rates versus exchange-traded futures contracts. The same essential differences apply to options. An over-the-counter (OTC) option can be written for any amount, at any strike price, with any expiration date. That's the good news. The bad news is that OTC options can be more expensive (due to the customization factor) and less liquid than the exchange-traded options. In most cases, an OTC option position has the best chance of being liquidated prior to expiration by buying from or selling back to the original counterparty. (This is particularly true as the terms of the option become more esoteric. We will discuss esoteric or *exotic* options in the next chapter.)

Exchange-traded options, like futures contracts, come with a specific strike price, size, and expiration date. Equity-based (stock) options are traded on many exchanges, although the largest arena is the Chicago Board Options Exchange (CBOE). Options on futures contracts are traded on the same exchanges as the underlying futures contracts. The main options-on-futures exchange players are the Chicago Mercantile Exchange (CME) and the Chicago Board of Trade (CBOT). Higher volume of option trading occurs in the more actively traded futures contracts. The Philadelphia Stock Exchange actively trades options on cash foreign currencies. (See Chapter 12 for a list of exchange Internet addresses. Additional information on these and other contracts traded on the various exchanges is available from those exchanges.)

OPTION STRATEGIES

A complete treatment of how options can be used in hedging and trading applications is beyond the scope of this book. This section highlights some of the more popular strategies for using options as a hedging tool and a speculative vehicle.

At this point, it is worthwhile reiterating one of the major differences between OTC and exchange-traded options: customization. Consider this analogy of the impact on hedge performance between OTC and exchange-traded options. In golf, hitting the ball on the green (exchange-traded options) is a good thing. But the pin is never in the same place, so the golfer is at the mercy of the greenskeeper. If the pin was never moved and the entire green acted as a funnel, pushing every ball that landed on the green into the hole (OTC options), there would be no need for putting! (Be still, my heart!) As was mentioned in Chapter 4, interest rate risk and basis risk are the two basic market-related risks in a fixed-income security. Hedging with exchange-traded options eliminates interest rate risk. Hedging with OTC options eliminates interest rate *and* basis risk.

Option Hedging Strategies

Two of the more popular hedging strategies using either exchange-traded or OTC options are *covered call writing* and *synthetic calls and puts.*

Covered Call Writing

Covered call writing is also viewed as an income enhancement tool. The strategy is to buy the underlying cash or futures market instrument and sell a call option against that position. The relation of the option's strike price to the underlying security price usually makes it either at-the-money or out-of-the-money.[1] An investor would execute this strategy if the projected price of the underlying instrument was unlikely to experience a sharp upward or downward movement over the life of the option. The premium received by the option seller is recorded as unearned income. If the seller is correct and the underlying security price remains relatively stable, the option will expire worthless and the option premium will become earned income. A sharp upward move in the underlying security would prompt exercise by the option buyer. In this case, the option seller would have to sell the underlying securities to the option buyer at the strike price, regardless of where the underlying security is currently trading. This limits the option seller's total sale proceeds to the initial premium received plus the strike price plus any accrued interest in the case of a fixed-income cash security. Exhibit 9.8 reflects a covered call option strategy along with the projected profit or loss (P/L) on the expiration date of the option. We use the expiration date because there is no time value left at an option's expiration.

Although the investor had to sell the stock to the call option buyer, he still made an additional $100 over what he would have made had he not sold the call. If the price of ABC had been $50 or lower by option expiration, the call option buyer would not have any economic

EXHIBIT 9.8   Covered call option

An investor purchases 100 shares of ABC stock @ $50 per share.
He also sells one 3-month $50 call option on 100 shares @ $3.
By option expiration, the price of ABC rises to $52 per share. The owner of the call option exercises the right to purchase ABC @ $50 from the investor.

The investor's P/L is calculated as:

Purchase 100 shares @ $50	= <$5,000>
Sell call option @ $3	= 300
At option expiration, sell 100 shares @ $50 to call option buyer =	5,000
P/L	$ 300

EXHIBIT 9.9   Covered call P/L chart

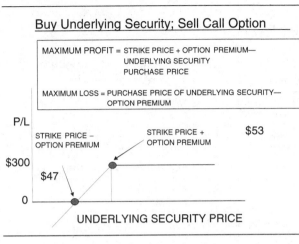

Buy Underlying Security; Sell Call Option

MAXIMUM PROFIT = STRIKE PRICE + OPTION PREMIUM—
UNDERLYING SECURITY
PURCHASE PRICE

MAXIMUM LOSS = PURCHASE PRICE OF UNDERLYING SECURITY—
OPTION PREMIUM

P/L

STRIKE PRICE –   STRIKE PRICE + $53
OPTION PREMIUM   OPTION PREMIUM

$300

$47

0

UNDERLYING SECURITY PRICE

incentive to exercise the option, and the investor would have kept the
$300 option premium as income. (See Exhibit 9.9.)

Synthetic Calls or Puts

A *synthetic call or put* combines a long option position with a long or
short position in the underlying security. A synthetic call is composed
of purchasing the underlying security and also purchasing a put option
on that security. The idea is simple. The investor believes the price of
the underlying security will rise but is looking for some degree of insurance in case the price moves in the other direction. With the synthetic call, the investor has, in essence, purchased a call option on the
security that includes any income-related benefits such as dividends or
interest accrued from owning the underlying security. The put option
limits the investor's losses on the underlying security to the difference
between the purchase price of the security and the option strike price,
plus the cost of purchasing the option. The degree of insurance is determined by the strike price and the expiration date of the put option.
The risk–return tradeoff is the option's cost versus the strike price.
For put options, the higher the strike, the more expensive the option.
For call options, it's the reverse. In a synthetic call, the higher the
put strike price, the greater the insurance. Determining the degree of

insurance (which strike price to buy) is a function of the degree of the investor's commitment to a specific directional price move in the underlying security, the size of that move, and the time frame necessary to achieve it.

Selling short the underlying security, and simultaneously purchasing a call option on that security, creates a synthetic put option. Here, the investor believes the underlying security will fall in value but wants some insurance in case this doesn't occur. The essence of the trade is to purchase a put option on the underlying security. The investor is protected against unlimited loss on the short position by owning the call option. The maximum loss in this instance is the difference

EXHIBIT 9.10a Synthetic call

Buy 100 shares of ABC Corp. at $50 per share.
Buy a 3-month put option on ABC $50 strike price @ $4.
Break-even is $54 per share ($50 + $4).

On the option expiration date, the price of ABC is $30 per share.
Stock value = $3,000 ($30 × 100 shares)
  Put value = $2,000 ($50 strike − $30 market price)
Total value = $5,000 ($3,000 + 2,000)
  Net loss = $400 ($5,400 − $5,000)

If ABC stock was $75 per share on the option expiration date, the value of the combined stock and option position would be $7,500 ($7,500 stock price − $0 put option value), with a net profit of $2,100 ($7,500 − $5,400).

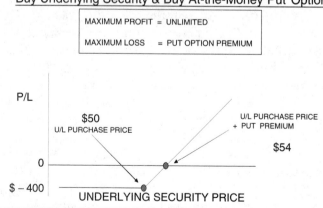

Buy Underlying Security & Buy At-the-Money Put Option

MAXIMUM PROFIT	= UNLIMITED
MAXIMUM LOSS	= PUT OPTION PREMIUM

P/L

$50
U/L PURCHASE PRICE

U/L PURCHASE PRICE
+ PUT PREMIUM

$54

0

$ − 400

UNDERLYING SECURITY PRICE

between the sale price on the underlying security and the strike price on the call option, plus the cost of the option. The higher the strike price on the call, the greater the potential loss. Exhibit 9.10 reflects a synthetic call and a synthetic put. The respective P/L charts on the option expiration date are shown.

Option Trading Strategies

Many other types of trading strategies are available with the use of options. To give the reader a glimpse at a few of the more straightforward applications, four are presented here: (1) bull spread, (2) bear spread, (3) short straddle, and (4) long straddle.

EXHIBIT 9.10b   Synthetic put

Sell short 100 shares of ABC Corp. at $50 per share.
Buy a 3-month call option on ABC $50 strike price @ $4.
Break-even is $46 per share ($50 − $4).

On the option expiration date, the price of ABC is $30 per share.
Stock value = $3,000
  Call value = $0 (out of the money)
Total value = $3,000
  Net profit = $1,600 ($4,600 − $3,000)

If ABC stock was $75 per share on the option expiration date, the combined stock and option position would be $5,000 ($7,500 stock price − $2,500 call option value) with a net loss of $400 ($5,000 − $4,600).

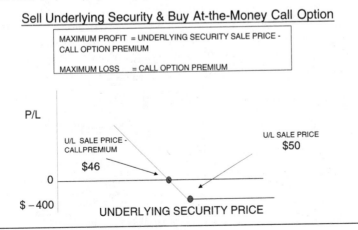

Sell Underlying Security & Buy At-the-Money Call Option

MAXIMUM PROFIT = UNDERLYING SECURITY SALE PRICE - CALL OPTION PREMIUM

MAXIMUM LOSS   = CALL OPTION PREMIUM

Bull Spread

A *bull spread* is either the purchase of a lower strike price call option and the sale of a higher strike price call option, or the sale of a higher strike price put option and the purchase of a lower strike price put option. In either case, the trader is anticipating higher prices in the underlying security but wants a way to defray part of the option cost and protect against extensive losses, in case prices move lower. The maximum amount of profit available on the trade is:

1. For the call option alternative, the spread between the strike prices, less the net premium paid. The lower strike call option will cost more than the higher strike price call.
2. For the put option alternative, the net premium received from the sale of the higher strike price put.

The maximum loss on the trade is:

1. For the call option alternative, the net premium paid.
2. For the put option alternative, the spread between the lower and higher strike prices, less the premium received.

Exhibit 9.11 reflects the bull spread and shows the P/L chart at the option expiration date.

Bear Spread

A *bear spread* is either the purchase of a higher strike call and the sale of a lower strike call, or the purchase of a higher strike put and the sale of a lower strike put. This is essentially the reverse of a bull spread. The trader is anticipating lower prices but wants a way to defray part of the option cost as well as guard against extensive losses if the expected outcome does not occur. Exhibit 9.12 reflects the bear spread and shows the P/L chart at the option expiration date.

Short and Long Straddles

A *short straddle* is executed when the trader believes the price of the underlying security will remain stable over the remainder of the option's

EXHIBIT 9.11   Bull spread

April 1998: Buy $105 strike price call @ $9.
            Sell $115 strike price call @ $7.
            Net payment of $2 per share, or $200 per contract. Strike price
            spread = $10 – $2 × 100 shares.

At the option expiration date, the maximum profit of the position is $8 per share, or $800. The maximum loss on the trade is $2 per share ($9 – $7 × 100 shares), or $200 per 100-share contract.

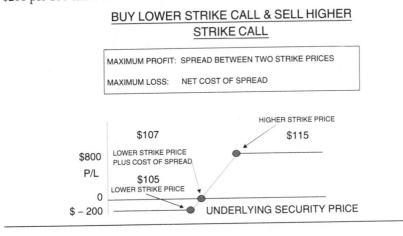

BUY LOWER STRIKE CALL & SELL HIGHER
STRIKE CALL

MAXIMUM PROFIT: SPREAD BETWEEN TWO STRIKE PRICES

MAXIMUM LOSS: NET COST OF SPREAD

life. The trader will sell an at-the-money put and call. The maximum profit is the total amount of premium taken in. The maximum loss is theoretically unlimited because both option positions are short and are subject to exercise at the demand of the option owner. A *long straddle* is the purchase of both an at-the-money put and an at-the-money call. This strategy is also referred to as a *volatility spread*. The trader doesn't care which way the price of the underlying security moves, as long as it is more than the total cost of the premiums paid for both the put and call options. Exhibit 9.13 reflects the short straddle and shows the P/L chart at the option expiration date.

P/L Short Straddle

The maximum profit on this position at the option expiration date is $600. This will occur *only* if the stock price is equal to $50 per share. Any other price would result in an exercise of one of the options. If the

EXHIBIT 9.12   Bear spread

April 1998:   Buy $50 strike price put @ $6.
Sell $40 strike price put @ $3.50.
Net payment of $2.50 ($6.00 - $3.50).

At the option expiration date, the maximum profit of the position is $7.50 (Strike price spread = $50 − $40 − $2.50 cost of spread) or $750 per 100-share contract. The maximum loss on the trade is $2.50 per share ($6.00 − $3.50), or $250 per 100-share contract. This is the cost of the spread.

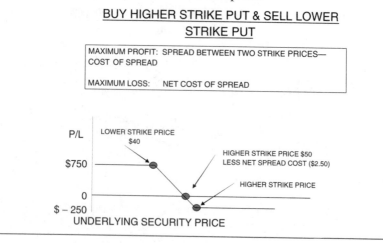

stock price were $49, the put owner would exercise the option. The short seller would buy the stock from the put owner at $50 and be able to sell it for only $49 in the marketplace. This $100 loss would reduce the total profit on the short straddle to $500 ($600 − $100). If the stock price were $51, the call owner would exercise the option. The option seller would have to sell the stock to the call owner at $50 and buy it back in the marketplace at $51, thereby generating a reduction of $100 from the total attainable profit.

Long Straddle

The trade is the same as for the short straddle, but instead of selling the call and the put, the investor buys the call and the put. Using the data from Exhibit 9.13, Exhibit 9.14 is created.

EXHIBIT 9.13   Short straddle

On 4/1/98, the market price of ABC stock is $50 per share.
Sell a July 1998 call $50 strike price @ $3.
Sell a July 1998 put $50 strike price @ $3.
Total premium received = $6 per share, or $600 for the position.
Break-even price of ABC at the option expiration date is either $44 or $56 per share.

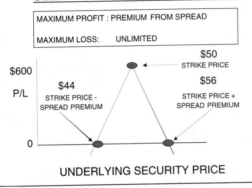

SELL AT THE MONEY CALL AND PUT

MAXIMUM PROFIT : PREMIUM FROM SPREAD

MAXIMUM LOSS: UNLIMITED

$600

P/L

$50
STRIKE PRICE

$44
STRIKE PRICE -
SPREAD PREMIUM

$56
STRIKE PRICE +
SPREAD PREMIUM

0

UNDERLYING SECURITY PRICE

EXHIBIT 9.14   Long straddle

On 4/1/98, the market price of ABC stock is $50 per share.
Buy a July 1998 call $50 strike price @ $3.
Buy a July 1998 put $50 strike price @ $3.
Total premium paid = $6 per share, or $600 for the position.
Break-even price of ABC at the option expiration date is, like the short straddle,
either $44 or $56 per share.

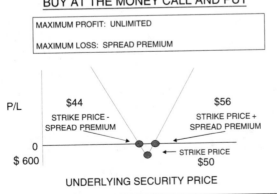

BUY AT THE MONEY CALL AND PUT

MAXIMUM PROFIT: UNLIMITED

MAXIMUM LOSS: SPREAD PREMIUM

P/L

$44
STRIKE PRICE -
SPREAD PREMIUM

$56
STRIKE PRICE +
SPREAD PREMIUM

0

$ 600

STRIKE PRICE
$50

UNDERLYING SECURITY PRICE

The combined premium paid for the options ($600) is the maximum loss, which *only* occurs if the stock price on the expiration date is exactly $50 per share. Any other price would result in the investor's exercising either the call or the put. This is why a long straddle is also referred to as a volatility spread. The more volatility in the underlying security price, the more likely it is to attain intrinsic value on or before the option expiration date. The P/L for a long straddle is shown in the accompanying chart.

The long straddle is a good segue into a practical discussion of option pricing. Underlying market price, strike price, number of days to expiration, underlying security volatility, and short-term risk-free rates have been mentioned as major determinants of an option's price. It is important to remember that financial markets trade not on the occurrence of actual events but on the *difference* between expectations and reality. The market for any security is made up of a pyramid of input factors of all kinds. At the peak of the pyramid is the bid and ask price for the security. The inside of the pyramid can be divided into two general sections:

1. Every public release, since the beginning of time, that has anything to do with the security in question.
2. Everything that a majority of your favorite economists and analysts think will happen until the end of time.

Whenever one of the two general sections is altered (historical information can be altered as a result of revisions to previous data releases), the pyramid shifts, thereby changing the price for the security. Anticipation is a key factor in option pricing because an option's cost reflects the *likelihood* that some security will achieve a specific price. The more significant an expected upcoming event is, in terms of a potential impact on securities pricing, the greater the anticipation. The greater the anticipation, the larger the option price. It is reasonable, therefore, to expect option volatility and option price to rise as a potential market-moving event draws close.

Option Trading Conventions

As we have discussed, options are traded either over the counter or on an organized exchange. A price unit is the main measure for options trading, but many market participants derive moment-to-moment pricing from the underlying security's implied price volatility measure. It is not uncommon to ask a trader where a particular option is trading and receive an answer like "12.3%." The trader is saying that the implied volatility in the underlying security—derived from the option price, security price, and an option pricing model—has been estimated to be 12.3%. This is the input I will use, along with the other necessary parameters, to determine the option's price. The volatility measure is the only subjective time value parameter of real substance. As the underlying security price moves up and down, the trader will, over the short term, use the same volatility estimate to price the option. Changes in investor demand for the option will have an impact on the volatility level. These changes are, in some cases, driven by economic factors such as results of anticipated events. They could also be driven by the submission of a large buy or sell order by one customer or a group of customers seeking a particular hedge or directional trade. Under these circumstances, an option's price may temporarily move higher or lower by a couple of ticks to accommodate the order.

It is important to consider the trading logic of most professional options traders: they are sellers of volatility. Any time an option's price moves higher than its current trading range, this sounds the alarm for a potential trade. There may be a very good reason why this has occurred. If it is due to what appears to be a secular, or longer-term move in the underlying security outside its current trading range, the trader may deem the option price change justifiable and not sell into the move. If, on the other hand, the option price rises in anticipation of some event, the trader may sell into the rise with no hedge, with a bull or bear spread, or by creating a synthetic put or call. As previously noted, the last two strategies provide the trader with insurance, should the short position rise in value.

Sell-side, over-the-counter options traders usually trade reactively. They must respond to the needs of their customers by providing bids and offers. Their goal is to put on a continuing stream of trades within two parameters. First, they cover the risk of the trade position for any underlying security not currently in inventory. In the case of over-the-counter options, purchasing the same option from someone else is unlikely because of the customized nature of the trade. One way to hedge is by buying or selling the underlying security, or a similar security in an offsetting direction to the option. For example, if a trader sells an uncovered call (no underlying security in inventory), the trader risks an unlimited loss if the price of the underlying security rises. In this instance, a purchase of the underlying security may be appropriate. Another possibility is to buy or sell a different class of security as a hedge. If a trader sells an uncovered put option on a particular Treasury bond, an offsetting transaction could be the sale of a T-bond futures contract. In this case, if the price of the underlying security fell, the put option would gain in value. By being short the futures contract, the profit from the futures market would offset the loss on the option. Be aware, however, of two associated risks: (1) any offsetting purchase or sale of a security not identical to the one on which the contract was written opens the trader to basis risk (Chapter 4); (2) the price of an option moves in a ratio to the price of the underlying security. This ratio continuously changes as the underlying security price changes. The hedge ratio, therefore, must be closely monitored to ensure against over- or undercoverage on the hedge. (We will discuss these hedge ratios in a later section on option price sensitivities.)

The second parameter of the trade must be to build into the option premium a sufficient cushion to allow for profit. This is where the option trader *should* be making money. We say *should* because the continuously increasing competitiveness of the financial markets forces traders to shave margins—in many instances, to bare bones. As a result, traders will sometime hold off hedging an unhedged option position if they feel the market is moving in their favor. For example, if a trader selling an uncovered call option feels the market in the underlying security is moving lower, the trader may wait several minutes, or even longer, in anticipation of purchasing the underlying security at a more favorable price.

Sell-side and proprietary options traders also spend more time studying the various price sensitivities of an option (covered in a later section of this chapter). They do this because of their greater interest in an option's short-term pricing characteristics. These traders are focusing either on extracting a profit from the order flow they handle for the customers of their firm, or on capitalizing on a perceived inefficiency or mispricing of a particular option or option spread.

Buy-side options users tend to take longer-term views of an option's value. They seek to hedge some future commercial or financial commitment, or they take a directional position in a one-or-more-options trading strategy. As a result, this group is not as sensitive to moment-to-moment pricing changes.

OPTION PRICING

Warning!!!! The next several pages are peppered with more formulae than we have used anywhere else in the book. While to a certain extent, this goes against the book's format, it is important in understanding the relationships in option pricing. Readers will find that some of the concepts discussed below have appeared in other sections of the book. Perhaps the best way to start is to remember the concept of efficient markets. If there is a way to lock in a risk-free profit over time, the markets will quickly spot it, and arbitrage forces will take over. So hold your nose and jump in. It's not as tough as you think.

At the beginning of this chapter, we mentioned that the factors that go into pricing an option vary to a certain extent, depending on the underlying security. However, these five factors are present in all valuations:

1. The price of the underlying security,
2. The strike price of the option,
3. The number of days to option expiration,
4. The level of price volatility in the underlying security,
5. The level of short-term risk-free interest rates.

The first two factors characterize an option's intrinsic value; the last three characterize the option's time value.

Prior to the mid-1970s, time value on options was determined more on subjective and intuitive bases. All this changed with the release of a paper written by Professors Fisher Black and Myron Scholes.[2] These two professors, who later became members of the Wall Street community, are responsible for the first widely recognized pass at defining an options value from a quantitative perspective. A host of option pricing models have been devised since the introduction of the Black–Scholes model. Some are interesting and informative, but a lengthy discussion of them would not serve the purpose of this book.

We will, however, do a cursory review of the structure of this landmark work, which serves as the base for most of the other models. We will also take a look at the Binomial method of pricing options.

The work of Black–Scholes depended on some basic assumptions about the price behavior of European-style options on non-dividend-paying stocks, and the behavior of the stocks themselves:

1. Stock prices are dynamic; they continually change.
2. Arbitrage forces prevent asset prices from moving out of equilibrium with each other.
3. The risk-free interest rate and price volatility of the underlying security remain constant over the life of the option.
4. Stock returns are distributed in a lognormal manner.
5. Trading and hedging activity is continuous.

Let's look at these assumptions more closely.

A security's price is a function of the marketplace. As we have outlined, a price can change for myriad reasons. Given the dynamic nature of the environment in which it exists, a security's price will change as the market environment changes.

In explaining the second assumption, it is important to examine another concept: *put–call parity*. This is a cornerstone to understanding the Black–Scholes valuation logic. To explain this, we need to look at two simultaneous investment strategies that have exactly offsetting cash flows. We will see that the net value of the portfolio of the two simultaneous investment strategies at option expiration is zero, regardless of the stock price at expiration. Its value at any time prior to option expiration must also be zero, to prevent arbitrage profits from being made. This will give us put–call parity.

The first investment is the purchase of a Call option and the sale of a Put option, both at the same strike price with the same expiration date. The strategy is subject to unlimited risk with the short Put. The payoff at option expiration for an in-the-money Call will be the Stock Price – Strike Price. In the case of the in-the-money put, the payoff will be the *negative* of the Strike Price – Stock Price (i.e., Stock Price – Strike Price) because the put position is short, not long. This means both the long Call and the short Put at the expiration date are valued with the same formula: Stock Price – Option Strike Price, regardless of the stock price at expiration.

The second investment is to sell short the underlying stock and buy a risk-free zero coupon bond with the proceeds of the stock sale. The maturity value of the bond is set equal to the strike price of the options in the other investment, and the bond's maturity date is equal to the option expiration date. At expiration:

1. The bond will have a value equal to the strike price of the options.
2. The short stock position will have a value equal to the negative of the Stock Price.
3. The second investment has the value of Strike Price − Stock Price, regardless of the stock price at that date.

At the expiration date, the portfolio consisting of both investments must have a zero value, regardless of the stock price. This means: Call Value − Put Value + Strike Price − Stock Price = 0 at expiration. To prevent riskless arbitrage, the portfolio value must also be zero at any time prior to expiration; that is, the Call Price − Put Price + present value of the Strike Price − Stock Price = 0 at any time prior to expiration. In other words, if we add the cash amount paid and received to set up the long call and short put position, to the cash amount received or paid to set up the short stock and long zero coupon bond position, the sum must be zero at any time prior to expiration. This is called a *self-financing* portfolio because the value of one investment is equal to and offset by the value of the other investment.

The net value of the stock and bond position will equal the stock price − option strike price for all values. From this, we can conclude that the call option price − the put option price = the Stock Price − the Strike Price at option expiration, and the Call price − the Put price = the Stock Price − the Present Value of the Strike Price during the life of the options. A simple way to look at these equations is to set the put price equal to zero. This would occur if the underlying security price were equal to or greater than the strike price. In this case, the call option equals the underlying security price − strike price.

1. At the option expiration date:

    Call − Put = Underlying stock − Underlying strike price.

2. During the life of the option:

    Call − Put = Underlying stock − Present value of the strike price.

EXHIBIT 9.15   Applying the arbitrage argument in option pricing

Given: ABC stock current market price = $100 per share.
6-month call option on 10 shares of ABC, 100 strike price = $100.
6-month put option on 10 shares of ABC, 100 strike price = $65.
6-month risk-free zero coupon bond rate 6% (annualized).

Price (present value) of zero coupon bond with $1,000 par value: $1,000/(1.06/2) = $970.90 6 months prior to option expiration.

According to put–call parity:

Call option – Put option = Stock price – Present value of bond price (Strike price of option)

A simple example of why the arbitrage argument must work is shown in Exhibit 9.15.

In Exhibit 9.15, the call option is $35 greater than the put option. The current market price of ABC stock is only $29.10 greater than the present value, or market price, of the risk-free zero coupon bond with a par value equal to $1,000, which is the strike price of the options.

An arbitrageur would take advantage of this situation by selling the call, buying the put, buying the stock, and selling the risk-free zero coupon bond. The cash flows would be:

$$+\$100 - \$65 = \$35 - \$1,000 + \$970.90$$

+$100	−$65		−$1,000	+$970.90	
Sell calls	Buy puts		Buy stock	Sell zero coupon bond	= −$29.10

Net credit = $5.90

The arbitrageur holds the portfolio until the option expiration date. The price of ABC stock is now $110 per share. The cash flows in the portfolio are:

−$100   Call is exercised as it is in-the-money (sell 10 shares for $1,000 to call option buyer; cover short in market at $1,100)

0   Put expires worthless as it is out of the money

+$1,100   Sell 10 shares ABC in market @ $110 per share

−$1,000   Purchase risk-free zero coupon bond to cover short position

0   Net difference at expiration date

With the zero net difference in cash flows at the option expiration date, the arbitrageur keeps the $5.90 as profit. If ABC was worth only $90 per share, or any other price, at the option expiration date, the net cash flow difference would still be $0, and the arbitrageur still would get to keep only the initial $5.90 profit. As we noted above, guaranteed profits of this nature will be attacked by market participants. This is why the arbitrage argument must work.

This concept of put–call parity is important in determining the value of an option. The seller of the option, who desires to completely hedge away the risk of the short option position, needs to create a parallel investment that will, in essence, replicate the payoff, or value, of the option over the option's life. Each time the value of the underlying security changes, the price of the option changes. The offsetting cash positions need to be adjusted to reflect the new option value. This adjustment consists of liquidating the existing positions and reestablishing new ones. According to the Black–Scholes set of assumptions, the adjustment will not require any additional out-of-pocket expense, thereby making this hedged portfolio self-financing. In this way, there is no additional cost for the hedge to the option short position any time the offsetting investment is rebalanced.

Neil Chriss[3] uses an excellent analogy for the self-financing transaction. A casino takes a $12,500 bet from a gambler. If, on the occurrence of three consecutive coin tosses, all three come up heads, the gambler will win $100,000. If not, the gambler will lose the entire $12,500.

Prior to the first coin toss, the gambler puts up the $12,500. The casino, not looking to make a profit on the game, uses it instead as a promotional ploy. It lays the $12,500 with a bookmaker and bets 2-to-1 on heads coming up on the first coin toss. If heads comes up, the casino will collect $25,000 ($12,500 + $12,500) from the bookmaker. If tails comes up, the casino loses the $12,500, but so does the gambler. The casino is economically indifferent to the coin toss outcome.

If heads comes up, the casino will bet the entire $25,000 on another heads coin toss. If heads comes up again, the casino will bet $50,000 on a third heads coin toss. The casino remains riskless in all three coin tosses because it is betting the gambler's money and the winnings from any heads coin tosses. If heads comes up all three times, the casino collects $100,000 from the bookmaker and pays the gambler.

As Exhibit 9.15 reflects, if, at any point in time, the riskless transaction situation didn't exist, arbitrage forces would be able to lock in what amounts to riskless profit over the remaining life of the option. Using the two-investment scenario, the profit would amount to the difference between the net option value (call−put) and the offsetting cash position (stock price−present value of risk-free bond). The arbitrage concept was discussed in a more simplified manner in Chapter 7. The investor could purchase either a 3-month investment and a 3-month forward or futures contract, or a 6-month investment. Both alternatives would generate the same return.

By now, some readers are saying to themselves, "This is great in the laboratory. But what about the real world?" We will return to the real world shortly.

The concept of continuous trading relates to the investor's ability to rebalance the investment positions as the price of the underlying security changes.

The Black–Scholes model presumes that the logarithm of stock price returns follows a normal distribution,[4] which is equivalent to assuming that percent changes in stock prices (not absolute, or arithmetic changes) follow a normal distribution. This type of probability distribution for stock prices is called a lognormal distribution,[5] and it generates random stock price paths over time that are often called geometric Brownian movement. Similar percentage price changes will create different actual price changes based on the price of the underlying security. For example, a 5% move in a $40 stock translates to a $2 price change. If the price of the stock were $20, 5% would indicate a $1 price change. The volatility of returns on the underlying security, therefore, is calculated from the percent price change, not the absolute change, on a period-to-period basis.

The lognormal distribution of stock price returns was used by Black and Scholes in order to ensure that stock prices could never be negative. If, instead, Black and Scholes had used a normal distribution for absolute, rather than lognormal, or percent stock price changes, it would have been possible for stock prices to become negative.

The levels of short-term interest rates and underlying security volatility are presumed constant in the formula. In hedging European-style options, the process presumes discounting of the risk-free bond at a specified risk-free rate. If this rate changes, the outcome of the hedge is no longer self-financing. Security volatility is presumed constant in the Black–Scholes model. Changes in the implied volatility could cause the price of the option to change even when the underlying security's price remains constant.

Structure of the Black–Scholes Pricing Model

The theoretical price of a European-style call is estimated as:

$$P_c = P_u \times N(d_1) - (S \times e^{-rt} \times N(d_2)).$$

The theoretical price of a European-style put is estimated as:

$$P_p = -P_u \times (1 - N(d_1)) + [S \times e^{-rt} \times (1 - N(d_2))]$$

$$d_1 = \frac{\log(P_u / S) + ((r + \sigma^2 / 2) \times t)}{\sigma\sqrt{t}}$$

$$d_2 = \frac{\log(P_u / S) + ((r - \sigma^2 / 2) \times t)}{\sigma\sqrt{t}}$$

$$d_2 = d_1 - \sigma\sqrt{t}$$

where: P_c = call option price,
P_p = put option price,
P_u = price of underlying security,
S = option strike price,
e^{-rt} = continuous compounding discount function (present value factor that discounts the strike or expiration price of the option back to its current value),
σ = implied volatility of P_u,
r = short-term risk-free interest rate,
t = time to expiration,
N = cumulative normal density function (As outlined below, we convert the values of d_1 and d_2 to where they would fall in a normal distribution. Remember, we are presuming all the observations we see are lognormally distributed.)

These formulae may seem a bit intimidating, but they are actually easy to use. Consider the following example:

Underlying stock price = 50
Call/Put option strike price = 45
Expiration = 3 months (.25 yr)
Volatility = 20%
Risk-free rate = 5%.

$$d_1 = \frac{\log (50 / 45) + ((.05 + .2^2 / 2) \times .25)}{.2\sqrt{.25}}$$

$$d_1 = \frac{.1053605 + ((.05 + .02) \times .25)}{.1} = 1.228605.$$

Under a normal distribution, 1.228605 = .89039.

$$d_2 = \frac{\log (50/ 45) + ((.05 - .20^2 / 2) \times .25)}{.2\sqrt{.25}} = 1.128605.$$

Under a normal distribution, 1.128605 = .87047.
Inserting the appropriate values in the call option formula, we get:

$$P_c = P_u \times N(d_1) - (S \times e^{-rt} \times N(d_2))$$

$$P_c = (50 \times .89039) - (45 \times .987578^\circ \times .87047) = 5.835.$$

Using the same parameters, let's calculate the value of a put option:

$$P_p = -P_u \times (1 - N(d_1)) + [S \times e^{-rt} \times (1 - N(d_2))]$$

$$P_p = -50 \times (1 - .89039) + (45 \times .987578) \times (1 - .87047) = .276.$$

Let's check these option values in the put–call parity equation:

Call option (long)	$5.835	Stock price (short)	−$50.000
Put option (short)	− .276	Bond present value (long)	44.441
	$5.559		−$ (5.559)

The transaction satisfies put–call parity.

° .987578 is the discount factor calculated by presuming 5% continuously compounded over a period of 3 months, or .25 year. $e^{-rt} = 2.71828^{(-.05^\circ.25)} = .987578.$

Calculating the Implied Volatility of an Option

As mentioned earlier in the chapter, many option traders quote an option's value in terms of its implied volatility rather than its price. The reason is that volatility, like yield spreads, is not as volatile as the actual change in the underlying security price or the option itself. As the underlying security trades up and down over short periods of time, the projected price volatility may not change; instead, it may remain relatively constant over the short run. Knowing the volatility of an option makes it easier to estimate its price during periods when the option is not trading. For example, if the implied volatility of a particular options price is 15% at the last traded price of the option, the investor can estimate the value of the option, given some upward or downward movement in the underlying security.

As with yield to maturity, there is no specific formula for calculating the implied volatility of an option. The most efficient method of calculation is to use an iterative technique similar to the one used to calculate yield to maturity, where implied volatilities are input to the pricing model until the price input is matched.

Relaxing the Assumptions behind the Black–Scholes Model

Now that we have seen the Black–Scholes model at work, let's take a look at the impact of relaxing the underlying economic assumptions of Black–Scholes.

1. *No transaction costs or taxes* are assumed in purchases and sales. Indeed, at least a few brokers we know would take issue with this. Adding these variables to the equation requires additional rebalancing for what amounts to uncertain cash flows due to changes in trade costs.

2. *Offsetting investment rebalancing is done on a continuous basis.* Every time the option values change, the offsetting cash securities change. Again, this process is not realistic.

3. *The risk-free rate of interest and the volatility of the underlying security remain constant over the life of the option.* Clearly, this

doesn't make sense in the real world. Interest rates change on a moment-to-moment basis, and implied volatility changes, causing the option price to move while the underlying security stays the same. As mentioned earlier in the chapter, anticipation of an upcoming event increases, the closer the event comes. This can generate increasing implied volatility with no change in the underlying security.

4. *No arbitrage is available to allow the trader to find buy/sell offsetting cash investments.* The fact is, arbitrage is still available, albeit at a much lower frequency than in the past, due to increased market efficiency.

5. *Markets are completely liquid.* In the trading world, only a small amount of the outstanding securities are actually traded on an active basis. This is particularly true for non-exchange-traded data. An attempt to execute a large order in a stock or bond with a thin market makes it more difficult to obtain the price needed to complete the required self-financing relationships assumed in the Black–Scholes model.

Despite all these caveats, the Black–Scholes pricing model remains the basis for most other option models and is used as a baseline for option valuation. The reason: the logic of the thought process used to create the model. There are weaknesses, but the approach to looking at an option's value is straightforward and logical. The fact that a majority of Wall Street continues to use variations of the Black–Scholes model is the best proof of its value and credibility.

Option Price Sensitivities

In Chapter 4, we discussed different measures of price/yield sensitivities in bonds. Options have their own set of sensitivity measurements, denoted by Greek letters.

Delta

Unquestionably, this is the most widely used sensitivity measurement. The delta of an option is the amount of change (measured in percent) experienced in an option price with respect to a one-unit price change in the underlying security. As we mentioned, the delta of an option is used to determine the hedging ratios with the underlying security. This concept, called *delta neutral hedging*, is used to determine the amount of an underlying security to be purchased or sold to mirror the value change in the option.

As a rule of thumb, the delta of an option is equal to 50% when the strike price of the option and the underlying security price are the same. Essentially, there is an equal likelihood the option will move in or out of the money. A block of 100 shares of an underlying stock will experience twice as much change in value as an option on 100 shares of the stock with a strike price equal to the underlying market price (at the money). As the option moves further in the money, the delta increases as the likelihood that the option will expire in the money increases. The delta, therefore, acts more like the underlying security in terms of size of price action. The delta decreases as the option moves further out of the money, and the likelihood of a worthless option at expiration increases.

Gamma

The gamma of an option measures the change in the option delta as the underlying security price changes. The graph of gamma value as the underlying security price changes looks something like a normal distribution curve. The largest gamma values appear around an at-the-money situation, when the option delta equals 50%. For example, if the call option delta of an option is 50% and the gamma is 3%, the value of the delta will move to 53%, given a one-point upward move in the underlying security price.

Theta

The change in an option's value is affected by the amount of time to expiration. Theta measures the daily amount of premium decay at any point in the option's life. For example, a theta of .07 creates a .07 of a point reduction in the value of the option for each day the underlying security price doesn't change. Time decay becomes much more significant on an option premium, the closer the option draws to expiration. Intuitively, this makes sense: the shorter the time to expiration, the less time the option has to achieve intrinsic value. Its value, therefore, decreases more rapidly as the expiration date approaches. Time decay also has the greatest impact on options with an at-the-money strike price. A popular measure using theta is the time decay on an option over a one-week (seven-day) period.

Vega

Vega measures the change in the value of an option, given a 1% change in the underlying volatility. The volatility of the underlying security is positively correlated to the price of the option. A vega measurement of .5 will generate a .5% change in an option premium for each 1% change in the option volatility. Consider an option written on two securities with equal strike price, underlying security price, and expiration date. Security A has a 10% volatility; security B has a 25% volatility. The larger volatility in security B raises the possibility that the option will achieve intrinsic value and expire in the money. As a result, the premium, or option cost, is greater for security B.

Many traders look at the historical volatility of a security as a measurement for current option pricing. It can be helpful to study these patterns, but it is important to remember that the current implied volatility of an option is a function of *expected* price volatility in the underlying security, not historical volatility. Option volatilities can differ, depending on the expiration period of the option. A one-week option can have a lower or higher level of volatility than a 3-month option based on recent trends, expectations, or a combination of both.

Rho

In our discussion of the Black–Scholes model, we determined that the value of an option is equal to the difference between the underlying security price and the present value of the risk-free bond. This present value is determined by discounting the par value of the bond by an appropriate risk-free rate. The value of a call option on a stock increases as the risk-free rate increases. The value of a put option on a stock decreases as the interest rate decreases.

The practical value of option price sensitivities is entirely a function of the amount of time an option is held. If an investor purchases or sells an option *with the intention of holding it until expiration*, it is irrelevant whether any of the sensitivities change during the holding period. For example, if an investor sells a call option against a long securities position and holds both positions until option expiration, the investor must be prepared to deliver the number of shares stated in the option. Otherwise, the option seller may be required to purchase additional shares in the market to satisfy exercise from the option owner. Option sensitivities are more relevant to options traders buying and selling options on an interim basis, prior to the expiration date.

Other Option Pricing Models

Binomial Model

In our discussion of securities with embedded options (Chapter 6), we modeled a binomial approach to valuation. The binomial model[6] for options valuation works essentially the same way. Unlike Black–Scholes, options on stocks that pay dividends, and both European- and American-style options, can be valued using the binomial approach. For a non-dividend-paying European-style call, the possible underlying security prices are determined through the use of a binomial tree. An equal probability for increase or decrease is presumed for the move in an underlying security's price at predetermined time periods. The amount of increase or decrease is a function of the volatility of price movement in the underlying security. The option value one period before expiration is determined to be the expected future value of the option discounted for one period by the risk-free rate. This process is used to work back through the tree to derive the current value of the option. The difference between this and the Black–Scholes model is that the latter presumes continuous compounding or adjustment, as opposed to the binomial method of periodic compounding adjustment. If the periodicity in the binomial model were increased to reflect extremely small time periods, the binomial valuation would essentially equal the Black–Scholes valuation. The rationale behind this statement is similar to the impact of changes in periodic compounding on a fixed-income security. The smaller the compounding periods become, the smaller the change in yield. The result of continuous compounding produces results very close to those from compounding on a daily basis.

Options on dividend-paying stocks require an adjustment to the binomial tree to account for the dividend cash flows (similar to the interest payments on callable bonds). These dividend payments have an impact on the value of the underlying stock at option expiration.

From a mathematical perspective, it can be proven that it is never optimal to exercise an option on a non-dividend-paying stock prior to expiration. Conceptually, the price of an American-style call option must be at least equal to the difference between the underlying security's market price and the present value of the strike price. A put option prior to expiration must be at least equal to the option strike price less the underlying market price. By exercising the option early, the option owner gives up all time value associated with the option; in other words, any time value is essentially disregarded. For example, should the volatility on the option rise between valuation periods, time value would increase. Exercise, however, is based on the spread between the strike price of the option and the underlying security's market price. The option price could triple from a volatility increase but have no impact on intrinsic value. As a result, the value of an American-style option will be close to the value of a European-style option.

As mentioned at the beginning of the pricing section, many different options pricing models are currently in use. With rare exception, however, they all relate back to the work of Fisher Black and Myron Scholes in the early 1970s. For readers interested in learning more about the mathematics of options, Appendix F lists texts that cover options and option pricing theory in much greater detail.

LEAPS

Long-term Equity AnticiPation Securities are options on stocks. The difference between LEAPS and ordinary options is the time to expiration. LEAPS are issued with multiple years between issuance and expiration; ordinary options are issued with expirations of less than a year. Introduced in 1990 at the Chicago Board Options Exchange, these long-term options are gaining in credibility with the investment public.

The structure of a LEAP is essentially the same as that of a shorter-term option. Strike price, time to expiration, underlying security volatility, and risk-free rate are all parameters in determining a LEAP's value. There are some differences, however, with regard to exchange listing conventions. Ordinary or shorter-term options have many more strikes and expiration months than LEAPS. Ordinary options offer four expiration months to choose from, with at least three strike prices: one in the money, one at the money, and one out of the money. LEAPS currently are listed with January expirations in one of two different years. Strike prices on LEAPS are also set wider apart than strike prices on shorter-term options.

Some question surrounds the use of conventional option pricing models for LEAP options. The extended time to expiration and the potentially higher level of underlying price volatility (compared to shorter-term options) could generate a fair value price well in excess of what seems reasonable, given the fundamentals of the underlying security. Currently, options of this length have not been introduced on nonequity underlying securities.

For traders and investors interested in learning more about LEAPS, Harrison Roth has written a book dedicated to LEAP options. See Appendix F for details.

SUMMARY

The concept of options—their structure, characteristics, and basic terminology—were covered in this chapter. Some basic trading and hedging option strategies were identified. The fundamentals of option pricing, as viewed in the Black–Scholes and binomial option pricing models, were outlined. The most important concepts in the Black–Scholes pricing model are: (1) the self-financing transaction and (2) the no-arbitrage availability with an efficiently priced option. The binomial model is essentially a period view of option pricing; the Black–Scholes model assumes continuous rebalancing.

Over the past 10 to 15 years, more innovative (some would say this is a diplomatic way of saying *more complicated*) options have been constructed. The name given these instruments is *exotic options*. They ultimately break down to some form of put and/or call, but they need to be segregated from the standard put and call option varieties. Option caps and floors also fall into this category. These option forms, along with interest rate swaps, will be discussed in the next chapter.

NOTES

1. The deeper an option is in the money, the more expensive it becomes, and the less likely that traders or investors will actively use it for either hedging or speculation.

2. Fisher Black and Myron Scholes, "The Pricing of Options and Corporate Liabilities," *Journal of Political Economy* (May–June 1973), pp. 637–654.

3. Neil Chriss, "Black–Scholes and Beyond" (John Wiley & Sons, 1997).

4. A normal distribution reflecting the differences between a series of observations (and the arithmetic average of those observations), when plotted on a graph, forms a bell-shaped curve. This relates to work done with the geometric Brownian movement.

5. A lognormal distribution is simply a normal distribution of the logarithmic values of the differences between a series of observations and the arithmetic average of those observations.

6. The binomial method for pricing options was developed by John Cox and Mark Rubenstein, in *Options Markets* (Prentice-Hall, 1985).

10 EXOTIC OPTIONS, INTEREST RATE SWAPS, AND OTHER INTEREST RATE DERIVATIVES

In Chapter 9, we discussed the basic principles and valuation techniques for options. As noted at the beginning of Chapter 7, one of the two basic types of derivatives measures the value of the likelihood that an underlying security will reach a specific value within a given period of time. This applies not only to basic options, but also to any derivative with option-type characteristics. In this chapter, we examine some instrument extensions to simple put and call options. We also look into the world of interest rate swaps and inverse floaters.

EXOTIC OPTIONS

Since the mid-1980s, financial engineers have worked hard to extend the principles of options to include an ever larger circle of applications. The primary motivation of these efforts was to create more efficient and more effective methods of financial risk management. The innovations generated from this research have been generically categorized as *exotic options*. The word *exotic* conjures up a number of different images; here, it means extended or additional variations on the same underlying theme. The value of most exotic options originates from what is

201

known as *path dependence:* the value of the option is a function of the movement of the underlying security over some determined period of time. There are many different types of exotic options—a testament to options' flexibility and humans' creativity—and they suggest an update to an old adage: "Necessity and profit are the parents of invention."

This book is not the correct venue for exposition of all known exotics' strategies. It is important, however, to get a flavor of the ways currently being used to hedge market risk. Our approach in discussing these instruments will continue to be more practical than quantitative. Remember that the basic option valuation principles discussed in Chapter 9 apply to the following exotic options as well.

COMPOUND OR SPLIT FEE OPTIONS

A compound or split fee option is essentially an option created by using another option as the deliverable security. Possible iterations of this strategy are: purchasing a call on a call, a call on a put, a put on a call, or a put on a put.

An excellent application of these options can be seen in the mortgage banking industry. The mid-1980s were good times for mortgage bankers; lenders were pushed to their limits from both new mortgage creations and refinancing of existing mortgages. The wide swing in long-term interest rates accounted for a large measure of this activity. Implicit in interest rate volatility, however, is the associated market risk. As we have studied, the shifting of the yield curve has the largest price impact on long-term interest rates. Mortgage bankers are in the business of making fixed interest rate commitments for long periods of time. These commitments may be made several months in advance of the actual funding of the mortgage. During the interim between commitment and funding, the mortgage banker is subject to financial market risk.

Traditionally, the lender could purchase a put option, thereby providing insurance against rising interest rates. However, a 2-month put option on a 30-year security can be pretty expensive, especially if volatility levels are high. The solution to this problem is the split fee option. Using 60 days as the necessary hedging window, the mortgage banker could purchase a 30-day call option on a 30-day put. The effects are:

- Purchasing the call gives the mortgage banker the right to buy a put option in 30 days.
- The call could be structured with the same strike price as the 60-day put option purchased today.
- The real value of the split fee option comes in the amount and timing of the premium payment for the option.
- The cost of the call option on the put option is flexible. The mortgage banker could choose to pay a very small amount for the call, making up the difference to fair value *if and when* the call option is exercised. This is the key.
- The mortgage banker can increase the size of the up-front payment if higher interest rates seem probable. If, on the other hand, higher rates are less likely, the mortgage banker can choose to pay a very low up-front fee. In either of these cases, the premium on the put option will be adjusted to reflect the amount of the call option premium.

As an example, in January, a mortgage lender commits to lending 30-year fixed-rate money at 7.5% during the month of March. Between January and March, however, 30-year mortgage borrowing rates might increase. The lender is still committed to funding at 7.5% even though the cost of funds increases. To hedge against a potential rise in rates, the mortgage banker could purchase (1) a 60-day put option, or (2) a call option to buy a 30-day put option in 30 days at the same, or a similar, strike price. Depending on the mortgage banker's views on the likelihood of a rise in interest rates, the cost of the 30-day call option could either be very low (rate rise is unlikely), or high (good chance for higher rates).

From a dollars-and-cents perspective, the cost of the 60-day put option will be lower than the overall cost of the split fee option if both legs are purchased (the banker pays for the additional flexibility). The difference in these costs, of course, is largely a function of the underlying security price and volatility (the price of the mortgage-backed security), and the strike prices of the options. If, however, interest rates remain stable or even decline, the mortgage banker has most likely purchased inexpensive insurance against rising interest rates. Additionally, if the put is not exercised and the mortgage banker wants to hedge the funding commitment for the remaining 30 days, it can be done as an at-the-money or out-of-the-money put. The strike price remains the same with an equal or higher underlying security price (the call wasn't exercised because the price of the underlying security was equal to or higher than the strike price) and a shorter number of days to expiration (30 versus 60 days).

Summary points of split fee options:

+ Potentially cheap insurance against a rise in borrowing cost or a decline in reinvestment rate.

− If the initial option is exercised, the overall cost may be significantly higher than the straight put.

Barrier Options

The concept of a barrier option is to specify a particular underlying security price either above or below the option strike price. Once this "barrier" is reached, the option will either attain value or expire worthless. Barrier options are also called *knock in* and *knock out* options. There are eight different kinds of barrier options:

Knock in	Knock out
Call: Down and in	Down and out
Up and in	Up and out
Put: Up and in	Up and out
Down and in	Down and out

Three examples of barrier options follow.

1. *Up-and-in put.* A borrower is looking to hedge a 3-month LIBOR repricing 2 months in the future. Current 3-month LIBOR is 5½%. The borrower feels there is a possibility LIBOR could jump as much as 1% by the next loan repricing date. To hedge against this possibility, the borrower purchases a 2-month up-and-in put option with a strike price of 6%, or 50 basis points over the current rate. If LIBOR

reaches 6%, the put turns into a straight put option with interest rate protection over 6%. If 6% is not reached, the put expires worthless. The difference between purchasing a straight put and an up-and-in put is that the up-and-in option has no value until LIBOR reaches 6%. Once 6% is reached, the up-and-in put has intrinsic value above this level and could have time value above, at, or below 6% if LIBOR drops below 6% before the expiration date of the put. Once the put is activated, it is valued the same way as a plain vanilla put. The no-value characteristic until 6% is penetrated for the first time results in a lower price for the up-and-in put.

It is important to remember the reason why the put is contingent on the underlying security's reaching a *higher* level. In the above case, strike prices are measured in yields, and yield varies inversely with price. Therefore, the higher the yield, the lower the dollar price.

2. *Up-and-in call.* A trader believes the price of XYZ stock is likely to experience a sharp upward price move in the next 30 days. Currently, the stock is trading at $50 per share. The trader purchases a 30-day up-and-in call option with a strike of $55 but a barrier of $60. If the price of the stock reaches $60 within the next 30 days, the option becomes vanilla with an immediate intrinsic value of $5 per share. If, however, the underlying price never reaches $60 and the option expires when the underlying security is at $59¾, the option expires worthless, despite the fact that there is $4¾ of intrinsic value (to $59¾ − $55). XYZ never reached $60 per share, so the option has no value. Similar to our up-and-in put example, the trader pays a cheaper premium for the additional contingency of XYZ's reaching $60 before the option attains any value.

3. *Down-and-out call.* The same trader also purchases a down-and-out call on XYZ, with the same $55 strike price and 30-day expiration. This time, however, if XYZ falls below $45 per share during the life of the option, it expires worthless. The option has immediate time value (and perhaps intrinsic value throughout its entire life) *provided* XYZ stock never falls below $45 per share. Again, the trader pays a cheaper premium than a plain call option because of the knock-out parameter at $45 per share.

The possible structures are virtually endless. The point to remember is that any contingency provision that automatically reduces or prevents value in an option prior to its expiration date results in a lower price than a standard vanilla option. Additionally, the option pricing factors (volatility, strike price, underlying security market price, time to expiration, risk-free rate) all play a role in any option's value.

Summary points of barrier options:

+ Like split fee options, barrier options can wind up cheaper than plain vanilla options. The user can generate a greater bang for a buck, in terms of size of underlying security coverage.

− Barrier options are essentially partial coverage options. For in-type options, coverage begins *after* some value in the underlying security is reached, even if intrinsic value exists prior to reaching that value level. Out-type options only provide coverage up to a particular value in the underlying security. If this value is exceeded, the option expires worthless, even if the underlying security returns to the range of coverage.

Lookback Options

Lookback options are a little different from the exotic options discussed thus far. In a lookback, the strike price is equal to either the lowest underlying security value (call option), or the highest underlying security value (put option) over some period of time ending on the option expiration date. As a result, lookback options are most often European-style and will almost always have intrinsic value on the expiration date. This characteristic makes the lookback option more valuable; it therefore commands a higher premium than a plain vanilla option. For example, a 2-month lookback call option with an underlying security price range of $45–$55 per share over the 2-month period, and a market price of $50 per share at option expiration, will have a strike price of $45 per share and intrinsic value of $5 per share on the expiration date.

Asian (Average) Options

Asian options are a specialized form of lookback option. The strike price is set at expiration from an arithmetical average price of the underlying security over some predetermined period of time. For example, a 3-month call option on XYZ stock could have a strike price of $50 per share, equal to the average price of the stock over the 3-month time frame of the option. On the expiration date, XYZ has a value of $57 per share. The intrinsic value in the option ($57 − $50 = $7 per share) will be determined by subtracting the 3-month average stock price from the current stock price. In a generic lookback call option, if the price range of XYZ was $40–$57 over the 3-month period, the option would have $17 of intrinsic value ($57 − $40). The averaging feature in Asian options helps prevent gains from call options on securities where prices were pushed to artificially high levels just prior to the option's expiration. Securities that are thinly traded would be more susceptible to this type of market manipulation.

Bermuda Options

Bermuda-style options are a mix of American- and European-style exercise options. A Bermuda option can be exercised on any one of several specified dates between purchase and expiration. The option premium could have slightly more time value than a European-style option, but not as much as an American-style option. Whether the underlying security has some form of cash throwoff during the option holding period (i.e., cash dividends or accrued interest) will also have an impact on the premium differential.

Another type of Bermuda option is a callable option. For example, the strike price on a 3-month put option could be reset at the end of the first and second months by raising or lowering the strike price by one point per month, but the option can be called at the issuer's discretion at either of the reset periods. If called, the writer pays the purchaser the intrinsic value. As a result, the option owner loses out on any further potential gains resulting from subsequent declines in the underlying security.

Appendix F lists other sources that contain comprehensive discussions and valuation techniques for exotic options.

Option Caps, Floors, and Collars

Caps

Interest rate caps represent a series of European-style (single expiration date) put options on the repricing dates of a stream of floating rate liabilities. Caps are used to hedge repricing against short-term rates used on the floating side of fixed/floating interest rate swaps (to be discussed later in the chapter) such as LIBOR, prime rate, commercial paper, and Treasury Bills. If, for example, a corporation has a liability stream of payments that are repriced every 3 months against 3-month LIBOR, a series of interest rate caps (also called *caplets*) could be set against each of the repricing dates to protect the corporation against a rise above the reference rate.

Like standard options, an interest rate cap requires several parameters to calculate the premium: the amount (principal) to be hedged, the strike price of the cap or *caplets* (which are largely struck at the same price), the term structure of interest rates, the current reference rate (e.g., LIBOR) and its implied volatility, the dates for the reset periods, and a short-term risk-free rate. The slope of the yield curve plays an important part in pricing the cap. If the strike price/yield of the cap is constant over its life and the yield curve is upward sloping, there is an increasing likelihood that the cap will attain intrinsic value as time progresses. The premium on the later segments of the cap, therefore, will take on increasing value. Conversely, a downward sloping yield curve will generate lower premiums for the later reset periods of the cap.

Another important difference between caps and standard options is that caps and floors use implied yield volatility rather than implied price volatility. This is because caps (and floors) are mostly quoted in yields, not prices. Nevertheless, the mathematical calculations are similar to using prices. At the beginning of each reset period, the reference rate is compared to the cap rate. If the reference rate is higher than the cap strike rate, the cap seller pays the purchaser the difference, calculated as follows:

$$\text{Cap payment} = \text{Principal amount} \times (\text{Reference rate} - \text{Cap rate}) \times (\text{Number of days in reset period} / 360).$$

For example, assume a $1,000,000 principal amount, a 90-day reset period, a reference rate of 6%, and a cap rate of 5½%. The calculation would be:

$$\text{Cap payment} = \$1,000,000 \times (6\% - 5\tfrac{1}{2}\%) \times (90/360) = \$1,250.$$

The cap seller pays the cap purchaser $1,250 at *the end* of the cap period—not at the beginning, as with a forward rate agreement (FRA) (see Chapter 7). With an FRA, the interest differential between contract and market rate at the beginning of the FRA is multiplied by the par value of the FRA and present valued at the current market rate for the FRA from the end of the FRA period to the beginning. The reason for using the present value is that the interest differential has not been earned at the beginning of the period. If the payment were to be made at the beginning of the period, it would have to equal the payment's present value, calculated by discounting the $1,250 back from the end to the beginning of the then-current period, at the market rate that was current at the beginning of the cap period.

If the reference (actual) rate is lower than the cap rate, that portion of the cap (or *caplet*) expires worthless. Remember what's going on. The cap purchaser is buying insurance against higher rates, presumably as some borrowing hedge. If the hedged or reference rate is lower than the strike rate on the cap, the cap buyer will be able to borrow at a rate below that of the cap during that period.

The number of structures for an interest rate cap is virtually endless. The cap yields could be varied, the principal amount (if amortizing) could vary, various knock-in or knock-out provisions could be added—and the list goes on. Exhibit 10.1 reflects the payoff matrix resulting from a $5,000,000 nonamortizing, 2-year interest rate cap set on 3/15/98, with a constant strike of 6%, and 3-month LIBOR resets every 3 months. In this transaction, there are 7 reset periods, starting 3

EXHIBIT 10.1   Interest rate cap payoff matrix

Start Date	Strike	Actual	End Date	Payment*
6/15/98	6.00%	6.20%	9/15/98	$ 2,555.56
9/15/98	6.00	6.10	12/15/98	1,263.89
12/15/98	6.00	5.95	3/15/99	0.00
3/15/99	6.00	6.25	6/15/99	3,194.44
6/15/99	6.00	6.30	9/15/99	3,833.33
9/15/99	6.00	6.50	12/15/99	6,319.44
12/15/99	6.00	6.40	3/15/00	5,055.56
				$22,222.22

*Interest basis is actual / 360.

months after the setting of the cap (3-month LIBOR on 3/15/98 is already known).

Floors

An interest rate floor is similar in concept to a cap, but it provides minimum rather than maximum rate protection. Floors are a series of European-style call options based on some floating rate index such as LIBOR, commercial paper, T-Bills, or the prime rate. Floors could be used to hedge resets on a floating rate asset or the floating side of a fixed/floating swap by protecting the swap buyer's reinvestment rates going forward. Exhibit 10.2 reflects a 2-year 6% interest rate floor on a floating rate investment with semiannual reset periods, beginning on 12/15/97. The same formula and par value used to calculate the cap payoff are used here, with the exception of reversing the reference rate and the floor rate.

$$\text{Floor payment} = \text{Principal amount} \times (\text{Floor rate} - \text{Reference rate})$$
$$\times (\text{Number of days in reset period} / 360).$$

In Exhibit 10.2, the last floor reset (on 12/15/99) resulted in no payment to the floor buyer because the reference (actual) rate was higher than the strike price/yield of the floor at the time of the reset. The buyer could invest at a higher rate than the 6% floor.

EXHIBIT 10.2 Interest rate floor payoff matrix

Start Date	Strike	Actual	End Date	Payment
6/15/98	6.00%	5.90%	12/15/98	$ 2,541.67
12/15/98	6.00	5.75	6/15/99	6,319.44
6/15/99	6.00	5.85	12/15/99	3,812.50
12/15/99	6.00	6.10	6/15/00	0.00
				$12,673.61

Collars

An interest rate collar is a combination of purchasing a cap and selling a floor. A borrower hedging a floating rate loan has concerns that short-term rates could move higher. To protect against this possibility, the borrower looks to purchase an interest rate cap with a series of expiration dates that are similar to the reset dates of the loan. Unfortunately, caps can be costly. To offset some of this expense, the borrower could sell a floor with a strike rate below the current borrowing rate. In analyzing this transaction, the higher the strike yield on the cap, the cheaper the price. The lower the strike yield on the floor, the cheaper the price. The collar could protect the borrower against higher interest rates with a cheaper cost than a simple cap.

It is important, however, to remember that the borrower is giving up some protection by selling the floor. Should interest rates experience a significant drop, the borrower would participate in the decline only down to the interest rate level of the floor. Below this level, the borrower would have to pay the purchaser of the floor the difference between the strike yield and the reference (actual) yield.

An investor could execute the reverse collar strategy from the borrower by buying a floor and selling a cap, thereby hedging a series of reset periods on a floating rate asset. For situations where two different floating rate indexes are being used (a prime rate-based asset versus a LIBOR-based funding), the purchase of a collar (buy a cap and a floor) also protects against basis risk, or the nonparallel shift in short-term rate relationships—in this case, prime versus LIBOR.

A *zero-cost collar* has received press coverage as a noncost way to hedge. The idea is to either buy a cap to protect against higher borrowing costs and sell a floor to pay for the cap, or buy a floor to protect against lower reinvestment rates and sell a cap to cover the cost of the floor. There are some issues to consider here:

1. Even if the cost of the cap is entirely offset by the proceeds from the sale of the floor, the bid–offer spread of the collar makes it more difficult to construct an efficient zero-cost collar. Additionally, should the investor want to liquidate the position, another bid–offer spread will be in effect.

2. Market risk is associated with the short sale in the collar. A borrower is at risk of declining interest rates (short floor), and an investor is at risk of rising interest rates (short cap).

It is important to go back to the customization-versus-cost tradeoff discussed in Chapter 7. A hedge can be structured to provide any level of protection against interest rate risk. However, as a general rule, the stronger, more "bullet-proof," or more flexible the hedge, the higher its cost. Investors need to closely examine their hedging needs before entering into what could amount to hunting for squirrel with an elephant gun.

INTEREST RATE SWAPS

Many books and articles have been published on interest rate swaps. Indeed, this has become a huge market segment, with applications to both large and small borrowers and investors. This section will analyze the basic characteristics of an interest rate swap. After defining the relevant terms and looking at the players in the market, we will examine how an interest rate swap is priced and quoted, review a basic swap structure, and discuss the different types of swaps. Later, we will look at *swaptions,* or options on swaps.

An interest rate swap is nothing more than the exchange of one stream of payments based on some rate or rate index for another based on a different rate or rate index. The first uses of a swap can be traced back to the early 1980s, a period of historically high interest rates in the United States. Here is a classic case of the financial markets' proving the old adage: Necessity is the mother of invention. The swap market evolved in the early 1980s as an outgrowth of borrowers' attempts to reduce their costs for fixed-rate loans by borrowing at a floating rate and then swapping that liability stream for a fixed-rate liability in the swap market. Borrowers with high credit ratings were able to swap lower fixed-rate funding available to them in the Eurobond market versus the domestic markets, for an even lower floating rate. The category of interest rate swaps structured at that time, which remains the most popular type of swap arrangement today, is termed a *fixed-floating* swap: a fixed-rate stream of cash flows is exchanged for a floating-rate stream with the same final maturity as the fixed rate. Implicit in these swap transactions is a significant level of market risk, which we will discuss in greater detail later in the chapter. Unless otherwise specified, applications and examples of interest rate swaps will be using the fixed/floating category of swap transaction.

Basic Swap Characteristics

1. There are two main functional types of interest rate swaps. An *asset swap* represents the exchange of two streams of assets or investment flows. A *liability swap* represents the exchange of two streams of liabilities, usually different types of borrowing.

2. Most swaps have a final maturity between 2 and 10 years, although transactions are structured from 1 year out to 30 years.

3. The principal amount of a swap is *notional,* except in cross-currency swaps (exchange of a stream of cash flows in one currency for a stream of cash flows in a different currency).

4. Payments between counterparties are made in arrears (at the end of each interest rate calculation period). For example, a 5-year fixed-rate payment stream based on a predetermined index is swapped for a 5-year floating-rate stream with floating-rate resets every 6 months (against some index specified in the swap agreement). At the end of each 6-month period, payment between parties is made based on the rates established on the reset date at the beginning of the period.

5. In a fixed/floating swap, the swap buyer or payer pays the fixed rate and receives the floating rate. The swap seller or receiver pays the floating rate and receives the fixed rate.

6. The institution that arranges the swap and sometimes acts as the "middleman" or *intermediary* in the transaction is either a swap dealer, normally residing within an investment or commercial bank, or a swap broker. About a half dozen major interdealer swap brokers are recognized by the financial community.

7. The fixed-rate cash flow of a fixed/floating swap is based on a widely followed benchmark or index. The most popular fixed-rate benchmarks in the U.S. dollar swap market are the active, or on-the-run, U.S. Treasury coupon issues, onto which a spread in basis

points is added. Treasury issues are used because of their high degree of liquidity and homogeneity of risk.

8. The floating-rate cash flow in an interest rate swap is also based on a widely followed benchmark or index. The most popular floating-rate index is *LIBOR* (**L**ondon **I**nterbank **O**ffered **R**ate), which is the major index for short-term commercial borrowing and lending transactions and for the liquidity of the Eurodollar time deposit market. Three- and 6-month rate reset periods are the most popular, again in direct relationship to commercial borrowing and lending transactions.

Market Participants

The main users of interest rate swaps are hedgers, speculators, or investors looking to exchange one series of cash flows for another. These include regional banks, domestic and international corporations, federal agencies, and state and local governments.

Quoting an Interest Rate Swap

Swaps are always quoted in terms of some form of yield measurement. A swap price can be quoted as all-in pricing or as a swap spread. *All-in pricing* represents the total cost of the fixed portion of the swap, including the fixed-rate benchmark and the swap spread over the benchmark. For example, a 5-year, fixed/floating swap could be quoted as 5.65%–5.67%, where the 5-year Treasury note yield is 5.41%, and the swap spread is 24 basis points on the bid side and 26 basis points on the offered side. The payer pays the offered side of the all-in quote as the fixed payment. The seller receives the bid side of the all-in quote as the fixed payment. The difference between the bid and offer of the quote is what the intermediary earns. (This is demonstrated in a swap example later in the chapter.)

Swaps are also quoted in terms of the *swap spread*—the difference between the fixed-rate index and the all-in fixed-rate cost of the swap charged to the payor. In the above example, the 5-year swap could be quoted 24–26, or 24 basis points over the 5-year Treasury yield on the bid side, and 26 basis points over the 5-year Treasury yield on the offer side.

How Swap Spreads Are Determined

The growing efficiency of the interest rate swap markets has translated into swap spread determinations primarily on a mathematical basis:

1. In the case of the standard fixed/floating swap, the yield on the on-the-run Treasury coupon security is compared to the yield on the corresponding strip of Eurodollar futures covering the same maturity as the Treasury security.

2. The yield on the Eurodollar futures strip is calculated by presuming reinvestment of each period rate at the following rate. For example, if the futures rate for a particular expiration within a strip of futures is 6% (100 − 94.00, the price of the contract), the proceeds from the previous contract period are presumed to be reinvested at 6%.

3. The time period between futures contract expirations is measured in the actual day count, on a 360-day basis, between the Wednesday in each contract expiration month.

4. The last trading day for each Eurodollar futures contract is the Monday preceding the third Wednesday of the expiration month. Payment on a cash Eurodollar deposit is due on the second business date following the trade date.

5. Presuming the last trading day to be the trade date for each successive Eurodollar futures contract, interest accruals are calculated between the Wednesdays. For example, in 1998, the day count between the contract expirations in March and June was calculated between March 18 and June 17, or 91 days. Note that yield calculations and differences in interest rate day count basis require some adjustment to the raw calculations. We will discuss this differentiation later in the chapter.

The interest rate swap market has picked up more of the trading characteristics of the U.S. Government securities market. There are effectively two segments to the interest rate swap market. The *sell-side* or interdealer market functions on the basis of being able to trade with a particular name. The participants need to have credit line facilities available to each other to be able to transact a swap. Either an institution is part of this segment of the market and is allowed to trade at the preferred rate levels, or it isn't. The members of this group are large international commercial and investment banks. Interdealer swap brokers handle a large portion of these trades. Plain vanilla fixed/floating swaps are structured on Treasury + spread versus LIBOR (usually, 3- or 6-month).

The *buy-side* is made up of the end users of interest rate swaps. These are small to medium size financial institutions, corporations, other institutional investors, and customer-related areas of the larger commercial banks. The end users structure their interest rate swap transactions with a member of the sell side. Here is where issues such as credit rating come into play. The sell-side dealer basically positions the swap in inventory, as either the swap payer or receiver. This is similar in concept to the way more conventional cash market securities dealers conduct business.

During many periods, the size of the swap spread was inversely related to the level of interest rates. Intuitively, when interest rates rise, fewer people should be interested in borrowing; the increasing cost should cause a decline in demand. The fact is, swap spreads have also experienced narrowing trends as interest rates moved lower, reflecting a decline in borrowing demand.

As we mentioned above, the most popular swap maturities are between 2 and 10 years. Pricing of these maturities is relatively easy because of the available active Treasury issues and the Eurodollar futures contracts with expirations out to 10 years. Interest rate swaps are quoted with maturities greater than 10 years. The liquidity for these instruments, however, is much less than for their shorter-term counterparts; relatively few dealers make active markets. The major problem in this maturity range is the inability to lay off the risk because of the lack of any actively traded benchmark cash or derivative market securities with maturities between 10 and 30 years.

The theoretical value of a swap spread should be the annualized percentage difference between the fixed-rate and floating-rate cash flows associated with the swap. The key word here is *theoretical.* Many factors go into determining a swap spread. Indeed, even break-even analysis can sometimes be set aside to satisfy exogenous supply or demand factors in a particular market.

The swap spread noted on the interdealer broker screens represents the difference between bid and offer. For example, if a swap spread quote in the interdealer market is 42–44, this means the swap payer pays the intermediary 44 basis points over the reference index and receives the floating-rate index. The receiver pays the floating-rate index and receives 42 basis points over the fixed-rate index. The 2-basis-point spread, like a price spread on an interdealer government securities broker, is simply the bid–offer spread in the interdealer broker swap market.

Interest Rate Swap Calculations

Interest rate swaps can be quoted in terms of a number of different day-count bases, discount versus coupon-bearing, and coupon frequency. Four basic interest calculation day counts are used in the swap markets (the day counts work in essentially the same manner as they do for different classes of bonds):

1. Semiannual compounded bond basis (s/a); 30-day month and 360-day year. This is the most popular of all the day-count conventions. U.S.-based fixed/floating swaps are calculated on an annual or semiannual bond basis.
2. Annually compounded bond basis; also 30-day month and 360-day year.
3. Semiannual money market basis; actual number of days in the month, 360 days in the year.
4. Annual money market: actual number of days in the month, 360 days in the year.

It is important to remember that where the instruments used as fixed or floating benchmarks have interest accrual bases different from the swap interest calculation, a conversion needs to be made to the swap day-count basis being used.

Risks Associated with Interest Rate Swaps

Like any other financial instruments, interest rate swaps contain a number of different types of risk.

Market Risk: Interest Rate and Basis Risk

The value of a swap is directly related to the prices of the underlying securities or indexes used to structure the swap. Changes in either of the rate indexes used to price the swap can have an effect on the swap's value. We will demonstrate these changes in the next section of this chapter. Exhibit 10.3 summarizes the interest rate risk characteristics of a fixed/floating interest rate swap, and shows how changes in them impact a normally sloped yield curve.

In reviewing Exhibit 10.3, keep in mind the cash flow parameters for both counterparties. The payor pays fixed and receives floating. The receiver pays floating and receives fixed. Exhibit 10.3 can be validated by simply calculating and comparing the basis point value (BPV) (see Chapter 4) for the fixed and floating sides of the swap.

In a 5-year fixed/floating (U.S. Treasury versus 6-month LIBOR) $1 million swap example, let's assume the coupon and yield of the 5-year Treasury note are both 5½%. The basis point value on our 5-year note is $432 BPV per million. The floating side of the swap is 6-month LIBOR, which has a BPV of $50 per million[1] (single cash flow due in .5

EXHIBIT 10.3   Interest rate risk characteristics of a fixed/floating interest rate swap

	Payors	Receivers
Change in the slope of the yield curve	Benefit from steeper yield curve (upward shift of fixed rate)	Benefit from flatter curve (downward shift of fixed rate)
Parallel shift in the yield curve	Benefit from upward shift	Benefit from downward shift
Swap spreads	Benefit from widening spread	Benefit from narrowing spread

year). Therefore, the BPV per million notional principal of the swap at its inception is $382 ($432 − $50). Note that:

1. A change in the slope of the curve due to a 10-bp increase in the 5-year rate would result in a swap value increase for the payer of $4,320 ($432 per million per bp × 10bp) because the cost of the fixed side of the swap has increased by 10 bps for any new transactions.

2. A change in the slope caused by a 10-bp decrease in 6-month LIBOR from one period to the next would result in a swap value decline to the payer of only $500 ($50 per million per bp × 10 bp). The payer is receiving the floating rate in the swap. As the floating rate declines, the payers' revenues decline.

3. A parallel shift of 10 bps upward in the curve would give the payer an immediate market value gain of $3,820 (($432 − $50) × 10 bps). The payer is saving $4,320 in fixed costs and would lose up to $500.[2] Additionally, at the following reset date, the payer will benefit from the 10 bps rise in the floating rate. A parallel shift 10 bps lower in the yield curve would result in the same levels of market value loss to the payer.

4. A widening in the swap spread results in a higher fixed rate. This change generates a value increase of $4,320 per basis point to the payer[3] ($432 per bp per million × 10 bps) on the swap, holding the floating rate constant. A narrowing in the swap spread reflects the same losses.

Counterparty/Credit Risk

Interest rate swaps, although becoming more and more liquid, are still over-the-counter instruments. Currently, no exchange is backing up transactions, although this may change in the future. Swap participants are subject to the payment/credit risk that the counterparty to a swap transaction may default. The International Swaps and Derivatives Association (ISDA), organized in 1985 as the trade group for the over-the-counter derivatives industry, has done a tremendous amount of work to establish a degree of consistency in executing swap transactions. Its master agreement for interest rate swaps has gone a long way toward creating an industry standard for swap documentation. Copies of this agreement are available from ISDA. For further information, the web site address is www.ISDA.org.

Changes in Consumer Tastes and Preferences

The swap market, like any other financial market segment, is subject to changes in demand generated by changes in consumer tastes and preferences. Different general levels of interest rates, for example, generate different strategies, which change as the rate levels change. This will have a direct impact on the demand for particular swap products and on the associated swap spreads.

Accounting and Taxation

Changes in accounting rules and tax laws covering swap products can clearly impact the hedge effectiveness of a swap. At the time of this writing, the Financial Accounting Standards Board (FASB) is embroiled in a battle to change the accounting treatment of many derivative products.

Staff Knowledge/Suitability

Perhaps the most important element of dealing with the operations of an interest rate swap is understanding the product. Unfortunately, many participants who have become involved in the swap market have lost money, largely because of their ignorance of the swap transaction. It would be unfair to exclude the sellers of interest rate swaps and other more complex derivatives from any of the blame. In some cases, derivative sales has become a case of the blind leading the deaf. The smartest and most prudent step a company can take is to make certain that trading, portfolio, sales, and operations staffs are fully educated on the workings of the swap market. *Caveat emptor.*

Exhibit 10.4 outlines the corporate participants and swap dealer in the structure of a sample fixed/floating liability swap. It also reflects the potential cost savings to both corporations by using a fixed/floating interest rate swap.

EXHIBIT 10.4   Liability swap sequence

Corporation A is Aaa rated; it can borrow 5-year fixed at 6.5% and 6-month floating at LIBOR.

Corporation B is Baa rated; it can borrow 5-year fixed at 7.25% and 6-month floating at LIBOR + 50 bps.

The 5-year swap spread is 25–30 bps. A 5-year Treasury note is 5.75%, and 6-month LIBOR is 5.25%.

Bank C brings A and B together through an exchange of payments, reducing the funding cost to both A and B. Bank C takes the other side of the transaction with each corporation. Bank C's profit is the swap spread (5 bps).

Interest Rate Swap Transaction

Corporation A borrows 5-year fixed at 6.5% in the market, pays 6-month LIBOR to Bank C, and receives 6% (5 year + 25 bps) from Bank C.

Corporation B borrows 5-year floating at LIBOR + 50 bps in the market, pays 6.05% (offered side of swap) to Bank C, and receives LIBOR from Bank C.

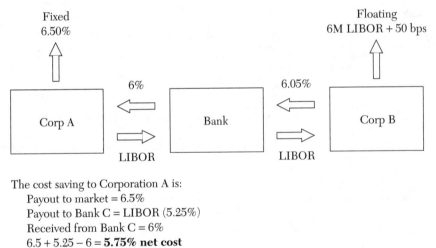

The cost saving to Corporation A is:
Payout to market = 6.5%
Payout to Bank C = LIBOR (5.25%)
Received from Bank C = 6%
6.5 + 5.25 − 6 = **5.75% net cost**
Result: (6.50 fixed − 5.75) = 75 bps savings

The cost saving to Corporation B is:
Payout to market = 5.75%
Payout to Bank C = 6.05%
Received from Bank C = 5.25%
5.75 + 6.05 − 5.25 = **6.55% net cost**
Result: (7.25 fixed − 6.55) = 70 bps savings

As Exhibit 10.4 indicates, the swap transaction saved funding costs for both corporations. The *market,* or *interest rate risk,* in the transaction *for Corporation A is an increase in 6-month LIBOR.* The *market risk for Corporation B* is a *decline in 6-month LIBOR.*

Exhibit 10.4 is a simplified version of a swap transaction, but it gets a message across. Proper use of the interest rate swap market can save an investor significant money as a borrower and protect future investment returns. The major caveat to this transaction, as with any other cash or derivatives market security, is: *The purchase or sale of any financial instrument results in taking a position in the market.* Perhaps the best way to remember this is: There is no free lunch. If there were, everyone would take part.

Like fixed-income cash markets, interest rate swaps are traded through a network of interdealer brokers. One of the most active interdealer brokers in the swaps market is Prebon Yamane. Exhibit 10.5 is a sample of a screen used internally by Prebon. The screen reflects both the current markets for actively traded interest rate swaps (and other related issues), as well as the implied value of swaps for which quotes may not be currently available.[4]

Settlement Price Quotes for Interest Rate Swaps

Most financial markets have what amounts to some measure of official closing, or settlement pricing, for some or all of their issues. Until recently, interest rate swaps were the exception to this rule. Now, through a combination of efforts by ISDA, Reuters, and a host of active swap dealers, daily closing/settlement prices will soon be available for a range of generic swap and swap-related instruments. The Reuters screen will reflect the U.S. dollar settlement rates for each generic swap maturity.

Other Types of Interest Rate Swaps

There are probably almost as many categories of swap transactions as there are players in the market. This is due to the degree of customization applied to many of the transactions. Here are a few of the more generic categories.

EXHIBIT 10.5   Interdealer broker-based pricing for interest rate swaps

Semi-Annual Pay Swap Spread Bid Offer

All-in Swap Spread Using Cash Market Yields

US Treasury Cash Market Bid-Offer Price

Yield Bid Offer

Annual Pay Swap Spreads vs 3- & 6-Month EURO Futures STRIPS Adjusted & Unadjusted for Convexity

All-in Rates Based on EURO Futures Contract Expirations (Forward Start-Annual Pay)

KeyQuote Analytics USD Swaps
0924 Today: 8/14/98 Spot: 8/18/98 3s ~ 5.6875 6s ~ 5.7188

Override Spreads in Yellow Cells

	Yield		Spread		Unadj	Adj	Unadj	Adj	A-MMKT	S-BOND	
2Y	99.314	99.316	5.382 5.378	41.25 42.50	0.405	0.399	0.406	0.400	5.785 5.802	5.791 5.807	
					5.788	5.782	5.789	5.783			
3Y	100.240	100.244	5.324 5.318	46.00 47.00	0.518	0.505	0.518	0.505	5.774 5.791	5.778 5.794	
					5.843	5.830	5.844	5.830			
4Y			5.357 5.353	49.75 50.75	0.536	0.514	0.537	0.514	5.849 5.863	5.850 5.864	
					5.896	5.873	5.896	5.873			
5Y	99.126	99.130	5.389 5.387	52.50 53.00	0.549	0.515	0.549	0.516	5.912 5.920	5.912 5.919	
					5.943	5.908	5.943	5.909			
6Y			5.400 5.398	54.50 55.50	0.583	0.536	0.584	0.536	5.942 5.954	5.943 5.955	
					5.988	5.940	5.989	5.941			
7Y			5.410 5.408	56.75 57.50	0.618	0.555	0.618	0.555	5.976 5.986	5.976 5.985	
					6.034	5.970	6.035	5.971			
8Y			5.421 5.419	57.75 58.75	0.652	0.572	0.652	0.572	5.998 6.010	5.996 6.008	
					6.080	5.998	6.080	5.998			
9Y			5.431 5.429	59.00 60.00	0.686	0.586	0.686	0.586	6.021 6.034	6.019 6.031	
					6.125	6.023	6.125	6.024			
10Y	101.114	101.120	5.442 5.440	60.50 61.25	0.718	0.597	0.718	0.598	6.046 6.056	6.045 6.055	
					6.168	6.046	6.168	6.046			

Interp / Over 10's

	Yield		Spread	Interp		A-MMKT	S-BOND
11Y	5.450	5.448	61.75 62.75	62.53 63.53		6.067 6.080	6.065 6.077
12Y	5.458	5.456	62.75 64.00	64.31 65.56		6.086 6.100	6.083 6.098
13Y	5.465	5.464	63.50 64.75	65.84 67.09		6.102 6.116	6.099 6.113
14Y	5.473	5.471	64.25 65.50	67.37 68.62		6.117 6.131	6.114 6.128
15Y	5.481	5.479	65.00 66.00	68.90 69.90		6.133 6.144	6.129 6.141
17Y	5.496	5.495	64.25 65.75	69.71 71.21		6.141 6.158	6.137 6.154
20Y	5.520	5.519	63.00 64.50	70.80 72.30		6.153 6.169	6.149 6.165
25Y	5.558	5.558	58.00 60.00	69.70 71.70		6.142 6.163	6.138 6.158
30Y	98.190 98.190		5.597 5.597	53.00 55.00	53.00 55.00	6.131 6.151	6.127 6.147

Forward Start Swap Rates from Spot Date (8/18/98):

	Sep	Dec	Mar	Jun
2Y	5.779	5.791	5.815	5.847
Sprd	5.787	5.779	5.776	5.790
3Y	5.831	5.847	5.871	5.898
Sprd	5.787	5.804	5.828	5.868
4Y	5.875	5.891	5.912	5.936
Sprd	5.861	5.880	5.903	5.939
5Y	5.911	5.926	5.946	5.969
Sprd	5.920	5.934	5.951	5.977

	1Y	2Y	3Y	4Y	5Y
1Y	5.811	5.871	5.917	5.953	5.984
Sprd	5.839	5.800	5.895	5.964	5.995
2Y	5.933	5.974	6.006	6.034	6.063
Sprd	5.761	5.927	6.011	6.041	6.074
3Y	6.019	6.045	6.072	6.100	6.126
Sprd	6.105	6.150	6.147	6.165	6.173
4Y	6.072	6.101	6.130	6.157	6.181
Sprd	6.197	6.169	6.188	6.192	6.207
5Y	6.131	6.162	6.189	6.212	6.232
Sprd	6.140	6.182	6.191	6.209	6.233

Basis Swaps vs 3-mo LIBOR:

	BILLS	PRIME	CP	FF
1Y	69-75	282-279	12-15	17-20
18M	69-75	280-275	12-15	18-22
2Y	69-75	281-276	11-14	19-22
3Y	69-75	279-275	11-14	19-23
4Y	69-75	278-274	11-14	20-24
5Y	69-75	277-273	11-14	21-25
7Y	69-75	277-272	11-14	21-25
10Y	69-75	276-271	11-14	22-26

All-in Swap Rates   Swap Spreads

Basis Swap

This is an exchange of one stream of floating-rate assets or liabilities for another. Both streams are based on one of a number of benchmark indexes. Examples include LIBOR, prime rate, commercial paper, federal funds, and 3- or 6-month U.S. Treasury Bills.

Currency Swap

This swap is the same as a dollar-denominated, fixed/floating interest rate swap, except that one or both legs of the swap are denominated in a currency other than the U.S. dollar.

Amortizing or Accreting Swap

The principal amount of the swap is periodically reduced or increased by a specific dollar amount, thereby reducing/increasing the potential interest rate exposure. A good example of a combination of both amortizing and accreting swaps in the same transaction is using an accreting swap in a construction loan, where more funding is required to continue building. Once construction is completed and the takeout mortgage is issued, an amortizing swap could be used as the principal declines over the life of the mortgage.

SWAPTIONS

A swaption is an over-the-counter option on an interest rate swap. In a nutshell, the math for the swaption price calculation is a little different because of the structure of the underlying security (interest rate swap) but the pricing parameter requirements are the same as for a standard option. Most swaptions are struck in a European style although some American-style agreements exist. Market price quotations for swaptions are generally in terms of volatility of the underlying fixed-rate portion of the swap. This volatility is then translated into the swaption premium through some designated option pricing model. Swaption prices will vary slightly from dealer to dealer, based on the volatility estimates and pricing models used.

   Generally speaking, swaptions are not very actively traded in the way standard options or futures contracts are traded. Additionally, time value in a swaption is expensive. As a result, swaptions are usually written around or in the money. Buy-siders entering into a swaption should have a reasonably strong conviction about the direction of interest rates. Make sure you look *before* you leap.

   Rather than looking at swaptions as puts or calls, it is easier to view them from the perspective of a swap buyer (payor) or seller (receiver). A buyer swaption allows the purchaser to pay fixed and receive floating. A seller swaption allows the purchaser to pay floating and receive fixed. The price (premium) of the swaption is quoted in basis points of the notional principal. For example, a 25-bp price on a $100 million swap translates to a premium of $250,000. The strike price of the swaption is the all-in fixed rate to be paid or received during the swap.

A swaption can also be cash-settled. For example, Corporation A purchases a 90-day swaption to pay a specified 5-year fixed rate of 6% and receive 6-month LIBOR on $10 million par value. On the expiration date of the swaption, the actual 5-year rate is 10 basis points higher than the 6% rate specified in the swaption. If the swaption were cash-settled, the swaption seller would pay the corporation the present value of the difference between the cash flows of what the corporation would have paid under the swaption (6%) and the current market rate (6.10%). This translates into a present value of 10 bps × $10 million (= $10,000) received every 6 months for the next 5 years. Present value is paid rather than nominal amount because the difference between the two rates has not yet been earned.

Exhibit 10.6 reflects the cash flows in a cash-settled swaption.

OTHER OPTIONS ON DERIVATIVES

The following over-the-counter instruments are options on other derivative securities. Like swaptions, their values are calculated with many of the same concepts used in pricing standard options. Although they are used for trading and hedging purposes, their popularity, particularly as

EXHIBIT 10.6   Cash settled swaption

Present value of 10 basis points on $10 million present value discounted @ 6.10% over 5 years:

Period	Cash Flow	Discount Factor	Present Value
6 months	10,000	1.0305	$ 9,704.03
12	10,000	1.06193025	9,416.81
18	10,000	1.094319123	9,138.10
24	10,000	1.127695856	8,867.64
30	10,000	1.162090579	8,605.18
36	10,000	1.197534342	8,350.49
42	10,000	1.23405914	8,103.34
48	10,000	1.271697943	7,863.50
54	10,000	1.310484731	7,630.76
60	10,000	1.350454515	7,404.91
Paid to swaption buyer			$85,084.76

trading vehicles, has remained limited—in part, because of a lack of liquidity in each respective market:

- *Captions:* Options written on interest rate caps.
- *Floortions:* Options written on interest rate floors.
- *Fraptions:* Options on forward rate agreements. Buy-side users of these instruments should have the intention of holding them until their expiration dates.

INVERSE FLOATERS

The concept of an inverse floater is yet another investment sales twist dreamed up on Wall Street. The idea is based on what is termed "coupon logic." The best way to explain it is with an example.

Federal Home Loan Bank (FHLB) has issued $100 million 7% noncallable notes, due in 10 years. Dealer X purchases the entire issue and restructures the interest payouts as follows: 75% or ¾ of the entire issue will be restructured to pay 6-month LIBOR over the entire maturity of the issue, and the remaining 25% or $25 million will pay 28% − (3 × 6-month LIBOR). The payouts are adjusted every 6 months in conjunction with LIBOR. The 28% is determined as follows: FHLB will pay $7 million in interest (the maximum amount of interest that can be paid) annually on the security. The $7 million in annual interest would represent 28% if it were paid entirely to the $25 million amount designated as the inverse floater. If LIBOR equals 5%, 75% of the issue ($75 million) would pay a rate of interest of 5%. The other $25 million (the inverse floater) would pay 28% − (3 × 5%), or 28 − 15 = 13%. If LIBOR increases to 6%, the inverse floater rate decreases to 10%. As readers can see, certain interest rate payout parameters must be set. The LIBOR receivers (75% of the issue) or the inverse floater portion (25%) can't receive more than $7 million. As a result, the maximum rate payable on the LIBOR portion is $7 million/$75 million, or 9.333%. If LIBOR were to rise to this rate, the inverse floater portion of the issue would receive 0% interest. As a general rule, the floater doesn't provide for the inverse floater portion of the issue to pay the difference over 9.333% to the LIBOR-paying portion.

EXHIBIT 10.7   Structure of an inverse floater

Given: $100,000,000 FHLB 7% notes due in 10 years
75% of the notes are converted to paying 6-month LIBOR
25% of the notes pay (7 × 4) 28% − 3 × LIBOR (inverse floater)

6-Month LIBOR	75% of Issue Pays	Inverse Floater Pays	
3 %	3 %	28 − (3 × 3)	= 19%
4	4	28 − (3 × 4)	= 16
5	5	28 − (3 × 5)	= 13
6	6	28 − (3 × 6)	= 10
7	7	28 − (3 × 7)	= 7
8	8	28 − (3 × 8)	= 4
9	9	28 − (3 × 9)	= 1
9.333%	9.333%	28 − (3 × 9.333) =	0%

The structure of the inverse floater makes it one of the few securities that attract attention from investors who believe interest rates will remain stable or rise, *and* from those who believe rates will remain stable or fall. Sort of something for everyone.

The risk in this investment really lies with the inverse floater portion of the security. The LIBOR-based investors are essentially purchasing a series of short-term investments based on LIBOR. The inverse floater portion runs the risk of losing some, or all, of the return on the investment, should short-term interest rates rise. Exhibit 10.7 summarizes the impact of LIBOR changes on an inverse floater.

SUMMARY

This chapter discussed a broad range of more complex derivatives. Exotic options, such as split fee and barrier options, extend the concept of the basic option to account for special types of exercise and expiration circumstances. Caps, floors, and collars are types of options used in hedging interest rate risk. Interest rate swaps represent the exchange of future cash flows with varying maturities. Swaptions are options on interest rate swaps. Finally, inverse floaters leverage returns to investors based on changes in short-term interest rates used to periodically reset returns on a floating rate security. The change in the floating rate reset results in some multiple of that change as an adjustment to the returns on the inverse floating portion of the security.

NOTES

1. LIBOR is calculated on an actual/360-day basis. The actual number of days in 6-month LIBOR will vary with the different number of days in each month over a 6-month period. Therefore, the BPV will vary slightly.
2. The shift occurred immediately after a reset date.
3. The $432 per million calculated from the 5½% yield to maturity will reflect a small change as the yield changes. The value difference given a 10 bp change is slightly more than $2 per million either up or down.
4. The generation of this type of comprehensive market information has enabled some interdealer brokers to offer their data on a subscription basis to the institutional investors via real-time information services.

11 RISK/RETURN

The first 10 chapters of this book focused on individual securities. We talked about the mechanics of various cash and derivative markets instruments, and how they are traded, quoted, and valued. This chapter takes a step back from the individual security and looks at the investment or borrowing portfolio and the decisions that go into structuring that portfolio. The continuing relevance of some of the more traditional methods for portfolio selection is discussed. Additionally, the concept of risk/return is examined as a yardstick for inclusion or exclusion of a security from any particular portfolio.

Robert Hagin[1] describes modern portfolio theory as "an investment decision process." It quantifies the risk–return relationship. This is perhaps the single biggest advance in the analysis of portfolio valuations. Traditional or classical equity portfolio theory proposed analyzing securities based on earnings estimates and price–earnings (P/E) ratios. By forecasting earnings and applying them to projected P/E ratios, an analyst could estimate the price of a particular security or a portfolio of securities. This seems reasonable, but it neglects one critically important factor: how to determine the price–earnings ratio—the relation of expected return, given a level of expected risk. An expected return on a security or portfolio is the weighted-average return

229

created by multiplying all possible returns by the probability of their occurrence. These returns are presumed to be normally distributed. Expected return on an equity can be loosely compared to yield to maturity on a bond.

Harry Markowitz,[2] credited with being the father of modern portfolio theory, observed that investors have the same preferences for risk (the less, the better) and return (the more, the better). What is missing from traditional portfolio theory is a connection between the way prices adjust and the way investors react. As noted above, there is no determination of how the price–earnings ratio is calculated. This is where the concept of capital market theory enters the picture. The fundamental principle of this theory is: Investors require an appropriate rate of return in conjunction with the risk they are assuming. The theory reflects the relationship between expected returns and the expected risk associated with these returns.

CAPITAL ASSET PRICING MODEL

The capital asset pricing model (CAPM) is, basically, a simplified extension of capital market theory. Initially discussed by William Sharpe,[3] the CAPM states that the relationship between expected risk and expected return can be quantified if the price-setting mechanism (higher return for higher risk) of the capital market theory is followed *and* investors react in the manner outlined by the theory.

A key concept in CAPM, as outlined by Markowitz, is the notion that an investor manages *expected utility*, as opposed to following rate of return. The concept of expected utility relates to the amount of return an investor is willing to accept relative to the amount of risk required to earn that return. In economics, there is a concept called *utiles*. A utile is the value derived from a good or service relative to the amount of resource required to obtain that good or service. I love banana cream pie, but it has too many calories. Not enough utiles. The analogies are endless.

This relationship between expected return and expected risk is most easily pictured through *indifference curves*. An indifference curve plots risk on the horizontal (X) axis and return on the vertical (Y) axis. Exhibit 11.1 reflects a sample indifference curve. The curve is

EXHIBIT 11.1   Indifference curve

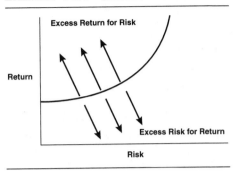

telling the investor that any point along this curve represents the investor's indifference to owning securities. In other words, any risk–return mix vertically up, or horizontally left, of the curve represents more than the minimal accepted return for the associated risk, or less than the maximum acceptable level of risk, given a specific level of expected return. Any risk–return mix vertically down, or horizontally right, of the curve represents either an unacceptably high level of risk relative to return, or an unacceptably low level of return relative to the expected level of risk. The steeper the curve, the more risk-averse the investor. The flatter the curve, the more aggressive the investor.

CAPM is called a single-factor model because it focuses on measuring the risk of a security simply by comparing it to the risk of the market. A simplified application of the model is done as follows. The expected return of a particular asset is equal to the risk-free rate (i.e., 3-month U.S. Treasury Bills) + a risk factor × the difference between the entire market rate of return and the risk-free rate. This risk factor is referred to as *Beta*. It is the relative level of volatility of a security's expected return as compared to that of the market as a whole. Betas can be derived from historical returns comparisons between the individual security and the market. Generally speaking, analysts believe that the longer the historical period used for the average, the more valid the comparison. According to CAPM, equilibrium of securities in a capital market will occur when the risk-free rate plus the beta of a security, multiplied by the expected return of the market, equals the expected returns on that security.

VALUATION THEORY

Here is a basic example of CAPM. The risk-free rate is 5%, the annualized market rate of return is 9%, and the beta on stock ABC is 1.5. The expected return on ABC is: $5\% + 1.5 \times (9\% - 5\%) = 11\%$. Now let's take this concept and apply it to stock price determination.

Valuation theory essentially uses a discount rate of a stock's future earnings to determine its fair value market price. As mentioned above, this discount rate can be loosely analogized to a bond's yield to maturity. In the case of equities, the expected return and the projected growth of the dividend stream are used to calculate price:

$$\text{Stock price today (\$)} = \frac{\text{Next year's dividend (\$)}}{\text{Expected return (\%)} - \text{Dividend growth rate (\%)}}.$$

$$\text{Expected return (\%)} = \frac{\text{Next year's dividend (\$)}}{\text{Stock price today (\$)}} + \text{Dividend growth rate (\%)}.$$

In theory, any difference between actual and calculated stock price would indicate an opportunity for a trade. Unfortunately, nothing in life is certain, except for death (we used to include taxes, but too many people have proven us incorrect). According to the old adage affectionately known as G.I.G.O. (garbage in, garbage out), any model is only as good as the data fed into it.

ARBITRAGE PRICE THEORY

Although it is conceptually valid and is an important tool in asset valuations, the CAPM has a weakness in that the only exogenous factor it relies on to determine securities value is the expected earnings of the market as a whole. Is beta a sufficiently valid proxy for risk? Damodaran[4] notes that studies conducted over the past two decades have created positive and negative schools of thought—both based on empirical evidence but using different statistical tests. Suffice it to say that the academic world does not speak in unison on the statistical validity of CAPM as an accurate pricing determination method.

The *arbitrage price theory* (APT) can be best described as a multifactor model for determining price.[5] It basically says that expected returns are a function of a number of factors, determined from the impact of exogenous data on historical returns. In English, expected returns are impacted by more than simply the expected return on the entire market. As a result, investors continuously adjust expected returns through arbitrage, based on dynamic changes impacting both the security in particular and the market as a whole. Intuitively, this makes more sense than the single-factor model. For example, changes in economic and financial indicators clearly have an impact on changes in securities pricing. The levels of gross domestic product, unemployment, inflation, short- and long-term interest rates, FX rates, and many other variables impact securities prices. The reality is that every market is related to every other market in one form or another. One of the most important concepts to keep in mind is: Markets trade on a "What's Hot–What's Not" basis. A case in point: Over the past two decades, it has been possible to relate changes in each major market segment to fixed-income securities. Inflation and precious-metal prices in the early 1980s; the stock market crash in 1987; energy prices during the Gulf War; the Maastricht Treaty relating to the introduction of the Euro as a single currency for Europe in 1992—all contributed to changes in the value investors placed on fixed-income securities.

The point is simple. Markets are dynamic, and they are affected by many different factors. Therefore, it makes sense to allow for numerous indicators to enter the securities valuation process. The apparent weakness, unfortunately, in the APT is that no series of factors has been specified to determine expected returns. That's the bad news. The good news is: There isn't a specified series of factors used to determine expected returns. Sound familiar? This allows each investor to establish personal parameters in value determination. It's what makes markets; in fact, this is also intuitive because no two portfolios are absolutely identical, and no two investors have absolutely identical indifference curves.

The concepts of risk and return have been intimated throughout the entire book. These are at the cornerstone of securities valuation. The capital asset pricing model, arbitrage price theory, various option pricing models, embedded options in bonds—all of these variations reflect value relative to some degree of perceived risk. The question really boils down to: What is each individual's required level of expected returns, given that person's tolerance for risk? In determining an answer, it is important to remember the role derivatives can play in mitigating market risks for what may turn out to be a relatively small portion of the actual returns on a security or portfolio. As we have mentioned, proper use of derivative securities can provide an effective hedge against loss in portfolio value. The valuation tools discussed in this book help the investor to quantify the actual value of a security or portfolio and to identify the potential risks to value-reduction faced in the real world. Sometimes, securities with returns significantly greater than those for other investments are, in fact, real bargains, despite the initially perceived degree of additional risk, if the investor knows how to accurately measure that risk. One example that immediately comes to mind is the issuance of corporate bonds with extended maturities over the 30 or 40 years traditionally issued. There are now a number of 100-year securities; in late 1997, Safra Republic Holdings issued $250 million of bonds maturing in 2997. That's right, 2997. One *thousand* years. When these securities were originally issued, the yield spread over the 30-year T-bond was 97 basis points. "It should be more," you say. These bonds don't mature until almost the end of the *next* millennium!

Interestingly enough, from a yield/duration perspective, these bonds were a real bargain. The difference between modified duration in a 30-year bond and in a 1000-year bond is a relatively minor 1½ years. In other words, a 100-basis-point yield move in the 1,000-year bond will move the price about 1.5% more, as a percentage of par, than the 30-year bond. The reason for this is the increasingly lower level of relative importance of cash flows in the present value weighting process. This concept was discussed in Chapter 4 ($2 - 1 = 1$, $3 - 2 = 1$, $101 - 100 = 1$, etc.).

Let's take another look at this risk/return tradeoff. Thirty years is a long time. Thirty years ago, Lyndon Johnson was president, the Beatles (Paul McCartney's, band before Wings) were still together, and PCs weren't even invented yet. Lots of things can happen in 30 years. A thousand years is another story; or is it? Lyndon Johnson, Paul McCartney, and PCs will be some form of artifact in an ancient-history museum. But, 970 years from now, our 1,000-year bond will have approximately the same modified duration as it does today (presuming the same general level of interest rates, or whatever people are using then as a measure of borrowing and lending). Taking a leap of faith on having a recognizable world at that point, and a financial structure that recognizes borrowing and lending in commercial transactions, our bond will still represent good value, especially if it has been held since issuance. Think about the reinvestment income on this bond.

Another interesting side note to this Methuselah-type issue is the lack of refinancing concerns on the part of the issuer, at least over the first several hundred years. Let's see, if we put a call feature in at the 500-year mark, will that afford the investor better opportunity for reinvestment by not locking in a "longer" term commitment?

The point of all of this jabbering is: Some basic assumptions must be made by an investor about risk and return to determine whether a 1,000-year bond—or, for that matter, any security—is right. There are many different analytical and securities-related applications one could use to make this determination. The concepts and instruments discussed in the earlier chapters provide the framework for a sufficient, yet for the most part practical, avenue to these answers. Portfolio application is just an extension of individual security analysis. *Portfolio duration and convexity* are simply weighted averages of these risk measurement statistics based on each security in the portfolio. *Realized compound portfolio yield* enables adjustments to expected portfolio returns based on projected reinvestment rates derived from either the current term structure of rates, or some outside source using a combination of term structure, changes in economic conditions, and perhaps internal forces such as changes in credit rating.

Bootstrapping to create an implied zero curve lets the investor analyze the true value of the market-observed term structure of rates. *Rich/cheap analysis* allows the investor to analyze the relative value of specific maturity sectors ranging from maturities at the same end of the yield curve to maturities at opposite ends of the curve. It also provides a crude, yet effective method, from a first-cut perspective, for singling out which individual or industry-related securities, with which maturities, in which credit ratings, provide the best bang for the buck (risk/return).

The world of *derivatives* lets the investor either protect the value of, or alter the actual streams of, revenues from securities in a portfolio, or costs from borrowing strategies. *Interest rate futures* contracts can be used as a quick and efficient method to temporarily adjust duration in a portfolio. *Options* are effective tools for immunizing a portfolio from market risk or a borrower from incremental funding costs resulting from changes in the level of interest rates. *Interest rate swaps* allow investors or borrowers to change the cash flow structure of receipts or disbursements at virtually any time during a borrowing or lending strategy.

The need to match the risk of an asset to the risk of a liability of equal maturity has been documented. The question now becomes: With what measures can one effectively complete this task, thereby achieving the best returns while staying within the associated risk parameters? To determine how well or how poorly an asset matches up with a liability in terms of return versus an equal amount of risk, it is necessary to create some sort of measuring stick from which to generate—as former New York City Mayor Ed Koch was fond of saying—a "How'm I doin'?" scale of performance.

ASSET–LIABILITY MONITOR: RELATING THE OBJECTIVE RISK TO ASSET RETURNS

Ryan Labs has an interesting method of comparing risk to return. It is titled Assets vs. Liabilities Monitor. The basic questions are:

1. What is the safest asset I can buy that will match up with the measured liability risk in question?
2. What is the risk of this asset?
3. How do other asset classes compare to the risk and return associated with these risk-free securities?

If the objective is to hedge against liabilities, the U.S. Treasury zero curve is the best alternative. Generically, the U.S.Treasury zero curve is the most popular risk-free benchmark because creditworthiness is homogeneous and there is no reinvestment risk on each individual zero security. Exhibit 11.2 reflects Ryan Labs' annualized total return (vertical axis) on Treasury zero coupon securities over a 10-year period ending 12/31/1997. It also reflects the annualized volatility (risk) of this return (horizontal axis) over the 10-year period. Each of the 30 points on the risk–return line represents a 1-year increment, from 1 to 30 years in Treasury STRIPS maturities. The volatility of their returns is measured on the horizontal axis. Reinvestment rates are presumed to be at the then-available rate for each specific asset class over the 10-year period.

EXHIBIT 11.2   Ryan Labs: Risk–return analysis

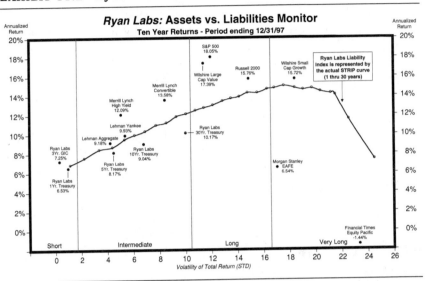

Ryan Labs: Assets vs. Liabilities Monitor
Ten Year Returns - Period ending 12/31/97

Sources: Ryan Labs, Inc. Standard & Poor's Corporation. Lehman Brothers. Merrill Lynch. Morgan Stanley. *Financial Times.* Frank Russell Company. Wilshire Asset Management. Crandell, Pierce & Company. The information presented herein was compiled from sources believed to be reliable. It is intended for illustrative purposes only, and is furnished without responsibility for completeness or accuracy. Past performance does not guarantee future results.

The idea behind the monitor is to reflect the relative risk of different classes of assets in relation to their return. Any points below the line indicates a lower total return was achieved over the 10-year period, compared to investing in Treasury zeros. Points above the line reflect better total returns than on the Treasury zeros.

We can use Exhibit 11.2 as follows. Let's assume a pension fund has a series of liabilities stretching out 30 years. Of those liabilities, 5% fall in the short range (< 1.5 years), 25% fall in the intermediate range (1.5–12 years), 50% fall in the long range (12–20 years) and 20% fall in the very long range (> 20 yrs). The pension fund would be better off using the S&P 500 stocks to invest in over the long section. The fund would be mismatching asset/liability risk/returns by using the 10-year Treasury notes as an investment for the long sector, because the 10-year note doesn't behave like the long-term liability against which it is being matched.

By matching up the asset and liability classes by the risk/return measures, the pension fund is effectively balancing its risk profile while identifying those asset classes most relevant to satisfying the objective (what is being hedged).

The annualized total returns used in Exhibit 11.2 were measured over 10 years. This is no magical number. Any number of years can be used, provided the user takes into account the positive and negative factors associated with using longer versus shorter time frames. Shorter time frames are easier to accumulate, although they are subject to greater degrees of volatility. Longer average returns will smooth out shorter-term fluctuations while masking, to some extent, the potential volatility in those shorter returns. Anyone can drown in an average of 4 feet of water.

VALUE AT RISK

Over the past several years, a new risk management technique has gained popularity. The concept has been embraced not only by buy and sell siders but by government regulators as well, as a tool for determining capital allocation. The technique is called *value at risk,* or simply VAR. The concept is quite simple. The percentage change in the value of a security, or an entire portfolio of securities, is measured on some periodic basis. Each percentage change is plotted in a distribution (presumed to be normally distributed) of all changes over the period under examination. From this distribution, the user selects a specific confidence interval that includes a worst-case scenario of the amount of value that could be lost over each designated holding period. This amount is called the value at risk.

Investment portfolios generally use percent change calculations over longer periods of time—say, 1 to 3 months—while changes in trading accounts with daily mark-to-market requirements are reviewed on a daily basis. For example, a bond-trading portfolio deals in daily purchase and sales of long-term U.S. Treasury bonds. An analysis of the daily percent price changes over the past 12 months reveals a 2 standard deviation, or approximately a 95% probability that long-term Treasury bonds won't lose more than 2% of their value on any one day. If the portfolio manager is comfortable with a 95% historical certainty of 2%

as the maximum potential daily loss, then 2% of the value of the portfolio becomes the daily value at risk. If the size of the portfolio is $500
million, then 2%, or $10 million, is the value at risk.

The percentage changes in value will be a function of the volatility
associated with the securities under analysis. Three-month T-bills will
have a lower holding-period price volatility than over-the-counter common stocks. Nevertheless, VAR can be used to evaluate risk in virtually
any type of cash or derivative instrument. J.P. Morgan took the early
lead in disseminating VAR information to the general public, beginning
in 1994. The bank's product, *Riskmetrics,* combines price volatility with
correlation measures to generate risk measurements over a wide variety
of financial instruments. This information is now available free via the
Internet, as well as on the networks of the larger real-time information
services providers (see Chapter 12). Other systems created since the introduction of *Riskmetrics* give users even more flexibility in the number
and type of instruments where risk can be effectively quantified. *Value
at Risk,* by Philippe Jorion (see Appendix F), is an excellent source for an
in-depth discussion of the value-at-risk concept.

SUMMARY

Many of the tools and applications used today by sophisticated investors to analyze and evaluate their portfolios are based on work done
decades ago. Why do we continue to use these tools? Because they still
work. It is important to remember that they are only tools. The best
portfolio mathematics in the world can tell an investor, in a multitude
of ways, whether—and sometimes even why—an investment is performing poorly or well. Mathematics can also tell an investor which
investments statistically look the most or least promising. But mathematics can't make a poorly performing investment turnaround, nor
can it tell the level of risk/return, or what investments to purchase,
unless fundamental input is received from the investor. In other
words, quantitative analysis is only one tool in the investment selection
process. The investor is responsible for providing the appropriate
input to the portfolio equation (remember G.I.G.O.). This input centers on an investment and/or borrowing strategy framed by a risk/re-
turn profile to structure that strategy. Chapter 12 deals with how

financial professionals implement a strategy by obtaining the right "gasoline" to power the analytical engines.

NOTES

1. Robert Hagin, "Modern Portfolio Theory and Management," in *Financial Handbook,* Fifth Edition, ed. Edwin Altman, Ch. 17 (New York: John Wiley & Sons, Inc., 1981).

2. Harry M. Markowitz, "Portfolio Selection," *Journal of Finance* (March 1952).

3. William F. Sharpe, "A Simplified Model for Portfolio Analysis," *Management Science,* Vol. 9, No. 2 (January 1963), pp. 277–293.

4. Aswath Damodaran, *Investment Valuation* (New York: John Wiley & Sons, 1996).

5. Arbitrage price theory was discussed by Stephen Ross, "The Arbitrage Theory of Capital Asset Pricing," *Journal of Economic Theory* (Dec. 1976).

12 INFORMATION LOCATION

The best subjective decision-making processes or analytical models in the world are virtually useless without some information on which to base decisions. This chapter is devoted to financial "gasoline stations," the providers of investment data and information. We will review the factors that move market prices and yields, and will then define and categorize the sources for obtaining this information.

WHAT MOVES THE MARKETS?

There are basically five different types of factors that cause market prices to change. Before evaluating these factors, it is important to understand how market prices are generated. Perhaps the most important issue to consider is: markets trade on the *differences* between expectations and reality. Any time an investor looks at a quote for a particular security, that quote represents all the available information on that security, plus everything the market consensus believes will happen to affect the price of that security in the future. When some data are released that contradict the expectations of the market, the quote will move to a new equilibrium level.

241

The basic categories of market-moving factors are:

1. Fundamental information—from a macro perspective, items such as economic indicators, and Federal Reserve policy and how it is executed.

2. Technical information—the price patterns observed on different types of technical price charts (i.e., bar charts and point and figure charts).

3. Specific information—credit ratings, management changes, and so on.

4. Liquidity of a particular issue or market—How long has the security been outstanding? How much par value is outstanding? What is the approximate tradable (easily accessible) amount of the issue? As a general rule, the longer the security has been outstanding, and the smaller the size or par value of the issue, the less liquid the security and, consequently, the wider the bid–offer spread.

5. Other "exogenous" factors over which the investor has little or no control—weather, environmental-related events, war, political unrest, and their effects.

Information is readily available for the first four categories. A host of different venues can be tapped for these data. The cost of this information runs from free to extremely expensive. Selecting a source can be as important as researching a specific risk/return profile or analytical application. It is up to the investor to determine which source(s) to consult. This chapter offers general categories of information sources; one service is not being promoted over another. The intent is to educate a novice investor on the key players in each category.

REAL-TIME INFORMATION SERVICES VENDORS

Real-time information services (I/S) vendors come in different sizes. The larger vendors sell market data and analytical applications over private networks. Several bill themselves basically as "one-stop" information services because they provide the four basic requirements for financial markets analysis: (1) news, (2) market commentary, (3) real-time securities pricing, and (4) value-added analysis. This last factor is the application of analytical routines to real-time and historical prices to create statistical data that can be used to gauge the absolute and relative attractiveness of an investment. The big three vendors are (in alphabetical order): Bloomberg Financial Markets, Telerate, and Reuters. All three provide information to all of the market segments, but each is known for a special strength. Bloomberg is particularly strong in investment analytics; Telerate has a strong real-time commodities and fixed-income pricing and financial news; Reuters is the foreign currency leader. Monthly subscriptions to these vendors are available at varying prices starting in the $200 to $300 range for a dial-up service (the user is charged for the connect time plus a basic monthly service fee). At the high end, a service can cost several thousand dollars a month for a single 24-hour, 7-day-week connection, with access to additional value-added commentary and technical-type charting services. Feeds for some of these services are available for distribution to multiple positions and entire trading floors.

A growing trend among real-time I/S vendors is the creation of interactive trading services. The user can establish an account with a participating securities dealer and then execute trades through a personal I/S vendor terminal. Trading by securities dealers, interdealer brokers, and their customers will continue to gravitate toward this method of trade execution as we move into the next millennium.

These monthly costs may seem a bit pricey, but the value derived from proper use of these services can more than compensate for the outlay. Consider an institutional investor who purchases $1 million par value of a U.S. Treasury note or bond. If the information taken from one of these services saves the even user $\frac{1}{32}$ of a point, the saving is equal to $312.50. Three to five of these $\frac{1}{32}$ savings will pay for the monthly cost of the service. A second consideration is the inevitable decline in these charges as the Internet becomes a more popular venue for conducting financial transactions and transmitting data. New services that have some of the same functionality as the I/S vendor products are popping up on the net at a small fraction of the current cost. Vendors themselves are establishing Websites. Nevertheless, the most comprehensive means of receiving and using data remains through the current subscription mechanisms of the vendor services.

The main information telephone numbers and Internet addresses for the big three information services vendors are:

Bloomberg	212-318-2000	www.bloomberg.com
Bridge Information Systems	212-372-7100	www.bridge.com
Reuters	212-593-5500	www.reuters.com

Smaller real-time information vendors are likely to provide only exchange-traded data, on a live or slightly delayed basis. The costs of these services are agreed on between the exchanges and the vendors. Charges will be considerably lower than for the major services noted above, but the data will probably be delayed by several minutes. One smaller vendor, Data Transmission Network (DTN), has created a good financial data product, including both exchange-traded and over-the-counter debt and equity data, access to interactive U.S. Treasury securities trading, news, and market commentary. The cost is under $100 per month. DTN is located in Omaha, Nebraska, and can be reached at 402-390-2328 or www.dtn.com.

ECONOMIC FORECASTING SERVICES

Financial market commentary and economic analysis can be delivered by the larger I/S vendors or on a stand-alone basis. Two large economic forecasting services that are delivered on a stand-alone basis are Data Resources Incorporated (DRI) and WEFA (formerly Wharton Econometric Forecasting Associates). Both services provide a broad range of historical economic and financial data, plus interactive analytics (the user can input proprietary data into an economic or financial forecasting model provided by the service), covering both domestic and international activity. The main information telephone numbers and Internet addresses for these services are:

DRI	781-863-5100	www. DRI.com
WEFA	610-490-4000	www. WEFA.com

SPREADSHEET "ADD-IN" ANALYTICAL SERVICES

As we mentioned earlier, more than three-fourths of financial services professionals use some form of spreadsheet application in their day-to-day work. Unfortunately, the spreadsheet developers included a minimum of investment analytical functions, and those that are provided are cumbersome to use. The inability to perform these calculations led to the creation of spreadsheet add-in vendors. One of the more popular names in the business is Tech Hackers. Don't let the name fool you. The company provides a broad range of accurate financial market cash and derivative calculation functions. The user simply enters the required parameters for a calculation, hits the <Enter> key, and the answer appears. These functions are much more efficient than those provided by other spreadsheet developers; many of the required parameters have been defaulted into the function. For example, yield to maturity requires at least nine different variables for calculation. The Tech Hacker "=byld" function for EXCEL asks only for coupon, maturity, settlement date, and security price. The default is to a U.S. Treasury note or bond, during a normal coupon period. If the user wishes to change the security type to, say, corporate, one more variable must be added. This will change the day count basis to $^{30}/_{360}$ from actual/actual.

A second value of these functions is their ability to be embedded into spreadsheet macro command language. Users can download either historical or real-time data into a spreadsheet, and perform various calculations using the embedded investment functions. For anyone who is not a spreadsheet programming wizard, Tech Hackers and some similar vendors provide consulting services to create customized spreadsheet applications. The cost is not cheap, but the rewards could far outweigh the charges.

Some spreadsheet add-in vendors are:

F.E.A., Berkeley, California	510-548-6200	www.fea.com
Glassco Park, Surrey, B.C., Canada		www.financialCAD.com
Montgomery Investment Technology, Randor, PA	610-688-8111	www.fintools.com

Morris Software,
    New York, NY   212-297-6115
Tech Hackers Inc.,
    New York, NY   212-344-9500   www.thi.com

EXCHANGES

The data used in the financial markets are predominantly taken from feeds provided by exchanges. Domestically, these represent the majority of equities, options on equities, and all the traded futures and options on futures. Following is a list of e-mail addresses for the major U.S. exchanges:

American Stock Exchange	www.ase.com
Chicago Board Options Exchange	www.cboe.com
Chicago Board of Trade	www.cbot.com
Chicago Mercantile Exchange	www.cme.com
New York Stock Exchange	www.nyse.com
Philadelphia Stock Exchange	www.phlx.com

GOVERNMENT STATISTICAL DATA

The U.S. Government is an excellent source for both historical economic and financial data. The online Commerce Department Bulletin Board contains a wide range of financial and economic data that can be downloaded onto a PC. Of particular value in the fixed-income area are *Constant Maturity Treasury* (CMT) issues. As discussed in Chapter 2, these are daily, weekly, and monthly yields on the on-the-run U.S. Treasury issues with the assumption that the maturity dates for each issue are exactly the number of years of the issue maturity sector. For example, on March 10, 1998, a 5-year constant maturity yield assumed the maturity on the Treasury issue was March 10, 2003, even though the actual maturity date for the on-the-run 5-year note was February 28, 2003. The yield is derived from a statistical technique using the actual on-the-run yields. The point of doing this is to create a consistent pattern of yields for a specific maturity with some statistical adjustment for the actual day counts. Time series of these data are often used in historical comparisons for both inter- and intra-market spread relationships. CMT yields are also used as the fixed benchmark in some fixed/floating interest rate swap transactions. The Treasury produces the weekly H.15 and monthly G.13 reports (both titled "Selected Interest Rates") that include the CMT yields. The available data go back more than 45 years. The phone number for the Commerce Dept. Bulletin Board is 202-482-1986. The G.13 and H.15 reports, as well as a multitude of other documents can be ordered from the Superintendent of Documents, U.S. Government Printing Office, Washington DC.

A second U.S. Government document well worth the money, is the Economic Report of the President. Published annually (the 1998 edition cost $20 at any U.S. Government bookstore), the report contains a statistical section of hundreds of economic and financial time series, some going back to the 1930s, and is an excellent reference.

Corporations with any publicly traded securities are required to file comprehensive annual and quarterly reports with the Securities Exchange Commission (SEC). These reports are available through the private sector or directly from the SEC.

NEWSPAPERS AND PERIODICALS

Daily publications of financial information include *The Wall Street Journal* and *Investor's Business Daily*. A widely read weekly published by Dow Jones, *Barron's*, provides numerous articles on corporate business and specific market commentary on the major market segments. It has a pull-out of approximately 100 pages containing statistical, financial, and economic data, including stock and bond prices, mutual fund valuations, and futures and exchange traded options. Generally speaking, financial newspapers provide more statistical data than their magazine counterparts.

APPENDIX A:
DAY COUNT BASIS
FOR DIFFERENT
TYPES OF BONDS

Type	Coupon Frequency	Day Count
U.S. Treasury	2	Actual/Actual
Federal agency	2	30/360
Corporation	2	30/360
Municipal	2	30/360
Mortgage-backed security	12	30/360
Australian Government	2	Actual/Actual[1]
Canadian Government	2	Actual/365[2]
Canadian Government (Bank of Canada)	2	Actual/Actual
French Government (OAT and BTAN)	1	Actual/Actual
German Government	2	30/360[3]
Italian Government (BTP)	2	Actual/365[2]
Italian Government (CTE)	1	Actual/365[2]
Japanese Government	2	Actual/365[2]
Swiss Government	1	30/360[3]
United Kingdom (Gilts)	2	Actual/365[1]
Eurobond	2	30/360[2]

[1] United Kingdom and Australian bonds trade with an "ex-dividend" date. This is a cutoff date for receiving the next coupon payment. In other words, for the purchaser of a bond to receive the interest payment on the next coupon date, the purchase must occur before the ex-dividend date. If the sale is made on or after the ex-dividend date, the seller receives the coupon payment. The price of bonds using this convention could include negative accrued interest because the buyer must be compensated for holding the bond for a portion of the coupon period.

[2] Actual/365 considers every year to have 365 days, ignoring the 366th day in a leap year. It is therefore possible, every four years, to have a day count fraction of 366/365.

[3] German and Swiss bonds and Eurobonds use a slightly varied version of the 30/360 day count. This basis calculates the difference between two dates as (Year 2 − Year 1) × 360 + (Month 2 − Month 1) × 30, + Day 2 − Day 1. The standard 30/360 says if Day 1 = 31, change Day 1 to 30. Also, if Day 2 = 31 and Day 1 = 31 or 30, change Day 2 to 30 or leave it at 31. For German and Swiss bonds and Eurobonds, if Day 2 = 31, change Day 2 to 30.

249

APPENDIX B: INTEREST CALCULATIONS FOR NORMAL, SHORT, AND LONG COUPON PERIODS

NORMAL COUPON PERIOD

$$\text{Accrued interest} = \frac{\text{Cpn}}{\text{Freq}} \times \frac{\text{D}_\#}{\text{D}_c}$$

where: Cpn = annual coupon rate,
 Freq = number of coupon periods per year,
  $\text{D}_\#$ = number of days from the last coupon date (or the dated date, if this is the first coupon period),
  D_c = number of days in the coupon period.

SHORT COUPON PERIOD

$$\text{Accrued interest} = \frac{\text{Cpn}}{\text{Freq}} \times \frac{\text{D}_{q\#}}{\text{D}_q}$$

where: $\text{D}_{q\#}$ = number of days from the last coupon date (or the dated date, if this is the first coupon period) to the settlement date,
  D_q = length of the quasi coupon period in which the settlement date falls.

The quasi coupon period is determined by the day count basis for the security. If, for example, the basis is 30/360, the coupon period will be 180 days.

If the basis is actual/actual, the coupon period will be the number of days from the previous quasi date to the first coupon date. For example, if the dated date is 9/1/98, the settlement date is 11/1/98, the first coupon date is 1/31/99, the previous quasi date would be 7/31/98, and the quasi coupon period would be 7/31/98–1/31/99.

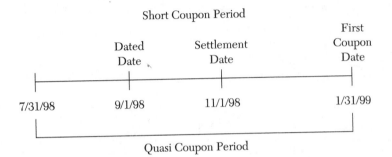

Short Coupon Period

Quasi Coupon Period

Example:

$$\text{Coupon} = 8\%$$

$$\text{Par value} = \$1,000,000$$

$$\text{Accrued interest} = \frac{8\%}{2} \times \frac{61 \text{ days } (11/1-9/1)}{184 \text{ days } (1/31/99-7/31)} = \$13,260.87$$

LONG COUPON PERIOD

$$\text{Accrued interest} = \text{Par value} \times \frac{\text{Cpn}}{\text{Freq}} \sum_{i=1}^{N} \frac{A_i}{D_q}$$

where: N = number of quasi coupon periods that fit between the previous coupon payment date (or the dated date) and the settlement date,

A_i = number of days between the previous coupon period (or the dated date) and the settlement date.

Example:

Dated date: 9/1/98
Settlement date: 3/20/99
First coupon date: 5/1/99
Coupon: 8%
Par value: 1,000,000
Basis: Actual/actual
Frequency: 2
5/1/98–11/1/98 = 183 days
11/1/98–5/1/99 = 182 days

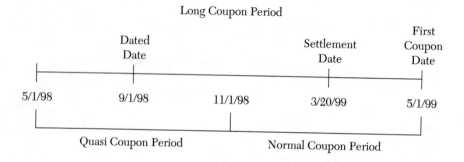

$$\text{Accrued interest} = 1,000,000 \times \frac{8\%}{2} \times \left[\frac{61}{184} + \frac{139}{181} \right] = \$43,979.10$$

APPENDIX C: U.S.TREASURY SECURITIES: HISTORICAL INTEREST RATES

Annual Maturity	3 Mos[1]	6 Mos[1]	1 Yr[2]	2 Yrs	3 Yrs	5 Yrs	10 Yrs	30 Yrs[3]
1970	6.59	6.79	6.90		7.29	7.38	7.35	6.86
1971	4.44	4.68	4.88		5.65	5.99	6.16	6.12
1972	4.17	4.65	4.96		5.72	5.98	6.21	6.01
1973	7.26	7.58	7.31		6.95	6.87	6.84	7.12
1974	8.10	8.39	8.18		7.82	7.80	7.56	8.05
1975	5.94	6.37	6.76		7.49	7.77	7.99	8.19
1976	5.10	5.47	5.88		6.77	7.18	7.61	7.86
1977	5.42	5.77	6.09	6.45	6.69	6.99	7.42	7.67
1978	7.43	7.99	8.34	8.34	8.29	8.32	8.41	8.49
1979	10.48	10.75	10.67	10.12	9.71	9.52	9.44	9.29
1980	11.89	12.18	12.00	11.73	11.51	11.45	11.43	11.27
1981	14.76	15.06	14.80	14.57	14.46	14.25	13.92	13.45
1982	11.05	11.88	12.27	12.80	12.93	13.01	13.01	12.76
1983	8.94	9.27	9.58	10.21	10.45	10.79	11.10	11.18
1984	9.91	10.43	10.91	11.67	11.92	12.26	12.46	12.41
1985	7.72	8.07	8.42	9.27	9.64	10.12	10.62	10.79
1986	6.15	6.30	6.45	6.86	7.06	7.30	7.67	7.78
1987	5.95	6.31	6.77	7.42	7.68	7.94	8.39	8.59
1988	6.88	7.26	7.65	8.10	8.26	8.47	8.85	8.96
1989	8.41	8.50	8.53	8.57	8.55	8.50	8.49	8.45
1990	7.75	7.86	7.89	8.16	8.26	8.37	8.55	8.61
1991	5.53	5.67	5.86	6.49	6.82	7.37	7.86	8.14
1992	3.51	3.65	3.89	4.77	5.30	6.19	7.01	7.67
1993	3.07	3.21	3.43	4.05	4.44	5.14	5.87	6.59
1994	4.36	4.82	5.32	5.94	6.27	6.69	7.09	7.37
1995	5.65	5.80	5.66	5.82	5.94	6.15	6.57	6.88
1996	5.15	5.29	5.52	5.84	5.99	6.18	6.44	6.71
1997	5.20	5.39	5.63	5.99	6.10	6.22	6.35	6.61

[1] Bank discount basis translated to bond equivalent yield.
[2] Quotes of actively traded issues adjusted to a constant maturity basis.
[3] 20-year maturity quoted through 1977; 30-year maturity thereafter.
Source: Federal Reserve Board, G.13.

APPENDIX D: YIELD SPREADS TO TREASURY BONDS ON LONG-TERM MUNICIPALS AND INVESTMENT GRADE CORPORATES

(In Basis Points)

Year	30-Year U.S. Treasury	Aaa Corporates	Baa Corporates	Moody's Aaa Municipals	Municipals/ Treasury[1]
1970	6.86	118	225	−74	80.5%
1971	6.12	127	244	−90	82.9
1972	6.01	120	215	−97	84.0
1973	7.12	32	112	−213	78.4
1974	8.05	52	145	−216	81.6
1975	8.19	64	242	−177	79.4
1976	7.86	57	189	−220	80.6
1977	7.67	35	130	−247	80.8
1978	8.49	24	100	−297	82.8
1979	9.29	34	140	−337	82.1
1980	11.27	67	240	−341	83.0
1981	13.45	72	259	−302	89.3
1982	12.76	103	335	−191	80.1
1983	11.18	86	237	−238	77.6
1984	12.41	30	178	−280	78.7
1985	10.79	58	192	−219	85.3
1986	7.78	124	261	−83	77.5
1987	8.59	79	199	−145	69.7
1988	8.96	75	187	−160	63.7
1989	8.45	81	173	−145	65.0
1990	8.61	80	209	−136	67.8
1991	8.14	63	166	−122	71.9
1992	7.67	47	131	−123	78.4

254

(In Basis Points)

Year	30-Year U.S. Treasury	Aaa Corporates	Baa Corporates	Moody's Aaa Municipals	Municipals/ Treasury[1]
1993	6.59	63	134	−100	73.2
1994	7.37	60	126	−118	70.1
1995	6.88	71	132	−93	83.9
1996	6.71	66	134	−95	85.3
1997	6.61	65	125	−109	89.2

[1] Aaa-rated municipals through 1989; mixed quality, 1990–1997.
Source: Moody's; Federal Reserve Board, G.13.

APPENDIX E: CREDIT RATING CATEGORIES FROM MOODY'S AND STANDARD & POOR'S

Corporate Bonds

Moody's		Standard & Poor's
Aaa	Top quality, gilt-edged	AAA
Aa[1]	High quality	AA
A1	Upper medium quality	A
Baa1	Medium quality	BBB
Ba1	Some speculative attributes	BB
B1	Lacks characteristics of desirable investment	B
Caa1	Poor standing; may be in default	CCC
Ca	Highly speculative	CC
C	Lowest rated class of bonds	C

Short-Term Debt
(Original Maturity < 1 year)

Moody's

PRIME-1	Superior ability for short-term debt repayment
PRIME-2	Strong ability for short-term debt repayment
PRIME-3	Acceptable ability for short-term debt repayment
NOT PRIME	Rated below the first three categories

Standard & Poor's

A-1+	Top degree of safety for short-term debt repayment
A-1	Strong degree of safety for short-term debt repayment
A-2	High degree of safety for short-term debt repayment
A-3	Acceptable degree of safety for short-term debt repayment

[1] Moody's rates corporate bonds with numerical modifiers from 1 to 3, ranging from Aa to Caa. For example, Aa2 is a higher rating than Aa3.

APPENDIX F: ADDITIONAL REFERENCES FOR SPECIFIED TOPICS

Chapter 4

Bond Risk Analysis, Livingston Douglas (New York Institute of Finance, 1990).

Yield Curve Analysis, Livingston Douglas (New York Institute of Finance, 1988).

Chapter 6

Handbook of Fixed-Income Securities, 5th Edition, ed. F. Fabozzi (Irwin, 1997).

Handbook of Mortgage-Backed Securities, 4th Edition, ed. F. Fabozzi (Irwin, 1995).

Mortgage-Backed Securities: Investment Analysis and Advanced Valuation Techniques, Andrew S. Davidson and Michael D. Herskovitz (Probus, 1994).

Mortgage-Backed Securities: Products, Analysis, and Trading, William W. Bartlett (New York Institute of Finance, 1988).

Chapter 7

The Treasury Bond Basis, Galen D. Burghardt and Terrence M. Belton (Irwin, 1993).

Chapter 8

Trading in the Global Currency Market, Cornelius Luca (New York Institute of Finance, 1995).

Chapter 9

Black–Scholes and Beyond, Neil Chriss (Wiley, 1997).

Complete Guide to Option Pricing Formulas, Espen Gaarder Haug (McGraw-Hill, 1997).

McMillan on Options, Lawrence McMillan (Wiley, 1996).

Chapter 10

Swap and Derivative Financing, Revised Edition, Satyajit Das (McGraw-Hill, 1994).

Chapter 11

Value at Risk, Philippe Jorion (McGraw-Hill, 1997).

Other Reference Books

After the Trade Is Made, David M. Weiss (New York Institute of Finance, 1993).

A Guide to Using The Wall Street Journal, 5th Edition, Michael Lehman (Irwin, 1996).

European Bond Markets, European Bond Commission (Probus, 1989).

Fixed-Income Mathematics, F. Fabozzi (Irwin, 1993, 1997).

Fundamentals of Municipal Bonds, Public Securities Association (PSA, 1990). (Now known as the Bond Market Association.)

Global Securities Processing, David M. Weiss (New York Institute of Finance, 1998).

Municipal Derivative Securities, Uses and Valuations, Gary Gray and Patrick Cusatis (Irwin, 1995).

Securities Operations, 2nd Edition, Michael T. Reddy (New York Institute of Finance, 1995).

Technical Analysis of the Futures Markets, John Murphy (New York Institute of Finance, 1986).

APPENDIX G: SPECIFICATIONS FOR SELECTED FUTURES CONTRACTS

Contract	Exch	Size	Tick Value	Expiration	Last Trading Day	Delivery
Treasury Futures						
2-Yr Note	CBOT	$200K	1/128 ($15.63)	Mar, Jun, Sep, Dec	8th to last bus day of month	Last bus day of month
5-Yr Note	CBOT	$100K	1/64 ($15.63)	Mar, Jun, Sep, Dec	8th to last bus day of month	Last bus day of month
10-Yr Note	CBOT	$100K	1/32 ($31.25)	Mar, Jun, Sep, Dec	8th to last bus day of month	Last bus day of month
T-Bond	CBOT	$100K	1/32 ($31.25)	Mar, Jun, Sep, Dec	8th to last bus day of month	Last bus day of month
Money Mkt Futures						
3-Month Eurodollar Time Deposit	CME	$1MM	.005 ($12.50)	Mar, Jun, Sep, Dec + 2 serial months	2nd London business day before 3rd Wednesday of contract month	Cash settled
13-Week T-Bill	CME	$1MM	.005 ($12.50)	Mar, Jun, Sep, Dec + 2 serial months	Bus day prior to issue date of 13-week T-Bills	3 successive days starting on bus day after last trading day
30-day interest rates	CBOT	$5MM	.0001 on 30-day basis ($41.67)	First seven consecutive calendar months + first two months of Mar, Jun, Sep, Dec cycle	Last bus day of contract month	Cash settled to average Fed funds rate for contract month as reported by NY Fed
1-month LIBOR	CME	$3MM	.0001 ($25.00)	All 12 months	2nd bus day before 3rd Wednesday of contract month	Cash settled
Currency Futures						
British Pound	CME	62,500 Pounds	.0002 ($12.50)	Jan, Mar, Apr, Jun, Jul, Sep, Oct, Dec, and Spot month	2nd bus day before 3rd Wednesday of contract month	3rd Wednesday of contract month
Canadian $	CME	100,000 CDollars	.0001 ($10)	Same	Same	Same
Deutsch Mark	CME	125,000 DM	.0001 ($12.50)	Same	Same	Same
Japanese Yen	CME	12.5MM Yen	.000001 ($12.50)	Same	Same	Same
Swiss Franc	CME	125,000 Sfrancs	.0001 ($12.50)	Same	Same	Same
Equities						
S&P 500 Index	CME	$250 × S&P index	.05 ($12.50)	Mar, Jun, Sep, Dec	Thursday prior to 3rd Friday of contract month	Cash settled
Dow Jones Industrial Average	CBOT	$10 × DJIA	1 point = $10	Mar, Jun, Sep, Dec	Bus day before 3rd Friday of contract month	Cash settled

Each of the above futures contracts has associated options listed on the same exchange as the futures contract. Many different futures contracts and options on futures contracts are traded on the CBOT, CME, and other exchanges, both domestically and abroad. For futher information, see Chapter 12.

APPENDIX H: CONVERSION FACTORS FOR TREASURY BOND FUTURES

Coupon	Maturity	9/1/98	12/1/98	3/1/99	6/1/99	9/1/99	12/1/99
11.250%	2/15/15	1.2924	1.2904	1.2879	1.2858	1.2832	1.2810
10.625	8/15/15	1.2397	1.2382	1.2361	1.2346	1.2325	1.2308
9.875	11/15/15	1.1726	1.1711	1.1701	1.1686	1.1676	1.1660
9.250	2/15/16	1.1156	1.1151	1.1140	1.1134	1.1123	1.1117
7.250	5/15/16	0.9300	0.9303	0.9310	0.9313	0.9319	0.9323
7.500	11/15/16	0.9527	0.9528	0.9533	0.9535	0.9540	0.9541
8.750	5/15/17	1.0718	1.0711	1.0709	1.0702	1.0700	1.0693
8.875	8/15/17	1.0840	1.0837	1.0830	1.0827	1.0820	1.0817
9.125	5/15/18	1.1102	1.1093	1.1089	1.1081	1.1077	1.1068
9.000	11/15/18	1.0990	1.0982	1.0979	1.0972	1.0968	1.0961
8.875	2/15/19	1.0868	1.0866	1.0859	1.0857	1.0850	1.0847
8.125	8/15/19	1.0124	1.0125	1.0122	1.0124	1.0121	1.0122
8.500	2/15/20	1.0505	1.0505	1.0500	1.0500	1.0495	1.0495
8.750	5/15/20	1.0764	1.0758	1.0757	1.0751	1.0750	1.0744
8.750	8/15/20	1.0765	1.0764	1.0758	1.0757	1.0751	1.0750
7.875	2/15/21	0.9869	0.9872	0.9870	0.9873	0.9871	0.9874
8.125	5/15/21	1.0130	1.0127	1.0128	1.0126	1.0127	1.0125
8.125	8/15/21	1.0128	1.0130	1.0127	1.0128	1.0126	1.0127
8.000	11/15/21	1.0000	0.9998	1.0000	0.9998	1.0000	0.9998
7.250	8/15/22	0.9206	0.9211	0.9212	0.9217	0.9218	0.9223
7.625	11/15/22	0.9603	0.9602	0.9605	0.9605	0.9608	0.9608
7.125	2/15/23	0.9068	0.9073	0.9074	0.9079	0.9081	0.9086
6.250	8/15/23	0.8125	0.8133	0.8137	0.8145	0.8150	0.8159
7.500	11/15/24	0.9456	0.9456	0.9460	0.9459	0.9463	0.9463
7.625	2/15/25	0.9589	0.9592	0.9592	0.9595	0.9594	0.9597
6.875	8/15/25	0.8765	0.8770	0.8771	0.8777	0.8779	0.8784
6.000	2/15/26	0.7793	0.7801	0.7805	0.7813	0.7817	0.7825
6.750	8/15/26	0.8613	0.8618	0.8620	0.8625	0.8628	0.8633
6.500	11/15/26	0.8334	0.8336	0.8342	0.8345	0.8351	0.8353
6.625	2/15/27	0.8467	0.8472	0.8475	0.8480	0.8482	0.8488
6.375	8/15/27	0.8180	0.8186	0.8189	0.8195	0.8198	0.8204
6.125	11/15/27	0.7897	0.7900	0.7907	0.7910	0.7917	0.7921

APPENDIX I: THE STANDARD NORMAL DISTRIBUTION

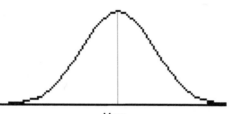

Mean

	0.0	0.01	0.02	0.03	0.04	0.05	0.06	0.07	0.08	0.09
0.0	0.0000	0.0040	0.0080	0.0120	0.0160	0.0199	0.0239	0.0279	0.0319	0.0359
0.1	0.0398	0.0438	0.0478	0.0517	0.0557	0.0596	0.0636	0.0675	0.0714	0.0753
0.2	0.0793	0.0832	0.0871	0.0910	0.0948	0.0987	0.1026	0.1064	0.1103	0.1141
0.3	0.1179	0.1217	0.1265	0.1293	0.1331	0.1368	0.1406	0.1443	0.1480	0.1517
0.4	0.1554	0.1591	0.1628	0.1664	0.1700	0.1736	0.1772	0.1808	0.1844	0.1879
0.5	0.1915	0.1950	0.1985	0.2019	0.2054	0.2088	0.2123	0.2157	0.2190	0.2224
0.6	0.2257	0.2291	0.2324	0.2357	0.2389	0.2422	0.2454	0.2486	0.2517	0.2549
0.7	0.2580	0.2611	0.2642	0.2673	0.2704	0.2734	0.2764	0.2794	0.2923	0.2852
0.8	0.2881	0.2910	0.2939	0.2967	0.2995	0.3023	0.3051	0.3078	0.3106	0.3133
0.9	0.3159	0.3186	0.3212	0.3238	0.3264	0.3289	0.3315	0.3340	0.3365	0.3389
1.0	0.3413	0.3438	0.3461	0.3485	0.3508	0.3531	0.3554	0.3577	0.3599	0.3621
1.1	0.3643	0.3665	0.3686	0.3708	0.3729	0.3749	0.3770	0.3790	0.3810	0.3830
1.2	0.3849	0.3869	0.3888	0.3907	0.3925	0.3944	0.3962	0.3980	0.3997	0.4015
1.3	0.4032	0.4049	0.4066	0.4082	0.4099	0.4115	0.4131	0.4147	0.4162	0.4177
1.4	0.4192	0.4207	0.4222	0.4236	0.4251	0.4265	0.4279	0.4292	0.4306	0.4319
1.5	0.4332	0.4345	0.4357	0.4370	0.4382	0.4394	0.4406	0.4418	0.4429	0.4441
1.6	0.4452	0.4463	0.4474	0.4484	0.4495	0.4505	0.4515	0.4525	0.4535	0.4545
1.7	0.4554	0.4564	0.4573	0.4582	0.4591	0.4599	0.4608	0.4616	0.4625	0.4633
1.8	0.4641	0.4649	0.4656	0.4664	0.4671	0.4678	0.4686	0.4693	0.4699	0.4706
1.9	0.4713	0.4719	0.4726	0.4732	0.4738	0.4744	0.4750	0.4756	0.4761	0.4767
2.0	0.4772	0.4778	0.4783	0.4788	0.4793	0.4798	0.4803	0.4808	0.4812	0.4817
2.1	0.4821	0.4826	0.4830	0.4834	0.4838	0.4842	0.4846	0.4850	0.4854	0.4857
2.2	0.4861	0.4864	0.4868	0.4871	0.4875	0.4878	0.4881	0.4884	0.4887	0.4890
2.3	0.4893	0.4896	0.4898	0.4901	0.4904	0.4906	0.4909	0.4911	0.4913	0.4916
2.4	0.4918	0.4920	0.4922	0.4925	0.4927	0.4929	0.4931	0.4932	0.4934	0.4936
2.5	0.4938	0.4940	0.4941	0.4943	0.4945	0.4946	0.4948	0.4949	0.4951	0.4952
2.6	0.4953	0.4955	0.4956	0.4957	0.4959	0.4960	0.4961	0.4962	0.4963	0.4964
2.7	0.4965	0.4966	0.4967	0.4968	0.4969	0.4970	0.4971	0.4972	0.4973	0.4974
2.8	0.4974	0.4975	0.4976	0.4977	0.4977	0.4978	0.4979	0.4979	0.4980	0.4981
2.9	0.4981	0.4982	0.4982	0.4983	0.4984	0.4984	0.4985	0.4985	0.4986	0.4986
3.0	0.4987	0.4987	0.4987	0.4988	0.4988	0.4989	0.4989	0.4989	0.4990	0.4990

APPENDIX J: U.S. GOVERNMENT SECURITIES PRIMARY DEALERS (AS OF 4/2/98)

Aubrey G. Lanston & Co., Inc.
BancAmerica Robertson Stephens
Bear Stearns
BT Alex Brown Incorporated
BZW Securities Inc.
Chase Securities Inc.
CIBC Oppenheimer Corp.
Citicorp Securities, Inc.
Credit Suisse First Boston Corporation
Daiwa Securities America Inc.
Dean Witter Reynolds Inc.
Deutsche Morgan Grenfel/C. J. Lawrence Inc.
Donaldson, Lufkin & Jenrette Securities Corporation
Dresdner Kleinwort Benson North America LLC.
Eastbridge Capital Inc.
First Chicago Capital Markets, Inc.
Fuji Securities Inc.
Goldman Sachs & Co.
Greenwich Capital Markets, Inc.
HSBC Securitie, Inc.
J. P. Morgan Securities, Inc.
Lehman Brothers Inc.
Merrill Lynch Government Securities Inc.
Morgan Stanley & Co. Incorporated

These are reporting dealers to the Market Reports Division of the Federal Reserve Bank of New York.

NationsBanc Montgomery Securities LLC
Nesbitt Burns Securities Inc.
Nikko Securities Co. International, Inc.
Nomura Securities International, Inc.
Paine Webber Incorporated
Paribas Corporation
Prudential Securities Incorporated
Salomon Brothers/Smith Barney Inc.°
Sanwa Securities (USA) Co., LP
SBC Warburg Dillon Read Inc.
UBS Securities LLC
Zions First National Bank

° Affiliated entities; the merger of these affiliates is expected to be completed by 11/30/98.

GLOSSARY

Adjusted Futures Price: The price of a Treasury note or bond futures contract adjusted for comparison to a particular deliverable cash market issue. The adjustment factor is known as a conversion factor published by the Chicago Board of Trade.

Asian Options: A specialized form of lookback option. The strike price is set at expiration from an arithmetic average price of the underlying security over some predetermined period of time.

At The Money: An option is considered to be at the money when the strike price is equal to the underlying commodity's market price.

Barrier Options: The concept of a barrier option is to specify a particular underlying security price either above or below the option strike price. Once this "barrier" is reached, the option will either attain value or expire worthless. Barrier options are also called "knock in" and "knock out" options.

Basis: A relationship between two securities, such as cash vs. cash or cash vs. futures. In cash vs. futures, the basis is the adjusted futures price compared to the corresponding cash market price:

$$Cash - (Futures\ price \times Conversion\ factor) = Basis.$$

Basis Point Value: The dollar price change in a security, given a one-basis-point change in the security's yield to maturity. Usually quoted in terms of $1 million par value. For example, the basis point value of a 6.25% T-Bond, due 8/15/2023, is $1,430 per $1 million par value, with a yield to maturity of 5.95%, and a settlement date of 11/1/1993.

Basis Swap: An interest rate swap where one floating stream of payments is exchanged for another stream of payments. An example of this type of swap would be three-month LIBOR against the three-month commercial paper rate. In this case, rates are adjusted quarterly.

Bermuda Options: A mix of American- and European-style exercise options. A Bermuda option can be exercised on any one of several specified dates between purchase and expiration.

Binomial Lattice: A pricing method for valuing securities with either fixed or stochastic (uncertain) cash flows. Also called Binomial Tree.

Binomial Option Model: One of the more popular methods used to price options. Both European- and American-style options are priced using this method.

Bond Equivalent Yield: The yield of a short-term, non-interest-bearing, discount security, or a short-term interest-at-maturity security, calculated so as to be comparable to yields quoted on coupon securities.

Break Even Repo Rate: A rate of financing that makes the investor indifferent to purchasing a particular Treasury security deliverable into the corresponding futures contract, and selling the futures contract. Also called implied repo rate.

Interest accrual − Basis = Money available for financing cost.

Call Option: The right to take delivery of a specified amount of a commodity, at a specified price, for a particular period of time. Investors buy call options when they believe the price in the underlying commodity will rise.

Cap: See **Interest Rate Cap.**

Cheapest-To-Deliver: (1)The eligible Treasury security that carries the least cost to the investor when delivering into the corresponding futures contract. (2) The note or bond that maximizes the return to buying the cash security, carrying the security to delivery, and delivering the security into the corresponding futures contract. The cheapest-to-deliver is identified as the issue that has the highest break-even repo rate.

Collar: See **Interest Rate Collar.**

Constant Maturity Treasury (CMT): Used by the U.S. Treasury Department, a CMT rate represents a daily determination of what the yield on a U.S. Treasury security would be for a particular maturity if it were issued on that day. CMT rates are published daily (H.15 Report) and weekly (G.13 Report) by the Treasury. These reports are titled "Selected Interest Rates."

Conversion Factor: The Chicago Board of Trade factor applied to each deliverable Treasury note and bond issue eligible for delivery into one of the listed futures contracts. This factor represents the price (in decimal) that would generate a yield of 8% for each respective security. For example, at the June 1995 (Jun '95) contract expiration(calculated to the first day of the expiration month), 1.0921 or 109.21 is the decimal price for the 8.875% T-Bond due 2/15/2019 that generates a yield of 8%. Another way of looking at this factor is that it converts the futures contracts underlying issue to each individual deliverable cash market security.

Convexity: The difference between the percentage price change of a security between two specific yield levels and the projected price change from modified duration. Mathematically, it is the second derivative of price with respect to yield. *Effective convexity* is the convexity measurement of securities with uncertain (callable or putable) cash flows.

Crossrates: The relationship between two currencies, both of which are not U.S. Dollars. Example: DEM/JPY (Deutschemark/Yen).

Currency Swaps: Currency swaps (as opposed to nondollar swaps) represent an exchange of cash flows in one currency for cash flows in another. Three basic types of currency swaps are available: (1) fixed interest payments for fixed interest payments; (2) fixed interest payments for floating interest payments; and (3) floating interest payments for floating interest payments (also known as a basis swap). Unlike interest rate swaps, currency swaps have an actual exchange of principal at the beginning and at maturity. Quoting conventions vary with each currency. Maturities of these types of transactions out as far as 10 years have become very popular in the financial community.

Current Yield: The coupon rate, or nominal return of a fixed-income security divided by its current market price.

Delta: An option delta is the percent of change in an options price, given a change in the price of the underlying commodity. For example, an option with delta of 50% will move half as fast, in terms of price, as its underlying commodity.

Discount Security: A security, usually less than 1 year, issued at a discount to par, paying no interest, and redeemed at maturity for full face or par value.

Duration: (1) The weighted average maturity of a security's cash flow stream, where the present values of the cash flows act as weights. (2) The future point in time at which, on average, an investor has received exactly half of the original investment in present value terms. Duration was developed by a statistician named Frederick Macaulay in the late 1930s. See also **Modified Duration.**

Eurodeposits: The money market yield curve for bank deposits denominated in Eurocurrencies. These could be any currency that trades in the Euromarket. The U.S. version is the Eurodollar. Eurodeposits are time deposits. They are not negotiable (transferable). Once you buy a Eurodeposit, you must hold it until the maturity date. Standard denomination in the Interbank market is 5 million units of currency. Active maturities run out as far as one year.

Eurodollar Futures Contract: The obligation to make or take delivery of a $1 million par value three-month Eurodollar time deposit. There is a cash settlement on the last trading day of each contract expiration. Eurodollar futures expire in March, June, September, and December, and in two serial months. Currently, Eurodollars have contract expirations out to 10 years.

Eurodollar Futures Strip: A series of Eurodollar contract expirations that can be substituted for a longer-term fixed-income maturity. Traders and hedgers use these instrument combinations interchangeably with longer-term, fixed-income securities based on the cost or return of each contract.

Exercise Price: See **Strike Price.**

Fixed-Income Security: A financial instrument that guarantees a fixed amount of periodic returns over a specified future time span. Interest is paid periodically over the life of the security.

Floating-Rate Security: A "floater" is a security with a variable-rate coupon, usually based on some money market index, such as LIBOR. The rate on the floater changes at some periodic interval, based on the change in the index. Three- and six-month interest rate resets are most popular.

Floor: See **Interest Rate Floor.**

Forward: The exchange rate for converting one currency into another at some predetermined time in the future. Forward prices are usually quoted in points, or pips, which represent 1/10,000 of a currency unit. For example, 1 point equals 1/10,000 of a dollar. *Forward points* are the premium or discount to a particular spot exchange rate that will offset any differential between borrowing and lending rates for two currencies during a specific period of time. If a trader could borrow in Currency A at 3% for 3 months, and lend in Currency B at 4% for 3 months, a profit of 1% could be earned. The forward points for 3 months would reflect a discount to Currency B (relative to Currency A) that is equivalent to the amount of money earned between the borrowing and lending transactions. Therefore, the trader would be indifferent to doing the transactions. This effective canceling of an arbitrage possibility is the result of the increased level of efficiency in the forward foreign exchange (FX) marketplace.

All FX trades assume settlement two business days after the actual trade date. Expiration periods are counted from the settlement date. Exceptions are: SPOT/NEXT and TOM NEXT (see below).

Forward Exchange Agreement (FXA): An instrument that is essentially a forward currency forward. For example, a 1×4 FXA indicates a 3-month forward rate differential beginning 1 month in the future. Unlike forward rates, FXAs are off-balance-sheet items. Pricing of FXAs is similar in concept to pricing of FRAs in terms of comparing a forward contract to the start of the FXA + the FXA, to the forward contract expiring at the end of the FXA. The comparison above would be the point sum of a one-month forward, and the points quoted in the FXA would be compared to the points quoted for a 4-month forward.

Forward Rate: The rate of exchange for a particular currency at some point in the future. The relationship between the current or spot rate and the forward rate is usually expressed in points (whole numbers are used, representing either .0001, or .01 of the base currency, depending on the quoting convention of each currency).

Forward Rate Agreement (FRA): A contract between two parties to lend or borrow a specified amount of money at a specified rate for a fixed period of time in the future. Essentially, it is an over-the-counter, customized Eurodollar futures contract with three notable exceptions: (1) unlike futures, FRAs have no margins; (2) FRAs allow a trader to hedge on any short-term rate, whereas a futures contract is limited to 3-month LIBOR; (3) futures contracts expire four times a year, and FRA expirations are established by the trading parties.

FRAs can be quoted in any maturity and amount, but the standard quoting conventions are maturities of 3 or 6 months. The fair value of an FRA should be the rate that would make a trader indifferent to either the total cost (return) of buying (selling) money to the beginning date of the FRA + the FRA, or of buying (selling) money directly to the end date of the FRA. For example, a 5-month cost plus the cost of the FRA should be approximately equal to an 8-month cost. Generally speaking, this value falls somewhere between the bid and offer of the FRA.

Forward Rate Points: The price differential between the current, or spot, rate of a foreign currency and a forward rate of that currency at some point in the future.

Future Value: Value of today's dollar at some point in the future.

Futures: An obligation to make or take delivery of a specific amount of a commodity at a specified price at a particular time in the future.

Gamma: The gamma of an option is a change in the change of its price. In other words, how fast does the option change as the underlying commodity's price moves up and down?

In the Money: An option is considered to be in the money when the strike price is less than the underlying commodity's market price (for a call option), or the strike price is greater than the underlying commodity's market price(in the case of a put option).

Interest-Bearing Security: A financial instrument issued at par with periodic interest payments, and redeemed at par, subject to call or amortizing provisions.

Interest Rate Basis: The number of days per month and days per year used in calculating accrued interest on fixed-income instruments. For example, Treasury note and bond interest is calculated on an actual/actual basis.

Interest Rate Cap: An option-based derivative used to hedge against higher borrowing costs. The underlying security or reference rate in the hedge is usually 3- or 6-month LIBOR. Interest rate caps are most often used to hedge a series of floating rate liabilities. Each maturity within the series is referred to as a caplet. An example of a cap could be a 2-year floating rate loan reset against 3-month LIBOR every 3 months.

Interest Rate Collar: A combination of an interest rate cap and floor. Collars can be used to hedge basis risk in a basis swap. They can also be used to reduce the cost of a cap or a floor. This is done by selling an out-of-the-money cap or floor in order to generate income to partially or totally offset the cost of the purchased cap or floor. A collar structured to totally offset the cost of the purchased leg (cap or floor) is called a zero cost collar.

Interest Rate Floor: An option-based derivative used to hedge against a series of lower floating reinvestment rates. Like interest rate caps, the underlying security or reference rate is usually 3- or 6-month LIBOR.

Interest Rate Swaps: Customized agreements that provide for an exchange of interest rate payments between two parties. Among the various types of payment exchanges, the most popular is the fixed–floating transaction. In this case, Party A agrees to pay a fixed rate of interest to Party B, who agrees to pay Party A a floating rate of interest, usually based on a specific LIBOR maturity. Like

FRAs, the principal amounts are notional (not exchanged). Settlement is effected through an exchange of interest checks at the resetting date after each period.

Fixed–Floating swaps are quoted either on a yield basis or a spread basis. In the case of yield, this is the fixed-rate leg of the spread. A 5-year quote of 5.10–5.15 indicates that the fixed-rate payer will pay a yield of 5.10% for 5 years, and will receive 5.15 as a fixed rate for 5 years. For spread quotes, the spreads are usually based off an active U.S. Treasury maturity. For example, a 3-year swap quoted at 31–34 indicates that the fixed-rate payer is willing to pay 31 basis points over the current 3-year Treasury yield, and will receive 34 basis points over the 3-year Treasury yield. The method of interest calculation and the LIBOR maturity being used are noted for each swap.

The above swaps are considered to be medium term. Short dated swaps are also traded actively. In many cases, the swap payment dates are tied to the expiration dates of the Euro futures contracts. For example, in the U.S. dollar market, a 12 V 3 swap sets a fixed rate for one year against 3-month LIBOR.

Intrinsic Value: An option is said to have intrinsic value when the strike(exercise) price on a put option is higher than the underlying commodity's market price, or, in the case of a call option, when the strike price is lower than the underlying commodity's market price. An option that is in the money has an intrinsic value equal to the positive difference between the strike price and the underlying market price.

Inverse Floater: A derivative-type security issued as a portion of a coupon security. The coupon security is broken up into floating rate and inverse floating rate securities. The sum of the interest payments on both of these securities must be less than or equal to the amount of interest generated by the coupon security. The coupons on inverse floating rate securities can change at a multiple to the floating rate security, based on the percentage of the original coupon security that is turned into a floating rate issue versus the portion that is turned into an inverse floater. For example, a coupon security with 75% of the principal allocated to floating rate and 25% to fixed rate would have a coupon on the inverse floater that changes three times as fast as the coupon rate on the floating portion.

LIBOR: London Interbank offered Rate. The offered side of the Eurodollar time deposit market. The British Bankers Association (BBA) is the official daily rate setting for LIBOR.

Lookback Options: The strike price is equal to either the lowest underlying security value (call option) or the highest underlying security value (put option) over some period of time ending on the option expiration date.

Mean Reversion: A statistical method used to curb,or dovetail, a series of estimated interest rate paths toward longer-term benchmarks or averages.

Modified Duration: A mathematical interpretation of the standard, or Macaulay, duration that adjusts this risk management tool for periodic compounding. The most popular adjustment is semiannual.

$$\text{Modified duration} \frac{\text{Duration}}{(1+i/2)}.$$

Modified duration is viewed as the negative first derivative of price, with respect to yield. *Effective duration* is the duration measurement for securities with uncertain (putable or callable) cash flows.

Monte Carlo Simulation: A quantitative technique used to estimate future interest rate paths for fixed-income securities.

On-the-Run Treasury Issues: The current or most recently issued Treasury securities for each maturity in the auction cycle. The on-the-run issues comprise the U.S. Treasury yield curve.

Options: An option owner has the *right* to make or take delivery of a specified amount of a commodity at a specified price for some period in the future. The underlying commodity for an options contract can be either a cash or a futures market instrument. Options are traded either over the counter or on an exchange. The over-the-counter variety provides significant incremental flexibility over exchange-traded instruments. Exchange-based options have a higher degree of liquidity and are usually less expensive.

Out of the Money: An option is considered to be out of the money when the strike price is greater than the underlying commodity's market price (for a call option), or the strike price is less than the underlying commodity's market price (in the case of a put option).

Present Value: The value today of one dollar received in the future.

Put Option: The right to make delivery of a specified amount of a commodity, at a specified price, for a particular period of time. Investors buy put options when they believe the price in the underlying commodity will fall.

Realized Compound Yield (RCY): Total return of a bond as expressed in an annualized form with semiannual compounding. RCY is the yield to maturity adjusted for the reality of the marketplace, through the input of externally specified principal and coupon reinvestment rates.

Split-Fee Options: Also known as compound options, these are options written on other options. For example, a split-fee option could be purchasing a call option to buy a put option at some time in the future.

Spot: The current exchange rate for converting one currency into another. Spot transactions settle two business days after the trade date.

Spot/Next: Assumes a trade date two business days from today, with a settlement on the following business day.

Strike Price: The strike (or exercise) price of an option is the price at which an investor can buy (call from) or sell (put to) a specified amount of a commodity for a particular period of time.

STRIPS: Separate Trading of Registered Interest and Principal Securities. Principal and interest payments representing portions of U.S. Treasury securities issued with an original minimum maturity of 10 years.

Swaption: An option written to buy or sell an interest rate swap that is usually fixed–floating in structure.

SWIFT Codes: Society for Worldwide International Financial Transactions codes, which use three letters to signify a particular currency, e.g., DEM = German (Deutsche) Mark. A standardized coding system for all foreign exchange currencies.

Time Value: In an option, the time value is a function of (1) the number of days to the option's expiration and (2) the price volatility in the underlying commodity. Time value is positively correlated to change in both of these factors.

Tom/Next: Abbreviation for tomorrow-next. Assumes trade date of next business day and settlement on the following business day.

Total Dollar Return: Change in the total value of an investment over a specified period. For a fixed-income security:

Total dollar return = Price return + Coupon return + Reinvestment return.

Treasury Bond Futures: The obligation to make or take delivery of $100,000 par value U.S. treasury bonds, notional coupon of 8%, with a minimum maturity of 15 years, net of call features.

Treasury Note Futures (10-Year): The obligation to make or take delivery of $100,000 par value U.S. Treasury notes, notional coupon of 8%, with a minimum maturity of 6.5 years. T-Note futures also trade in 5-year and 2-year maturities.

Weighted Average Cash Flow: The maturity of a bond, using both principal and interest cash flows as weights. Note: duration is the present value equivalent of weighted average cash flow.

Weighted Average Maturity: The maturity of a bond, using the principal repayment schedule as the weight.

Yield to Call: The yield to maturity of a security that equates the present value of the cash flows received through a specified call date(s) to the security's current market price.

Yield to Maturity: A rate of discount that equates the present value of all cash flows associated with a particular coupon security to its current market price.

Yield Value of a 32nd: The change in yield to maturity of a particular coupon-bearing security, given a 1/32 change in price.

INDEX

273

EXAMINE WILEY'S
COST MANAGEMENT SERIE
of Books & Journals and Stay Ahead of Your Competitio